Volume 8, 1821:

'Born for Opposition'

Born for Opposition opens with Byron in Ravenna, in 1821. His passion for the Countess Guiccioli is subsiding into playful fondness, and he confesses to his sister Augusta that he is not "so furiously in love as at first." Italy, meanwhile, is afire with the revolutionary activities of the Carbonari, which Byron sees as "the very *poetry* of politics." His Journal, written while the insurrection grew, is a remarkable record of his reading and reflections while awaiting the sounds of gunfire. In spite of the turmoil, Byron stuck fast to his work. By the end of this volume, in October 1821, he is established in Pisa, having written *Sardanapalus, Cain,* and *The Vision of Judgement.*

Mr. Marchand's unexpurgated edition of Byron's letters has won high praise from all quarters. The *New Spectator* writes: "He was an epic liver, having a genuis for life and making life into poetry and wit and passion . . . To read Byron in his letters is to fall in love—with Byron."

Leslie A. Marchand, author of *Byron: A Biography* and *Byron: A Portrait,* is Professor of English, Emeritus, Rutgers University.

'Born for opposition'

BYRON'S LETTERS AND JOURNALS
VOLUME 8
1821

A modest hope—But Modesty's my forte,
   And Pride my feeble:—let us ramble on.
I meant to make this poem very short,
   But now I can't tell where it may not run.
No doubt, if I had wished to pay my court
   To critics, or to hail the setting sun
Of Tyranny of all kinds, my concision
Were more;—but I was born for opposition.

DON JUAN 15, 22

BYRON. Marble bust by Lorenzo Bartolini, 1822

Reproduced by courtesy of the
National Portrait Gallery, London

'Born for opposition'

BYRON'S LETTERS AND JOURNALS

Edited by

LESLIE A. MARCHAND

VOLUME 8
1821

*The complete and unexpurgated text of
all the letters available in manuscript and
the full printed version of all others*

THE BELKNAP PRESS OF
HARVARD UNIVERSITY PRESS
CAMBRIDGE, MASSACHUSETTS

1978

ISBN 0-674-08948-0

Library of Congress Catalog
Card Number 73-81853

Printed in the United States
of America

CONTENTS

EDITORIAL NOTE

The statement concerning editorial principles, here repeated as in previous volumes, is intended to make the volume as self-contained as possible. The Byron Chronology, the index of proper names, and the appendixes are also designed to aid the reader in like manner. The general index and subject index will appear in the last volume.

ACKNOWLEDGMENTS. (Volume 8). I am continually amazed and delighted with the personal attention given by my publisher John Murray to this project and his enthusiasm and success in finding new letters. The National Endowment for the Humanities, already generous in its support, has given me a three-year Grant to complete the research for this edition. The Harvard University Press, and all its staff, has been zealous in promoting the American edition. I am again indebted to the staff of the Carl H. Pforzheimer Library for help of various kinds, and for supplying me with photocopies of its numerous Byron letters. For this I want to thank particularly the Librarian, Mihai Handrea. Donald H. Reiman, editor of *Shelley and his Circle* for the Library, and his assistant Doucet D. Fischer, have given me much valuable help and advice. I am again indebted to the Marchesa Iris Origo for her permission to use her translations of Byron's Italian letters, and to Professor Nancy Dersofi of Bryn Mawr College and Ricki B. Herzfeld of the Carl H. Pforzheimer Library for other translations from the Italian. John Gibbins of the Murray editorial staff has given meticulous attention to the copy and proofs and has helped me to avoid many errors. And I want to thank Stewart Perowne for reading the proofs and making corrections and suggestions for notes, and Sir Rupert Hart-Davis for his help in locating some of Byron's obscure references.

For permission to get photocopies of letters in their possession and to use them in this volume I wish to thank the following libraries and individuals: The late Countess of Berkeley and her son Francis V. Lloyd: Biblioteca Classense, Ravenna; Biblioteca Nazionale Centrale, Florence; British Library (Department of Manuscripts); Fales Collection, New York University; Historical Society of Pennsylvania; Houghton Library, Harvard University; Henry E. Huntington Library; Lord Kinnaird; University of Leeds Library; The Earl of

Lytton; Lord Mersey; Meyer Davis Collection, University of Pennsylvania Library; Pierpont Morgan Library; John Murray; Harry Oppenheimer; Carl H. Pforzheimer Library; Stark Library, University of Texas; Texas Christian University Library; Watson Library, University College London.

For assistance of various kinds I wish to thank the following; Walter Jackson Bate; John Buxton; Cecil Clarabut; John Clubbe; Mrs. H. N. Colvin; Mrs. E. E. Duncan-Jones; Gwynne Evans; Mrs. James Edward Fitzgerald; Paul Fussell; Diana Goldsborough; Leon Guilhamet; Danny Karlin; Jerome J. McGann; Mary Millard; Rae Ann Nager; Simon Nowell-Smith; AntonyPeattie; Gordon N. Ray; Mrs. E. T. Wilcox; Carl Woodring.

* * * * * *

EDITORIAL PRINCIPLES. With minor exceptions, herein noted, I have tried to reproduce Byron's letters as they were written. The letters are arranged consecutively in chronological order. The name of the addressee is given at the top left in brackets. The source of the text is indicated in the list of letters in the Appendix. If it is a printed text, it is taken from the first printed form of the letter known or presumed to be copied from the original manuscript, or from a more reliable editor, such as Prothero, when he also had access to the manuscript. In this case, as with handwritten or typed copies, or quotations in sale catalogues, the text of this source is given precisely.

When the text is taken from the autograph letter or a photo copy or facsimile of it, the present whereabouts or ownership is given, whether it is in a library or a private collection. When the manuscript is the source, no attempt is made to indicate previous publication, if any. Here I have been faithful to the manuscript with the following exceptions:

1. The place and date of writing is invariably placed at the top right in one line if possible to save space, and to follow Byron's general practice. Fortunately Byron dated most of his letters in this way, but occasionally he put the date at the end. Byron's usual custom of putting no punctuation after the year is followed throughout.

2. Superior letters such as S^r or 30th have been lowered to Sr. and 30th. The & has been retained, but &^{c} has been printed &c.

3. Byron's spelling has been followed (and generally his spelling is good, though not always consistent), and *sic* has been avoided except in a few instances when an inadvertent misspelling might

change the meaning or be ambiguous, as for instance when he spells *there* t-h-e-i-r.

4. Although, like many of his contemporaries, Byron was inconsistent and eccentric in his capitalization, I have felt it was better to let him have his way, to preserve the flavour of his personality and his times. With him the capital letter sometimes indicates the importance he gives to a word in a particular context; but in the very next line it might not be capitalized. If clarity has seemed to demand a modification, I have used square brackets to indicate any departure from the manuscript.

5. Obvious slips of the pen crossed out by the writer have been silently omitted. But crossed out words of any significance to the meaning or emphasis are enclosed in angled brackets ⟨ ⟩.

6. Letters undated, or dated with the day of the week only, have been dated, when possible, in square brackets. If the date is conjectural, it is given with a question mark in brackets. The same practice is followed for letters from printed sources. The post mark date is given, to indicate an approximate date, only when the letter itself is undated.

7. The salutation is put on the same line as the text, separated from it by a dash. The complimentary closing, often on several lines in the manuscript, is given in one line if possible. The P.S., wherever it may be written in the manuscript, follows the signature.

8. Byron's punctuation follows no rules of his own or others' making. He uses dashes and commas freely, but for no apparent reason, other than possibly for natural pause between phrases, or sometimes for emphasis. He is guilty of the "comma splice", and one can seldom be sure where he intended to end a sentence, or whether he recognized the sentence as a unit of expression. He does at certain intervals place a period and a dash, beginning again with a capital letter. These larger divisions sometimes, though not always, represented what in other writers, particularly in writers of today, correspond to paragraphs. He sometimes uses semicolons, but often where we would use commas. Byron himself recognized his lack of knowledge of the logic or the rules of punctuation. He wrote to his publisher John Murray on August 26, 1813: "Do you know anybody who can *stop*—I mean point—commas and so forth, for I am I fear a sad hand at your punctuation". It is not without reason then that most editors, including R. E. Prothero, have imposed sentences and paragraphs on him in line with their interpretation of his intended meaning. It is my feeling, however, that this detracts from the im-

pression of Byronic spontaneity and the onrush of ideas in his letters, without a compensating gain in clarity. In fact, it may often arbitrarily impose a meaning or an emphasis not intended by the writer. I feel that there is less danger of distortion if the reader may see exactly how he punctuated and then determine whether a phrase between commas or dashes belongs to one sentence or another. Byron's punctuation seldom if ever makes the reading difficult or the meaning unclear. In rare instances I have inserted a period, a comma, or a semicolon, but have enclosed it in square brackets to indicate it was mine and not his.

9. Words missing but obvious from the context, such as those lacunae caused by holes in the manuscript, are supplied within square brackets. If they are wholly conjectural, they are followed by a question mark. The same is true of doubtful readings in the manuscript.

Undated letters have been placed within the chronological sequence when from internal or external evidence there are reasonable grounds for a conjectural date. This has seemed more useful than putting them together at the end of the volumes. Where a more precise date cannot be established from the context, these letters are placed at the beginning of the month or year in which they seem most likely to have been written.

ANNOTATION. I have tried to make the footnotes as brief and informative as possible, eschewing, sometimes with reluctance, the leisurely expansiveness of R. E. Prothero, who in his admirable edition of the *Letters and Journals* often gave pages of supplementary biographical information and whole letters *to* Byron, which was possible at a time when book publishing was less expensive, and when the extant and available Byron letters numbered scarcely more than a third of those in the present edition. Needless to say, I have found Prothero's notes of inestimable assistance in the identification of persons and quotations in the letters which he edited, though where possible I have double checked them. And I must say that while I have found some errors, they are rare. With this general acknowledgment I have left the reader to assume that where a source of information in the notes is not given, it comes from Prothero's edition, where additional details may be found.

The footnotes are numbered for each letter. Where the numbers are repeated on a page, the sequence of the letters will make the reference clear.

In an appendix in each volume I have given brief biographical sketches of Byron's principal correspondents first appearing in that volume. These are necessarily very short, and the stress is always on Byron's relations with the subject of the sketch. Identification of less frequent correspondents and other persons mentioned in the letters is given in footnotes as they appear, and the location of these, as well as the biographical sketches in the appendix, will be indicated by italic numbers in the index. Similarly italic indications will refer the reader to the principal biographical notes on persons mentioned in the text of the letters.

With respect to the annotation of literary allusions and quotations in the letters, I have tried to identify all quotations in the text, but have not always been successful in locating Byron's sources in obscure dramas whose phrases, serious or ridiculous, haunted his memory. When I have failed to identify either a quotation or a name, I have frankly noted it as "Unidentified". When, however, Byron has quoted or adapted some common saying from Shakespeare or elsewhere, I have assumed that it is easily recognizable and have passed it by. I have likewise passed by single words or short phrases (quoted or not quoted) which may have had a source in Byron's reading or in conversation with his correspondents, but which it is impossible to trace. And when he repeats a quotation, as he frequently does, I have not repeated the earlier notation except occasionally when it is far removed from its first occurrence in the letters, hoping that the reader will find it in the general index or the subject index in the last volume. No doubt readers with special knowledge in various fields may be able to enlighten me concerning quotations which may have baffled me. If so, I shall try to make amends with notes in later volumes.

Since this work will be read on both sides of the Atlantic, I have explained some things that would be perfectly clear to a British reader but not to an American. I trust that English readers will make allowance for this. As Johnson said in the Preface to his edition of Shakespeare: "It is impossible for an expositor not to write too little for some, and too much for others ... how long soever he may deliberate, [he] will at last explain many lines which the learned will think impossible to be mistaken, and omit many for which the ignorant will want his help. These are censures merely relative, and must be quietly endured."

I have occasionally given cross references, but in the main have left it to the reader to consult the index for names which have been identified in earlier notes.

SPECIAL NOTES. The letters to Thomas Moore, first published in his *Letters and Journals of Lord Byron* (1830), were printed with many omissions and the manuscripts have since disappeared. Moore generally indicated omissions by asterisks, here reproduced as in his text.

Byron's letters in Italian to the Countess Guiccioli (and a few other correspondents) I have transcribed from the original autograph manuscripts, most of them now in the Biblioteca Classense, Ravenna. A few are in the Carl H. Pforzheimer Library. I have tried to be faithful to Byron's Italian script so far as possible. His chief slips are to be seen in his carelessness with accents and his tendency to excessive elision with the apostrophe. His spelling is generally good, but he sometimes leaves the English consonant as in *circo(n)stanza*. The Italian text is followed immediately by the English translation as printed by Iris Origo in *The Last Attachment*. The translations of other letters, not translated or not included in that volume, have been made for me by Professor Nancy Dersofi and Ricki B. Herzfeld.

Beginning with Volume 7, I have divided some of Byron's longer letters into paragraphs, where a pause or change of subject is indicated. This helps with the proof-correcting, and makes easier the reading of the text, without detracting significantly from the impression of Byron's free-flowing and on-rushing style of composition.

BYRON CHRONOLOGY

1821 Jan. 4—Began "Ravenna Journal".

Jan.—Began *Sardanapalus*.

Feb. 10—Finished first letter on Bowles-Pope controversy.

Feb. 24—Plan of Carbonari uprising failed and leaders betrayed.

March—Wrote second letter on Bowles.

March 1—Put daughter Allegra in convent school at Bagna-cavallo.

April 25—*Marino Faliero* put on stage at Drury Lane in spite of Byron's protests.

May—Disturbed by false report that the play had been "hissed off the stage".

May 27—finished *Sardanapalus*.

June 12—Began *The Two Foscari*.

June 22—Byron's servant Tita arrested for quarrel with soldier.

July—Promised Teresa not to continue *Don Juan*.

July 10—Pietro Gamba arrested and banished—his father banished soon after.

July 16—Started drama of *Cain*.

July 25—Teresa left to join her father and brother in Florence.

Aug. 6—Shelley arrived in Ravenna for visit to Byron.

Aug.—Wrote *The Blues*.

Sept.—Wrote *The Vision of Judgment*.

Oct. 9—Began *Heaven and Earth*.

Oct.—Preparations for leaving Ravenna.

Oct. 29—Left Ravenna for Pisa to join Gambas and Teresa.

Oct. 29–30—Met Rogers at Bologna and travelled with him to Florence.

BYRON'S LETTERS AND JOURNALS

RAVENNA JOURNAL

January 4–February 27, 1821

[Moore's transcription]

Ravenna, January 4th, 1821

"A sudden thought strikes me." Let me begin a Journal once more.[1] The last I kept was in Switzerland, in record of a tour made in the Bernese Alps, which I made to send to my sister in 1816, and I suppose that she has it still, for she wrote to me that she was pleased with it. Another, and longer, I kept in 1813–1814, which I gave to Thomas Moore in the same year.

This morning I gat me up late, as usual—weather bad—bad as England—worse. The snow of last week melting to the sirocco of to-day, so that there were two d—d things at once. Could not even get to ride on horseback in the forest. Stayed at home all the morning —looked at the fire—wondered when the post would come. Post came at the Ave Maria, instead of half-past one o'clock, as it ought. Galignani's Messengers, six in number—a letter from Faenza, but none from England. Very sulky in consequence (for there ought to have been letters), and ate in consequence a copious dinner; for when I am vexed, it makes me swallow quicker—but drank very little.

I was out of spirits—read the papers—thought what *fame* was, on reading, in a case of murder, that "Mr. Wych, grocer, at Tunbridge, sold some bacon, flour, cheese, and, it is believed, some plums, to some gypsy woman accused. He had on his counter (I quote faithfully) a *book*, the Life of *Pamela*, which he was *tearing* for *waste* paper, &c., &c. In the cheese was found, &c., and a *leaf* of *Pamela wrapt round the bacon.*" What would Richardson, the vainest and luckiest of *living* authors (i.e. while alive)—he who, with Aaron Hill,[2] used to prophesy and chuckle over the presumed fall of Fielding (the *prose* Homer of

---

[1] All that we have of this journal is what Moore published as "Extracts from a Diary of Lord Byron, 1821". (Moore, II, 395 ff.) In deference to Hobhouse, who wanted no life of Byron written, he cut out some parts and then apparently destroyed it altogether, for it has not survived. (See Doris Langley Moore, *The Late Lord Byron*, p. 273). The quotation at the beginning is from *The Rovers* by George Canning, which appeared in the *Anti-Jacobin*.

[2] Aaron Hill (1685–1750), dramatist, satirized Pope in his "Progress of Wit" (1730) and flattered Richardson.

11

human nature)[3] and of Pope (the most beautiful of poets)—what would he have said, could he have traced his pages from their place on the French prince's toilets (see Boswell's Johnson) to the grocer's counter and the gipsy-murderess's bacon!!!

What would he have said? What can anybody say, save what Solomon said long before us? After all, it is but passing from one counter to another, from the bookseller's to the other tradesman's—grocer or pastry-cook. For my part, I have met with most poetry upon trunks; so that I am apt to consider the trunk-maker as the sexton of authorship.

Wrote five letters in about half an hour, short and savage, to all my rascally correspondents. Carriage came. Heard the news of three murders at Faenza and Forli—a carabinier, a smuggler, and an attorney—all last night. The two first in a quarrel, the latter by premeditation.

Three weeks ago—almost a month—the 7th it was—I picked up the Commandant, mortally wounded, out of the street; he died in my house; assassins unknown, but presumed political. His brethren wrote from Rome last night to thank me for having assisted him in his last moments. Poor fellow! it was a pity; he was a good soldier, but imprudent. It was eight in the evening when they killed him. We heard the shot; my servants and I ran out, and found him expiring, with five wounds, two whereof mortal—by slugs they seemed. I examined him, but did not go to the dissection next morning.

Carriage at 8 or so—went to visit La Contessa G.—found her playing on the piano-forte—talked till ten, when the Count, her father, and the no less Count, her brother, came in from the theatre. Play, they said, Alfieri's Filippo[4]—well received.

Two days ago the King of Naples passed through Bologna on his way to congress.[5] My servant Luigi brought the news. I had sent him to Bologna for a lamp. How will it end? Time will show.

Came home at eleven, or rather before. If the road and weather are

[3] Byron was a great admirer of Fielding, and he was inclined to ridicule Richardson.

[4] The scene of *Filippo* is laid in Madrid in 1608, and the principal character is Philip II, the "Spanish Tiberius". Byron later thought of writing a tragedy based on the life of Tiberius. See Journal, Jan. 28, 1821.

[5] The Congress at Laibach (modern Ljubljana, Yugoslavia) was called by the Czar of Russia, the Emperor of Austria, and the Prince of Prussia in January, 1821. King Ferdinand of Naples was invited to attend. The purpose of it was to suppress the Neapolitan revolt and to declare that the powers would not tolerate a constitution which sprang from a revolution, and that the country would be occupied by the Austrian army.

conformable, mean to ride to-morrow. High time—almost a week at this work—snow, sirocco, one day—frost and snow the other—sad climate for Italy. But the two seasons, last and present, are extraordinary. Read a Life of Leonardo da Vinci by Rossi[6]—ruminated—wrote this much, and will go to bed.

January 5th, 1821

Rose late—dull and drooping—the weather dripping and dense. Snow on the ground, and sirocco above in the sky, like yesterday. Roads up to the horse's belly, so that riding (at least for pleasure) is not very feasible. Added a postscript to my letter to Murray. Read the conclusion, for the fiftieth time (I have read all W. Scott's novels at least fifty times) of the third series of "Tales of my Landlord",— grand work—Scotch Fielding, as well as great English poet—wonderful man! I long to get drunk with him.

Dined versus six o' the clock. Forgot that there was a plum-pudding, (I have added, lately, *eating* to my "family of vices,") and had dined before I knew it. Drank half a bottle of some sort of spirits—probably spirits of wine; for what they call brandy, rum, &c. &c., here is nothing but spirits of wine, coloured accordingly. Did *not* eat two apples, which were placed by way of dessert. Fed the two cats, the hawk, and the tame (but *not tamed*) crow. Read Mitford's History of Greece— Xenophon's Retreat of the Ten Thousand. Up to this present moment writing, 6 minutes before eight o' the clock—French hours, not Italian.

Hear the carriage—order pistols and great coat, as usual— necessary articles. Weather cold—carriage open, and inhabitants somewhat savage—rather treacherous and highly inflamed by politics. Fine fellows, though,—good materials for a nation. Out of chaos God made a world, and out of high passions comes a people.

Clock strikes—going out to make love. Somewhat perilous, but not disagreeable. Memorandum—a new screen put up to-day. It is rather antique, but will do with a little repair.

Thaw continues—hopeful that riding may be practicable to-morrow. Sent the papers to Al[borghett]i.—grand events coming.

11 o' the clock and nine minutes. Visited La Contessa G[uiccioli] Nata G[hiselli] G[amba]. Found her beginning my letter of answer to the thanks of Alessio del Pinto of Rome for assisting his brother the

[6] Probably a misreading for Giuseppe Bossi who wrote *Del Cenacolo di Leonardo da Vinci*, Milano, 1810, and *Delle Opinioni di Leonardo da Vinci . . .*, 1811.

late Commandant in his last moments, as I had begged her to pen my reply for the purer Italian, I being an ultramontane, little skilled in the set phrase of Tuscany. Cut short the letter—finish it another day. Talked of Italy, patriotism, Alfieri, Madame Albany,[1] and other branches of learning. Also Sallust's Conspiracy of Catiline, and the War of Jugurtha.[2] At 9 came in her brother, Il Conte Pietro—at 10, her father, Conte Ruggiero.

Talked of various modes of warfare—of the Hungarian and Highland modes of broad-sword exercise, in both whereof I was once a moderate "master of fence". Settled that the R[evolution]. will break out on the 7th or 8th of March, in which appointment I should trust, had it not been settled that it was to have broken out in October, 1820. But those Bolognese shirked the Romagnuoles.

"It is all one to Ranger,"[3] One must not be particular, but take rebellion when it lies in the way. Came home—read the "Ten Thousand" again, and will go to bed.

Mem.—Ordered Fletcher (at four o'clock this afternoon) to copy out 7 or 8 apophthegms of Bacon, in which I have detected such blunders as a school-boy might detect rather than commit. Such are the sages! What must they be, when such as I can stumble on their mistakes or misstatements? I will go to bed, for I find that I grow cynical.

January 6th, 1821

Mist—thaw—slop—rain. No stirring out on horseback. Read Spence's Anecdotes. Pope a fine fellow—always thought him so. Corrected blunders in *nine* apophthegms of Bacon—all historical—and read Mitford's Greece. Wrote an epigram. Turned to a passage in Guinguené[1]—ditto in Lord Holland's Lope de Vega. Wrote a note on Don Juan.

[1] The Comtesse d'Albany, née Stolberg (1753–1824) married the Young Pretender, Charles Edward Stuart, in 1772. After his death in 1788 she lived with Alfieri in Paris and later in Florence, and was said to have had considerable influence on his literary work. After Alfieri's death in 1803, she became attached to a French painter, François Fabre, to whom she left the library and manuscripts of Alfieri.

[2] Jugurtha, King of Numidia, warred against several Roman consuls sent into Africa to defeat him until he was finally captured and brought to Rome in 104 B.C. where he died in prison.

[3] Benjamin Hoadly, *The Suspicious Husband* (1747), Act. V, scene 2.

[1] Pierre Louis Ginguené (1748–1816), once French ambassador at Turin, published the beginning of his *Histoire Littéraire de l'Italie* in 1811. After his death the work was completed, in 14 volumes, by Salfi by 1835.

At eight went out to visit. Heard a little music—like music. Talked with Count Pietro G. of the Italian comedian Vestris,[2] who is now at Rome—have seen him often act in Venice—a good actor—very. Somewhat of a mannerist; but excellent in broad comedy, as well as in the sentimental pathetic. He has made me frequently laugh and cry, neither of which is now a very easy matter—at least, for a player to produce in me.

Thought of the state of women under the ancient Greeks—convenient enough. Present state, a remnant of the barbarism of the chivalry [chivalric?] and feudal ages—artificial and unnatural. They ought to mind home—and be well fed and clothed—but not mixed in society. Well educated, too, in religion—but to read neither poetry nor politics—nothing but books of piety and cookery. Music—drawing—dancing—also a little gardening and ploughing now and then. I have seen them mending the roads in Epirus with good success. Why not, as well as hay-making and milking?

Came home, and read Mitford again, and played with my mastiff—gave him his supper. Made another reading to the epigram, but the turn the same. To-night at the theatre, there being a prince on his throne in the last scene of the comedy,—the audience laughed, and asked him for a *Constitution*. This shows the state of the public mind here, as well as the assassinations. It won't do. There must be an universal republic,—and there ought to be.

The crow is lame of a leg—wonder how it happened—some fool trod upon his toe, I suppose. The falcon pretty brisk—the cats large and noisy—the monkeys I have not looked to since the cold weather, as they suffer by being brought up. Horses must be gay—get a ride as soon as weather serves. Deuced muggy still—an Italian winter is a sad thing, but all the other seasons are charming.

What is the reason that I have been, all my lifetime, more or less *ennuyé*? and that, if any thing, I am rather less so now than I was at twenty, as far as my recollection serves? I do not know how to answer this, but presume that it is constitutional,—as well as the waking in low spirits, which I have invariably done for many years. Temperance and exercise, which I have practiced at times, and for a long time together vigorously and violently, made little or no difference. Violent passions did;—when under their immediate influence—it is odd, but—I was in agitated, but *not* in depressed spirits.

[2] Luigi Vestri (1781–1841) was chosen by Alfieri to act the part of Gomez in *Filippo*. He played parts also in Goldoni's comedies in Venice.

A dose of salts has the effect of a temporary inebriation, like light champagne, upon me. But wine and spirits make me sullen and savage to ferocity—silent, however, and retiring, and not quarrelsome, if not spoken to. Swimming also raises my spirits,—but in general they are low, and get daily lower. That is *hopeless*: for I do not think I am so much *ennuyé* as I was at nineteen. The proof is, that then I must game, or drink, or be in motion of some kind, or I was miserable. At present, I can mope in quietness; and like being alone better than any company —except the lady's whom I serve. But I feel a something, which makes me think that, if I ever reach near to old age, like Swift, "I shall die at top"[3] first. Only I do not dread idiotism or madness so much as he did. On the contrary, I think some quieter stages of both must be preferable to much of what men think the possession of their senses.

January 7th, 1821, Sunday

Still rain—mist—snow—drizzle—and all the incalculable combinations of a climate, where heat and cold struggle for mastery. Read Spence, and turned over Roscoe,[1] to find a passage I have not found. Read the 4th vol. of W. Scott's second series of "Tales of my Landlord". Dined. Read the Lugano Gazette. Read—I forget what. At 8 went to conversazione. Found there the Countess Geltrude,[2] Betti V. and her husband, and others. Pretty black-eyed woman that—*only* twenty-two[3]—same age as Teresa, who is prettier, though.

The Count Pietro G[amba] took me aside to say that the Patriots have had notice from Forli (twenty miles off) that to-night the government and its party mean to strike a stroke—that the Cardinal here has had orders to make several arrests immediately, and that, in consequence, the Liberals are arming, and have posted patroles in the streets, to sound the alarm and give notice to fight for it.

He asked me "what should be done?" I answered, "Fight for it, rather than be taken in detail;" and offered, if any of them are in immediate apprehension of arrest, to receive them in my house

---

[3] Edward Young, in his *Conjectures on Original Composition* (1759) recorded that while he was walking with Swift near Dublin, the Dean "earnestly gazing upward at a noble elm, which in its uppermost branches was much withered, and decayed," pointed to it and said: "I shall be like that tree, I shall die at top."

[1] William Roscoe (1753–1831) published *The Life of Lorenzo de Medici, called the Magnificent* in 1796, and *The Life and Pontificate of Leo the Tenth* in 1805.

[2] Geltrude Vicari, Teresa's friend.

[3] Prothero has changed this to "nineteen".

(which is defensible), and to defend them, with my servants and themselves (we have arms and ammunition), as long as we can,—or to try to get them away under cloud of night. On going home, I offered him the pistols which I had about me—but he refused, but said he would come off to me in case of accidents.

It wants half an hour of midnight, and rains;—as Gibbet says, "a fine night for their enterprise—dark as hell, and blows like the devil."[4] If the row don't happen *now*, it must soon. I thought that their system of shooting people would soon produce a reaction—and now it seems coming. I will do what I can in the way of combat, though a little out of exercise. The cause is a good one.

Turned over and over half a score of books for the passage in question, and can't find it. Expect to hear the drum and the musquetry momently (for they swear to resist, and are right,)—but I hear nothing, as yet, save the plash of the rain and the gusts of the wind at intervals. Don't like to go to bed, because I hate to be waked, and would rather sit up for the row, if there is to be one.

Mended the fire—have got the arms—and a book or two, which I shall turn over. I know little of their numbers, but think the Carbonari strong enough to beat the troops, even here. With twenty men this house might be defended for twenty-four hours against any force to be brought against it, *now* in this place, for the same time; and, in such a time, the country would have notice, and would rise,—if ever they *will* rise, of which there is some doubt. In the mean time, I may as well read as do any thing else, being alone.

January 8th, 1821, Monday

Rose, and found Count P.G. in my apartments. Sent away the servant. Told me that, according to the best information, the Government had not issued orders for the arrests apprehended; that the attack in Forli had not taken place (as expected) by the Sanfedisti—opponents of the Carbonari or Liberals—and that, as yet, they are still in apprehension only. Asked me for some arms of a better sort, which I gave him. Settled that, in case of a row, the Liberals were to assemble *here* (with me), and that he had given the word to Vincenzo G. and others of the *Chiefs* for that purpose. He himself and father are going to the chase in the forest; but V[incenzo]. G[allina]. is to come to me,

---

[4] Farquhar, *The Beaux' Strategem*, Act. IV, scene 2.

and an express to be sent off to him, P. G., if any thing occurs. Concerted operations. They are to seize—but no matter.

I advised them to attack in detail, and in different parties, in different *places* (though at the *same* time), so as to divide the attention of the troops, who, though few, yet being disciplined, would beat any body of people (not trained) in a regular fight—unless dispersed in small parties, and distracted with different assaults. Offered to let them assemble here if they choose. It is a strongish post—narrow street, commanded from within—and tenable walls. * * * * * *

Dined. Tried on a new coat. Letter to Murray, with corrections of Bacon's Apophthegms and an epigram—the *latter not* for publication. At eight went to Teresa, Countess G. * * * * * * At nine and a half came in Il Conte P. and Count P. G. Talked of a certain proclamation lately issued. Count R. G. had been with * * (the * *), to sound him about the arrests. He, * *,[1] is a *trimmer*, and deals, at present, his cards with both hands. If he don't mind, they'll be full. * * pretends (*I* doubt him—*they* don't—we shall see) that there is no such order, and seems staggered by the immense exertions of the Neapolitans, and the fierce spirit of the Liberals here. The truth is, that * * cares for little but his place (which is a good one), and wishes to play pretty with both parties. He has changed his mind thirty times these last three moons, to my knowledge, for he corresponds with me. But he is not a bloody fellow—only an avaricious one.

It seems that, just at this moment (as Lydia Languish says) "there will be no elopement after all."[2] I wish that I had known as much last night—or, rather, this morning—I should have gone to bed two hours earlier. And yet I ought not to complain; for, though it is a sirocco, and heavy rain, I have not *yawned* for these two days.

Came home—read History of Greece—before dinner had read Walter Scott's Rob Roy. Wrote address to the letter in answer to Alessio del Pinto, who has thanked me for helping his brother (the late Commandant, murdered here last month) in his last moments. Have told him I only did a duty of humanity—as is true. The brother lives at Rome.

Mended the fire with some "sgobole" (a Romagnuole word) and gave the falcon some water. Drank some Seltzer-water. Mem.— received to-day a print, or etching, of the story of Ugolino, by an Italian painter—different, of course, from Sir Joshua Reynolds's, and I

---

[1] Count Giuseppe Alborghetti, the Secretary to the Papal Legate in Ravenna.
[2] Sheridan, *The Rivals*, Act. IV, scene 2.

think (as far as recollection goes) *no worse*, for Reynolds's is not good in history. Tore a button in my new coat.

I wonder what figure these Italians will make in a regular row. I sometimes think that, like the Irishman's gun (somebody had sold him a crooked one), they will only do for "shooting round a corner;" at least, this sort of shooting has been the late tenor of their exploits. And yet, there are materials in this people, and a noble energy, if well directed. But who is to direct them? No matter. Out of such times heroes spring. Difficulties are the hot-beds of high spirits, and Freedom the mother of the few virtues incident to human nature.

Tuesday, January 9th, 1821

Rose—the day fine. Ordered the horses; but Lega (my *secretary*, an Italianism for steward or chief servant) coming to tell me that the painter had finished the work in fresco for the room he has been employed on lately, I went to see it before I set out. The painter has not copied badly the prints from Titian, &c., considering all things.

* * * * * * * * * * * * * *

Dined. Read Johnson's "Vanity of Human Wishes,"—all the examples and mode of giving them sublime, as well as the latter part, with the exception of an occasional couplet. I do not so much admire the opening. I remember an observation of Sharpe's[1] (the *Conversationist*, as he was called in London, and a very clever man) that the first line of this poem was superfluous, and that Pope (the best of poets, *I* think,) would have begun at once, only changing the punctuation—

"Survey mankind from China to Peru!"

The former line, "Let observation." &c., is certainly heavy and useless. But 'tis a grand poem—and *so true!*—true as the 10th of Juvenal himself. The lapse of ages *changes* all things—time—language—the earth—the bounds of the sea—the stars of the sky, and every thing "about, around, and underneath"[2] man, *except man himself*, who has always been, and always will be, an unlucky rascal. The infinite variety of lives conduct but to death, and the infinity of wishes lead but to

[1] Richard Sharp (1759–1835), a prominent figure in political, social and literary life in London, knew most of the interesting men of his day and talked so well about them that he gained the name of "Conversation Sharp".

[2] cf. Milton, *Il Penseroso:* "Above, about, or underneath".

disappointment. All the discoveries which have yet been made have multiplied little but existence. An extirpated disease is succeeded by some new pestilence; and a discovered world has brought little to the old one, except the p[ox]—first and freedom afterwards—the *latter* a fine thing, particularly as they gave it to Europe in exchange for slavery. But it is doubtful whether "the Sovereigns" would not think the *first* the best present of the two to their subjects.

At eight went out—heard some news. They say the King of Naples has declared, by couriers from Florence, to the *Powers* (as they call now those wretches with crowns) that his Constitution was compulsive, &c., &c., and that the Austrian barbarians are placed again on *war* pay, and will march. Let them—"they come like sacrifices in their trim,"[3] the hounds of hell! Let it still be a hope to see their bones piled like those of the human dogs at Morat,[4] in Switzerland, which I have seen.

Heard some music. At nine the usual visitors—news, *war*, or rumours of war. Consulted with P. G., &c., &c. They mean to *insurrect* here, and are to honour me with a call thereupon. I shall not fall back; though I don't think them in force or heart sufficient to make much of it. But, *onward!*—it is now the time to act, and what signifies *self*, if a single spark of that which would be worthy of the past can be bequeathed unquenchedly to the future? It is not one man, nor a million, but the *spirit* of liberty which must be spread. The waves which dash upon the shore are, one by one, broken, but yet the *ocean* conquers, nevertheless. It overwhelms the Armada, it wears the rock, and, if the *Neptunians* are to be believed, it has not only destroyed, but made a world. In like manner, whatever the sacrifice of individuals, the great cause will gather strength, sweep down what is rugged, and fertilize (for *sea-weed* is *manure*) what is cultivable. And so, the mere selfish calculation ought never to be made on such occasions; and, at present, it shall not be computed by me. I was never a good arithmetician of chances, and shall not commence now.

January 10th, 1821

Day fine—rained only in the morning. Looked over accounts. Read Campbell's Poets[1]—marked errors of Tom (the author) for correction.

[3] *Henry IV*, Part I, Act IV, scene 1.
[4] Byron recovered some bones from the field of Morat near Avenches where the Swiss defeated the Burgundians in the fifteenth century. See Vol. 5, p. 78.
[1] Campbell's *Specimens of the British Poets* (9 vols., 1819) was prefixed by an *Essay on English Poetry*.

Dined—went out—music—Tyrolese air, with variations. Sustained the cause of the original simple air against the variations of the Italian school. * * * * * * *

Politics somewhat tempestuous, and cloudier daily. To-morrow being foreign post-day, probably something more will be known.

Came home—read. Corrected Tom Campbell's slips of the pen. A good work, though—style affected—but his defence of Pope is glorious. To be sure, it is his *own cause* too,—but no matter, it is very good, and does him great credit.

Midnight

I have been turning over different *Lives* of the Poets. I rarely read their works, unless an occasional flight over the classical ones, Pope, Dryden, Johnson, Gray, and those who approach them nearest (I leave the *rant* of the rest to the *cant* of the day), and—I had made several reflections, but I feel sleepy, and may as well go to bed.

January 11th, 1821

Read the letters. Corrected the tragedy and the "Hints from Horace". Dined, and got into better spirits.—Went out—returned—finished letters, five in number. Read Poets, and an anecdote in Spence.

Al[borghett]i writes to me that the Pope, and Duke of Tuscany, and King of Sardinia, have also been called to Congress; but the Pope will only deal there by proxy. So the interests of millions are in the hands of about twenty coxcombs, at a place called Leibach![1]

I should almost regret that my own affairs went well, when those of nations are in peril. If the interests of mankind could be essentially bettered (particularly of these oppressed Italians), I should not so much mind my own "sma' peculiar". God grant us all better times, or more philosophy.

In reading, I have just chanced upon an expression of Tom Campbell's;—speaking of Collins, he says that "no reader cares any more about the *characteristic manners* of his Eclogues than about the authenticity of the tale of Troy". 'Tis false—we *do* care about "the authenticity of the tale of Troy". I have stood upon that plain *daily*, for more than a month, in 1810; and, if any thing diminished my pleasure, it was

[1] See Diary, Jan. 4, 1821, note 5.

21

that the blackguard Bryant[2] had impugned its veracity. It is true I read "Homer Travestied"[3] (the first twelve books), because Hobhouse and others bored me with their learned localities, and I love quizzing. But I still venerated the grand original as the truth of *history* (in the material *facts*) and of *place*. Otherwise, it would have given me no delight. Who will persuade me, when I reclined upon a mighty tomb, that it did not contain a hero?—its very magnitude proved this. Men do not labour over the ignoble and petty dead—and why should not the *dead* be *Homer's* dead? The secret of Tom Campbell's defence of *inaccuracy* in costume and description is, that his Gertrude,[4] &c., has no more locality in common with Pennsylvania than with Penmanmaur. It is notoriously full of grossly false scenery, as all Americans declare, though they praise parts of the Poem. It is thus that self-love for ever creeps out, like a snake, to sting anything which happens, even accidentally, to stumble upon it.

January 12th, 1821

The weather still so humid and impracticable, that London, in its most oppressive fogs, were a summer-bower to this mist and sirocco, which now has lasted (but with one day's interval), chequered with snow or heavy rain only, since the 30th of December, 1820. It is so far lucky that I have a literary turn;—but it is very tiresome not to be able to stir out, in comfort, on any horse but Pegasus, for so many days. The roads are even worse than the weather, by the long splashing, and the heavy soil, and the growth of the waters.

Read the Poets—English, that is to say—out of Campbell's edition. There is a good deal of taffeta in some of Tom's prefatory phrases, but his work is good as a whole. I like him best, though, in his own poetry.

Murray writes that they want to act the Tragedy of Marino Faliero;—more fools they, it was written for the closet. I have protested against this piece of usurpation, (which, it seems, is legal for managers over any printed work, against the author's will) and I

---

[2] Jacob Bryant, *Dissertation concerning the war of Troy, and the expedition of the Grecians, as described by Homer; showing that no such expedition was ever undertaken, and that no such city of Phrigia existed*, 1796. Byron protested against Bryant's view in *Don Juan*, Canto IV, stanza 101.

[3] *Homer Travestie; Being a new translation of that great poet* was published anonymously in 1720. A third edition with the title *A Burlesque Translation of Homer* appeared with the name of the author, T. Bridges, in 1770.

[4] Campbell's *Gertrude of Wyoming* was published in 1809.

hope they will not attempt it. Why don't they bring out some of the numberless aspirants for theatrical celebrity, now encumbering their shelves, instead of lugging me out of the library? I have written a fierce protest against any such attempt; but I still would hope that it will not be necessary, and that they will see, at once, that it is not intended for the stage. It is too regular—the time, twenty-four hours —the change of place not frequent—nothing *melo*dramatic—no surprises, no starts, nor trap-doors, nor opportunities "for tossing their heads and kicking their heels"—and no *love*—the grand ingredient of a modern play.

I have found out the seal cut on Murray's letter. It is meant for Walter Scott—or Sir Walter—he is the first poet knighted since *Sir* Richard Blackmore. But it does not do him justice. Scott's—particularly when he recites—is a very intelligent countenance, and this seal says nothing.

Scott is certainly the most wonderful writer of the day. His novels are a new literature in themselves, and his poetry as good as any—if not better (only on an erroneous system)—and only ceased to be so popular, because the vulgar learned were tired of hearing "Aristides called the Just", and Scott the Best, and ostracised him.

I like him, too, for his manliness of character, for the extreme pleasantness of his conversation, and his good-nature towards myself, personally. May he prosper!—for he deserves it. I know no reading to which I fall with such alacrity as a work of W. Scott's. I shall give the seal, with his bust on it, to Madame la Comtesse G. this evening, who will be curious to have the effigies of a man so celebrated.

How strange are my thoughts!—The reading of the song of Milton, "Sabrina fair"[1] has brought back upon me—I know not how or why— the happiest, perhaps, days of my life (always excepting, here and there, a Harrow holiday in the two latter summers of my stay there) when living at Cambridge with Edward Noel Long,[2] afterwards of the Guards,—who, after having served honourably in the expedition to Copenhagen (of which two or three thousand scoundrels yet survive in plight and pay), was drowned early in 1809, on his passage to Lisbon with his regiment in the St. George transport, which was run foul of, in the night, by another transport. We were rival swimmers— fond of riding—reading—and of conviviality. We had been at Harrow

---

[1] *Comus*, line 859 ff.
[2] Long was at Harrow and Cambridge with Byron. He is the "Cleon" of "Childish Reflections" and the subject of a separate poem, "To Edward Noel Long, Esq.".

together; but—*there*, at least—his was a less boisterous spirit than mine. I was always cricketing—rebelling—fighting—*rowing* (from *row*, not *boat*-rowing, a different practice), and in all manner of mischiefs; while he was more sedate and polished. At Cambridge—both of Trinity—my spirit rather softened, or his roughened, for we became very great friends. The description of Sabrina's seat reminds me of our rival feats in *diving*. Though Cam's is not a very "translucent wave," it was fourteen feet deep, where we used to dive for, and pick up—having thrown them in on purpose—plates, eggs, and even shillings. I remember, in particular, there was the stump of a tree (at least ten or twelve feet deep) in the bed of the river, in a spot where we bathed most commonly, round which I used to cling, and "wonder how the devil I came there".[3]

Our evenings we passed in music (he was musical, and played on more than one instrument, flute and violoncello), in which I was audience; and I think that our chief beverage was soda-water. In the day we rode, bathed, and lounged, reading occasionally. I remember our buying, with vast alacrity, Moore's new quarto[4] (in 1806), and reading it together in the evenings.

We only passed the summer together;—Long had gone into the Guards during the year I passed in Notts, away from college. *His* friendship, and a violent, though *pure*, love and passion[5]—which held me at the same period—were the then romance of the most romantic period of my life.

* * * * * * * * * * * * * * * *

I remember that, in the spring of 1809, H[obhouse] laughed at my being distressed at Long's death, and amused himself with making epigrams upon his name, which was susceptible of a pun—*Long, short*, &c. But three years after, he had ample leisure to repent it, when our mutual friend, and his, H[obhouse]'s particular friend, Charles Matthews, was drowned also, and he, himself, was as much affected by a similar calamity. But *I* did not pay him back in puns and epigrams, for I valued Matthews too much, myself, to do so; and, even if I had not, I should have respected his griefs.

---

[3] cf. Pope, Epistle to Dr. Arbuthnot (line 172): "But wonder how the devil they got there."

[4] *Epistles, Odes, and other Poems* (1806).

[5] An obvious reference to his attachment to John Edleston, the Cambridge chorister. See Marchand, I, 107–108. The asterisks indicate that Byron wrote more of this attachment in his journal, but Moore omitted it.

Long's father wrote to me to write his son's epitaph. I promised—but I had not the heart to complete it. He was such a good, amiable being as rarely remains long in this world; with talent and accomplishments, too, to make him the more regretted. Yet, although a cheerful companion, he had strange melancholy thoughts sometimes. I remember once that we were going to his uncle's, I think—I went to accompany him to the door merely, in some Upper or Lower Grosvenor or Brook Street, I forget which, but it was in a street leading out of some square,—he told me that, the night before, he "had taken up a pistol—not knowing or examining whether it was loaded or no—and had snapped it at his head, leaving it to chance whether it might not be charged." The letter, too, which he wrote me on leaving college to join the Guards, was as melancholy in its tenour as it could well be on such an occasion. But he showed nothing of this in his deportment, being mild and gentle;—and yet with much turn for the ludicrous in his disposition. We were both much attached to Harrow, and sometimes made excursions there together from London to revive our schoolboy recollections.

Midnight

Read the Italian translation by Guido Sorelli of the German Grillparzer[6]—a devil of a name, to be sure, for posterity; but they *must* learn to pronounce it. With all the allowance for a *translation*, and above all, an *Italian* translation (they are the very worst of translators, except from the Classics—Annibale Caro,[7] for instance—and *there*, the bastardy of their language helps them, as, by way of *looking legitimate*, they ape their fathers' tongue)—but with every allowance for such a disadvantage, the tragedy of *Sappho* is superb and sublime! There is no denying it. The man has done a great thing in writing that play. And *who is he*? I know him not; but *ages will*. 'Tis a high intellect.

I must premise, however, that I have read *nothing* of Adolph Müllner's[8] (the author of "Guilt"), and much less of Goëthe, and Schiller, and Wieland, than I could wish. I only know them through the medium of English, French, and Italian translations. Of the *real*

---

[6] Franz Grillparzer (1791–1872), a German poet born in Vienna, published his *Sappho* in 1819 and in the same year appeared Guido Sorelli's *versione italiana*.

[7] Annibale Caro (1507–1566) translated the *Æneid* into blank verse (published at Venice in 1581).

[8] Adolf Müllner (1774–1829) published *Die Schuld* in 1812. It was one of the "Fate Tragedies" of the German Romantic School.

language I know absolutely nothing,—except oaths learned from postillions and officers in a squabble. I can *swear* in German potently, when I like—"Sacrament—Verfluchter—Hundsfott"—and so forth; but I have little of their less energetic conversation.

I like, however, their women, (I was once *so desperately* in love with a German woman, Constance,)[9] and all that I have read, translated, of their writings, and all that I have seen on the Rhine of their country and people—all, except the Austrians, whom I abhor, loathe, and—I cannot find words for my hate of them, and should be sorry to find deeds correspondent to my hate; for I abhor cruelty more than I abhor the Austrians—except on an impulse, and then I am savage—but not deliberately so.

Grillparzer is grand—antique—*not so simple* as the ancients, but very simple for a modern—too Madame de Stael-*ish*, now and then—but altogether a great and goodly writer.

January 13th, 1821, Saturday

Sketched the outline and Drams. Pers. of an intended tragedy of Sardanapalus, which I have for some time meditated. Took the names from Diodorus Siculus, (I know the history of Sardanapalus, and have known it since I was twelve years old), and read over a passage in the ninth vol. octavo of Mitford's Greece, where he rather vindicates the memory of this last of the Assyrians.

Dined—news come—the *Powers* mean to war with the peoples. The intelligence seems positive—let it be so—they will be beaten in the end. The king-times are fast finishing. There will be blood shed like water, and tears like mist; but the peoples will conquer in the end. I shall not live to see it, but I foresee it.

I carried Teresa the Italian translation of Grillparzer's Sappho, which she promises to read. She quarrelled with me, because I said that love was *not the loftiest* theme for true tragedy; and, having the advantage of her native language, and natural female eloquence, she overcame my fewer arguments. I believe she was right. I must put more love into "Sardanapalus" than I intended. I speak, of course, *if* the times will allow me leisure. That *if* will hardly be a peace-maker.

---

[9] Constance Spencer Smith, with whom Byron fell in love at Malta in 1809.

Turned over Seneca's tragedies. Wrote the opening lines of the intended tragedy of Sardanapalus. Rode out some miles into the forest. Misty and rainy. Returned—dined—wrote some more of my tragedy.

Read Diodorus Siculus—turned over Seneca, and some other books. Wrote some more of the tragedy. Took a glass of grog. After having ridden hard in rainy weather, and scribbled, and scribbled again, the spirits (at least mine) need a little exhilaration, and I don't like laudanum now as I used to do. So I have mixed a glass of strong waters and single waters, which I shall now proceed to empty. Therefore and thereunto I conclude this day's diary.

The effect of all wines and spirits upon me is, however, strange. It *settles*, but it makes me gloomy—gloomy at the very moment of their effect, and not gay hardly ever. But it composes for a time, though sullenly.

Weather fine. Received visit. Rode out into the forest—fired pistols. Returned home—dined—dipped into a volume of Mitford's Greece—wrote part of a scene of "Sardanapalus". Went out—heard some music—heard some politics. More ministers from the other Italian powers gone to Congress. War seems certain—in that case, it will be a savage one. Talked over various important matters with one of the initiated. At ten and half returned home.

I have just thought of something odd. In the year 1814, Moore ("the poet", *par excellence*, and he deserves it) and I were going together, in the same carriage, to dine with Earl Grey, the Capo Politico of the remaining whigs. Murray, the magnificent (the illustrious publisher of that name), had just sent me a Java gazette—I know not why, or wherefore. Pulling it out, by way of curiosity, we found it to contain a dispute (the said Java gazette) on Moore's merits and mine. I think, if I had been there, that I could have saved them the trouble of disputing on the subject. But, there is *fame* for you at six and twenty! Alexander had conquered India at the same age; but I doubt if he was disputed about, or his conquests compared with those of Indian Bacchus, at Java.

It was a great fame to be named with Moore; greater to be compared with him; greatest—*pleasure*, at least—to be *with* him; and, surely, an odd coincidence, that we should be dining together while they were quarrelling about us beyond the equinoctial line.

Well, the same evening, I met Lawrence the painter, and heard one of Lord Grey's daughters (a fine, tall, spirit-looking girl, with much of the *patrician, thorough-bred look* of her father, which I dote upon) play on the harp, so modestly and ingenuously, that she *looked music.* Well, I would rather have had my talk with Lawrence (who talked delightfully) and heard the girl, than have had all the fame of Moore and me put together.

The only pleasure of fame is that it paves the way to pleasure; and the more intellectual our pleasure, the better for the pleasure and for us too. It was, however, agreeable to have heard our fame before dinner, and a girl's harp after.

January 16th, 1821

Read—rode—fired pistols—returned—dined—wrote—visited—heard music—talked nonsense—and went home.

Wrote part of a Tragedy—advanced in Act 1st with "all deliberate speed."[1] Bought a blanket. The weather is still muggy as a London May—mist, mizzle, the air replete with Scotticisms, which, though fine in the descriptions of Ossian, are somewhat tiresome in real, prosaic perspective. Politics still mysterious.

January 17th, 1821

Rode i' the forest—fired pistols—dined. Arrived a packet of books from England and Lombardy—English, Italian, French, and Latin. Read till eight—went out.

January 18th, 1821

To-day, the post arriving late, did not ride. Read letters—only two gazettes instead of twelve now due. Made Lega write to that negligent Galignani, and added a postscript. Dined.

At eight proposed to go out. Lega came in with a letter about a bill *unpaid* at Venice which I thought paid months ago. I flew into a

---

[1] *Merchant of Venice*, Act III, scene 4: "With all convenient speed."

paroxysm of rage, which almost made me faint. I have not been well ever since. I deserve it for being such a fool—but it *was* provoking—a set of scoundrels! It is, however, but five and twenty pounds.

January 19th, 1821

Rode. Winter's wind somewhat more unkind than ingratitude itself, though Shakespeare says otherwise.[1] At least, I am so much more accustomed to meet with ingratitude than the north wind, that I thought the latter the sharper of the two. I had met with both in the course of the twenty-four hours, so could judge.

Thought of a plan of education for my daughter Allegra, who ought to begin soon with her studies. Wrote a letter—afterwards a postscript. Rather in low spirits—certainly hippish—liver touched—will take a dose of salts.

I have been reading the Life, by himself and daughter, of Mr. R. L. Edgeworth,[2] the father of *the* Miss Edgeworth. It is altogether a great name. In 1813, I recollect to have met them in the fashionable world of London (of which I then formed an item, a fraction, the segment of a circle, the unit of a million, the nothing of something) in the assemblies of the hour, and at a breakfast of Sir Humphry and Lady Davy's, to which I was invited for the nonce. I had been the lion of 1812: Miss Edgeworth and Madame de Staël, with "the Cossack," towards the end of 1813, were the exhibitions of the succeeding year.

I thought Edgeworth a fine old fellow, of a clarety, elderly, red complexion, but active, brisk, and endless. He was seventy, but did not look fifty—no, nor forty-eight even. I had seen poor Fitzpatrick[3] not very long before—a man of pleasure, wit, eloquence, all things. He tottered—but still talked like a gentleman, though feebly. Edgeworth bounced about, and talked loud and long; but he seemed neither weakly nor decrepit, and hardly old.

He began by telling "that he had given Dr. Parr[4] a dressing, who had taken him for an Irish bogtrotter," &c., &c. Now I, who know Dr.

---

[1] *As You Like It*, Act II, scene 7.

[2] Richard Lovell Edgeworth (1744–1817) was the father of Maria Edgeworth, the Irish novelist. His *Memoirs*, completed by Maria, were published in 1820.

[3] General Richard Fitzpatrick (1747–1813), a politician and wit, was a lifelong intimate friend of Charles James Fox, and held various ministerial posts. He was a contributor to the *Rolliad*.

[4] Samuel Parr (1747–1825) known as the Whig Dr. Johnson, was a teacher and writer, noted for his conversation. He at one time became closely associated with the radical Joseph Priestley. Byron met him as an associate of Rogers and Moore.

Parr, and who know (*not* by experience—for I never should have presumed so far as to contend with him—but by hearing him *with* others, and *of* others) that it is not so easy a matter to "dress him," thought Mr. Edgeworth an assertor of what was not true. He could not have stood before Parr for an instant. For the rest, he seemed intelligent, vehement, vivacious, and full of life. He bids fair for a hundred years.

He was not much admired in London, and I remember a "ryghte merrie" and conceited jest which was rife among the gallants of the day,—viz. a paper had been presented for the *recall of Mrs. Siddons to the stage*, (she having lately taken leave, to the loss of ages,—for nothing ever was, or can be, like her), to which all men had been called to subscribe. Whereupon, Thomas Moore, of profane and poetical memory, did propose that a similar paper should be *sub*scribed and *circum*scribed "for the recall of Mr. Edgeworth to Ireland."[5]

The fact was—everybody cared more about *her*. She was a nice little unassuming "Jeanie Deans'-looking bodie," as we Scotch say—and, if not handsome, certainly not ill-looking. Her conversation was as quiet as herself. One would never have guessed she could write *her name*; whereas her father talked, *not* as if he could write nothing else, but as if nothing else was worth writing.

As for Mrs. Edgeworth,[6] I forget—except that I think she was the youngest of the party. Altogether, they were an excellent cage of the kind; and succeeded for two months, till the landing of Madame de Staël.

To turn from them to their works, I admire them; but they excite no feeling, and they leave no love—except for some Irish steward or postillion. However, the impression of intellect and prudence is profound—and may be useful.

January 20th, 1821

Rode—fired pistols. Read from Grimm's Correspondence. Dined—went out—heard music—returned—wrote a letter to the Lord Chamberlain to request him to prevent the theatres from representing the Doge, which the Italian papers say that they are going to act. This is pretty work—what! without asking my consent, and even in opposition to it!

[5] Moore disclaimed the *bon mot*.
[6] Edgeworth's fourth wife, née Beaufort.

Fine, clear frosty day—that is to say, an Italian frost, for their winters hardly get beyond snow; for which reason nobody knows how to skate (or skait)—a Dutch and English accomplishment. Rode out, as usual, and fired pistols. Good shooting—broke four common, and rather small, bottles, in four shots, at fourteen paces, with a common pair of pistols and indifferent powder. Almost as good *wafering* or shooting—considering the difference of powder and pistol,—as when, in 1809, 1810, 1811, 1812, 1813, 1814, it was my luck to split walking-sticks, wafers, half-crowns, shillings, and even the *eye* of a walking-stick, at twelve paces, with a single bullet—and all by *eye* and calculation; for my hand is not steady, and apt to change with the very weather. To the prowess which I here note, Joe Manton and others can bear testimony;—for the former taught, and the latter has seen me do, these feats.

Dined—visited—came home—read. Remarked on an anecdote in Grimm's Correspondence, which says that "Regnard[1] et la plûpart des poètes comiques étaient gens bilieux et mélancoliques; et que M. de Voltaire, qui est très gai, n'a jamais fait que des tragedies—et que la comedie gaie est le seul genre où il n'ait point réussi. C'est que celui qui rit et celui qui fait rire sont deux hommes fort differens."—Vol. VI.

At this moment I feel as bilious as the best comic writer of them all, (even as Regnard himself, the next to Moliere, who has written some of the best comedies in any language, and who is supposed to have committed suicide), and am not in spirits to continue my proposed tragedy of Sardanapalus, which I have, for some days, ceased to compose.

To-morrow is my birthday—that is to say, at twelve o' the clock, midnight, i.e. in twelve minutes, I shall have completed thirty and three years of age!!!—and I go to my bed with a heaviness of heart at having lived so long, and to so little purpose.

It is three minutes past twelve.—"'Tis the middle of the night by the castle clock,"[2] and I am now thirty-three!

> "Eheu, fugaces, Posthume, Posthume,
> Labuntur anni;"—[3]

[1] Jean François Regnard (1655–1709), a French writer of comedies, wrote both for the Italian and the French theatre.
[2] Coleridge, *Christabel*, Part I, line 1.
[3] Horace, *Carmina*, II, xiv, 1–2: "Ah me, Postumus, Postumus, the fleeting years are slipping by."

but I don't regret them so much for what I have done, as for what I *might* have done.

> Through life's road, so dim and dirty,
> I have dragg'd to three-and-thirty.
> What have these years left to me?
> Nothing—except thirty-three.

January 22d, 1821

1821.
Here lies
interred in the Eternity
of the Past,
from whence there is no
Resurrection
for the Days—whatever there may be
for the Dust—
the Thirty-Third Year
of an ill-spent Life,
Which, after
a lingering disease of many months
sunk into a lethargy,
and expired,
January 22d, 1821, A. D.
Leaving a successor
Inconsolable
for the very loss which
occasioned its
Existence.

January 23d, 1821

Fine day. Read—Rode—fired pistols, and returned. Dined—read. Went out at eight—made the usual visit. Heard of nothing but war,— "the cry is still, They come."[1] The Car[bonar]i seem to have no plan— nothing fixed among themselves, how, when, or what to do. In that case, they will make nothing of the project, so often postponed, and never put in action.

[1] *Macbeth*, Act V, scene 5.

Came home, and gave some necessary orders, in case of circumstances requiring a change of place. I shall act according to what may seem proper, when I hear decidedly what the Barbarians mean to do. At present, they are building a bridge of boats over the Po, which looks very warlike. A few days will probably show. I think of retiring towards Ancona, nearer the northern frontier; that is to say, if Teresa and her father are obliged to retire, which is most likely, as all the family are Liberals. If not, I shall stay. But my movements will depend upon the lady's wishes—for myself, it is much the same.

I am somewhat puzzled what to do with my little daughter, and my effects, which are of some quantity and value,—and neither of them [will] do in the seat of war, where I think of going. But there is an elderly lady who will take charge of *her*, and T. says that the Marchese C. will undertake to hold the chattels in safe keeping. Half the city are getting their affairs in marching trim. A pretty Carnival! The blackguards might as well have waited till Lent.

January 24th, 1821

Returned—met some masques in the Corso—"Vive la bagatelle!"[1]— the Germans are on the Po, the Barbarians at the gate, and their masters in council at Leybach (or whatever the eructation of the sound may syllable into a human pronunciation), and lo! they dance and sing, and make merry, "for to-morrow they may die." Who can say that the Arlequins are not right? Like the Lady Baussiere, and my old friend Burton—I "rode on."[2]

Dined—(damn this pen!)—beef tough—there is no beef in Italy worth a curse; unless a man could eat an old ox with the hide on, singed in the sun.

The principal persons in the events which may occur in a few days are gone out on a *shooting party*. If it were like a *"highland* hunting," a pretext of the chase for a grand re-union of counsellors and chiefs, it would be all very well. But it is nothing more or less than a real snivelling, popping, small-shot, water-hen waste of powder, ammunition, and shot, for their own special amusement:—a rare set of fellows for "a man to risk his neck with," as "Marishal Wells" says in the Black Dwarf.[3]

---

[1] See *Hints from Horace*, line 344: "Swift's motto 'Vive la bagatelle!'"
[2] "The Lady Baussiere rode on". *Tristram Shandy*, Book V, chap. 1.
[3] Scott's *The Black Dwarf* (first of the *Tales of My Landlord*, 1816, chap. 13).

If they gather,—"whilk is to be doubted,"—they will not muster a thousand men. The reason of this is, that the populace are not interested,—only the higher and middle orders. I wish that the peasantry *were*; they are a fine savage race of two-legged leopards. But the Bolognese won't—the Romagnuoles can't without them. Or, if they try—what then? They will try, and man can do no more—and, if he *would* but try his utmost, much might be done. The Dutch, for instance, against the Spaniards—*then*, the tyrants of Europe—since, the slaves—and, lately, the freedmen.

The year 1820 was not a fortunate one for the individual me, whatever it may be for the nations. I lost a lawsuit, after two decisions in my favour. The project of lending money on an Irish mortgage was finally rejected by my wife's trustee after a year's hope and trouble. The Rochdale lawsuit had endured fifteen years, and always prospered till I married; since which, every thing has gone wrong—with me at least.

In the same year, 1820, the Countess T. G. *nata* G[amb]a G[hisell]i, in despite of all I said and did to prevent it, *would* separate from her husband, Il Cavalier Commendatore G[uicciol]i, &c. &c. &c., and all on the account of "P. P. clerk of this parish."[4] The other little petty vexations of the year—overturns in carriages—the murder of people before one's door, and dying in one's beds—the cramp in swimming—colics—indigestions and bilious attacks, &c. &c. &c.—

> "Many small articles make up a sum,
> And hey ho for Caleb Quotem, oh!"[5]

January 25th, 1821

Received a letter from Lord S. O.,[1] state secretary of the Seven Islands—a fine fellow—clever—dished in England five years ago, and came abroad to retrench and to renew. He wrote from Ancona, in his way back to Corfu, on some matters of our own. He is son of the late Duke of L[eeds] by a second marriage. He wants me to go to Corfu. Why not?—perhaps I may, next spring.

Answered Murray's letter—read—lounged. Scrawled this addi-

4 Pope's *Memoirs of P. P. Clerk of this Parish.*
5 George Colman the Younger, *The Review, or the Wags of Windsor*, scene 4.
1 Lord Sidney Godolphin Osborne (1789–1861) was the son of the second wife of the Duke of Leeds whom the Duke married after divorcing Augusta Leigh's mother, the Marchioness of Carmarthen, who eloped with and later married Byron's father.

tional page of life's log-book. One day more is over of it, and of me;—but "which is best, life or death, the gods only know," as Socrates said to his judges, on the breaking up of the tribunal.[2] Two thousand years since that sage's declaration of ignorance have not enlightened us more upon this important point; for, according to the Christian dispensation, no one can know whether he is *sure* of salvation—even the most righteous—since a single slip of faith may throw him on his back, like a skaiter, while gliding smoothly to his paradise. Now, therefore, whatever the certainty of faith in the facts may be, the certainty of the individual as to his happiness or misery is no greater than it was under Jupiter.

It has been said that the immortality of the soul is a "grand peut-être"—[3] but still it is a *grand* one. Every body clings to it—the stupidest, and dullest, and wickedest of human bipeds is still persuaded that he is immortal.

January 26th, 1821

Fine day—a few mares' tails portending change, but the sky clear, upon the whole. Rode—fired pistols—good shooting. Coming back, met an old man. Charity—purchased a shilling's worth of salvation. If that was to be bought, I have given more to my fellow-creatures in this life—sometimes for *vice*, but, if not more *often*, at least more *considerably*, for virtue—than I now possess. I never in my life gave a mistress so much as I have sometimes given a poor man in honest distress;—but no matter. The scoundrels who have all along persecuted me (with the help of * * who has crowned their efforts) will triumph;—and, when justice is done to me, it will be when this hand that writes is as cold as the hearts which have stung me.

Returning, on the bridge near the mill, met an old woman. I asked her age—she said "Tre croci".[1] I asked my groom (though myself a decent Italian) what the devil *her* three crosses meant. He said, ninety years, and that she had five years more to boot!! I repeated the same three times—not to mistake—ninety-five years!!!—and she was yet rather active—*heard* my question, for she answered it—*saw* me, for

---

[2] In Plato's *Phaedo* (62) Socrates is quoted as saying that "at some times and to some persons it is better to die than to live".

[3] This was one of the apocryphal legends about the death-bed utterances of Rabelais: "La farce est jouée", "Je vais chercher un grand peut-être."

[1] A *croce* is ten years; *tre croce* would be thirty years (i.e., XXX). But it is suggested that what she said was *tre tre croce*, ninety years. Byron gave her a pension for the rest of her life.

she advanced towards me; and did not appear at all decrepit, though certainly touched with years. Told her to come to-morrow, and will examine her myself. I love phenomena. If she *is* ninety-five years old, she must recollect the Cardinal Alberoni,[2] who was legate here.

On dismounting, found Lieutenant E.[3] just arrived from Faenza. Invited him to dine with me to-morrow. Did *not* invite him for to-day, because there was a small *turbot*, (Friday, fast regularly and religiously,) which I wanted to eat all myself. Ate it.

Went out—found T. as usual—music. The gentlemen, who make revolutions and are gone on a shooting, are not yet returned. They don't return till Sunday—that is to say, they have been out for five days, buffooning, while the interests of a whole country are at stake, and even they themselves compromised.

It is a difficult part to play amongst such a set of assassins and blockheads—but, when the scum is skimmed off, or has boiled over, good may come of it. If this country could but be freed, what would be too great for the accomplishment of that desire? for the extinction of that Sigh of Ages? Let us hope. They have hoped these thousand years. The very revolvement of the chances may bring it—it is upon the dice.

If the Neapolitans have but a single Massaniello[4] amongst them, they will beat the bloody butchers of the crown and sabre. Holland, in worse circumstances, beat the Spains and Philips; America beat the English; Greece beat Xerxes; and France beat Europe, till she took a tyrant; South America beats her old vultures out of their nest; and, if these men are but firm in themselves, there is nothing to shake them from without.

January 28th, 1821

Lugano Gazette did not come. Letters from Venice. It appears that the Austrian brutes have seized my three or four pounds of English powder. The scoundrels!—I hope to pay them in *ball* for that powder. Rode out till twilight.

Pondered the subjects of four tragedies to be written (life and circumstances permitting) to wit, Sardanapalus, already begun, Cain, a metaphysical subject, something in the style of Manfred, but in five

[2] Cardinal Alberoni was legate in the Romagna from 1734 to 1739.

[3] Probably Giovanni Battista Elisei, with whom Byron used to ride in the Pineta during the summer of 1820.

[4] Tommaso Aniello (1623–1647) headed an uprising of the Neapolitans in 1647. But after seven days he had alienated his followers by his cruelty and was assassinated.

acts, perhaps, with the chorus; Francesca of Rimini, in five acts; and I am not sure that I would not try Tiberius. I think that I could extract a something, of *my* tragic, at least, out of the gloomy sequestration and old age of the tyrant—and even out of his sojourn at Caprea—by softening the *details*, and exhibiting the despair which must have led to those very vicious pleasures. For none but a powerful and gloomy mind overthrown would have had recourse to such solitary horrors,— being also, at the same time, *old*, and the master of the world.

Memoranda.

What is Poetry?—The feeling of a Former world and Future.

Thought Second.

Why, at the very height of desire and human pleasure,—worldly, social, amorous, ambitious, or even avaricious,—does there mingle a certain sense of doubt and sorrow—a fear of what is to come—a doubt of what *is*—a retrospect to the past, leading to a prognostication of the future? (The best of Prophets of the future is the Past.) Why is this? or these?—I know not, except that on a pinnacle we are most susceptible of giddiness, and that we never fear falling except from a precipice—the higher, the more awful, and the more sublime; and, therefore, I am not sure that Fear is not a pleasurable sensation; at least, *Hope* is; and *what Hope* is there without a deep leaven of Fear? and what sensation is so delightful as Hope? and, if it were not for Hope, where would the Future be?—in hell. It is useless to say *where* the Present is, for most of us know; and as for the Past, *what* predominates in memory?—*Hope baffled*. Ergo, in all human affairs, it is Hope—Hope—Hope. I allow sixteen minutes, though I never counted them, to any given or supposed possession. From whatever place we commence, we know where it all must end. And yet, what good is there in knowing it? It does not make men better or wiser. During the greatest horrors of the greatest plagues, (Athens and Florence, for example—see Thucydides and Machiavelli) men were more cruel and profligate than ever. It is all a mystery. I feel most things, but I know nothing, except

———— ———— ———— ———— ———— ———— ———— ————

———— ———— ———— ———— ———— ———— ———— ————

———— ———— ———— ———— ———— ———— ————   ————[1]

---

[1] "Thus marked, with impatient strokes of the pen, in the original". (Moore, II, 420.)

Thought for a Speech of Lucifer, in the Tragedy of Cain:—
Were *Death* an *evil*, would *I* let thee *live?*
Fool! live as I live—as thy father lives,
And thy son's sons shall live for evermore.

I have been reading W. F. S. * *[2] (brother to the other of the name) till now, and I can make out nothing. He evidently shows a great power of words, but there is nothing to be taken hold of. He is like Hazlitt, in English, who *talks pimples*—a red and white corruption rising up (in little imitation of mountains upon maps), but containing nothing, and discharging nothing, except their own humours.

I dislike him the worse (that is, S[chlegel],) because he always seems upon the verge of meaning; and, lo, he goes down like sunset, or melts like a rainbow, leaving a rather rich confusion,—to which, however, the above comparisons do too much honour.

Continuing to read Mr. F[rederick] S[chlegel]. He is not such a fool as I took him for, that is to say, when he speaks of the North. But still he speaks of things *all over the world* with a kind of authority that a philosopher would disdain, and a man of common sense, feeling, and knowledge of his own ignorance, would be ashamed of. The man is evidently wanting to make an impression, like his brother,—or like George in the Vicar of Wakefield, who found out that all the good things had been said already on the right side, and therefore "dressed up some paradoxes" upon the wrong side—ingenious, but false, as he himself says—to which "the learned world said nothing, nothing at all, sir."[3] The "learned world," however, *has* said something to the brothers S[chlegel].

It is high time to think of something else. What they say of the antiquities of the North is best.

January 29th, 1821

Yesterday, the woman of ninety-five years of age was with me. She said her eldest son (if now alive) would have been seventy. She is thin—short, but active—hears, and sees, and talks incessantly. Several

---

[2] Karl Wilhelm Friedrich Schlegel (1772–1829) published his *History of Literature* (lectures delivered at Vienna) in 1814. Byron was probably reading the translation published in Edinburgh in 1818.
[3] *Vicar of Wakefield*, Chap. 20.

teeth left—all in the lower jaw, and single front teeth. She is very deeply wrinkled, and has a sort of scattered grey beard over her chin, at least as long as my mustachios. Her head, in fact, resembles the drawing in crayons of Pope the poet's mother, which is in some editions of his works.

I forgot to ask her if she remembered Alberoni (legate here), but will ask her next time. Gave her a louis—ordered her a new suit of clothes, and put her upon a weekly pension. Till now, she had worked at gathering wood and pine-nuts in the forest—pretty work at ninety-five years old! She had a dozen children, of whom some are alive. Her name is Maria Montanari.

Met a company of the sect (a kind of Liberal Club) called the "Americani" in the forest, all armed, and singing, with all their might, in Romagnuole—"*Sem* tutti soldat' per la liberta" ("we are all soldiers for liberty"). They cheered me as I passed—I returned their salute, and rode on. This may show the spirit of Italy at present.

My to-day's journal consists of what I omitted yesterday. To-day was much as usual. Have rather a better opinion of the writings of the Schlegels than I had four-and-twenty hours ago; and will amend it still farther, if possible.

They say that the Piedmontese have at length risen—*ça ira*!

Read S[chlegel]. Of Dante he says that "at no time has the greatest and most national of all Italian poets ever been much the favourite of his countrymen." 'Tis false! There have been more editors and commentators (and imitators, ultimately) of Dante than of all their poets put together. *Not* a favourite! Why, they talk Dante—write Dante—and think and dream Dante at this moment (1821) to an excess, which would be ridiculous, but that he deserves it.

In the same style this German talks of gondolas on the Arno[1]— a precious fellow to dare to speak of Italy!

He says also that Dante's chief defect is a want, in a word, of gentle feelings. Of gentle feelings! and Francesca of Rimini—and the father's feelings in Ugolino—and Beatrice—and "La Pia!" Why, there is gentleness in Dante beyond all gentleness, when he is tender. It is true that, treating of the Christian Hades, or Hell, there is not much

---

[1] Speaking of Tasso, Schlegel says: "Individual parts and episodes of his poem [*Gerusalemme Liberata*] are frequently sung in the gondolas of the Arno and the Po." See Byron's lines in *Childe Harold* IV, stanza 3:

"In Venice Tasso's echoes are no more,
And silent rows the songless Gondolier"

and Hobhouse's note.

scope or site for gentleness—but who *but* Dante could have introduced any "gentleness" at all into *Hell?* Is there any in Milton's? No—and Dante's Heaven is all love, and glory, and majesty.

1 o'clock

I have found out, however, where the German is right—it is about the Vicar of Wakefield. "Of all romances in miniature (and, perhaps, this is the best shape in which Romance can appear) the *Vicar of Wakefield* is, I think, the most exquisite." He thinks!—he might be sure. But it is very well for a S[chlegel]. I feel sleepy, and may as well get me to bed. To-morrow there will be fine weather.

"Trust on, and think to-morrow will repay."[2]

January 30th, 1821

The Count P. G. this evening (by commission from the C[arbonar]i. transmitted to me the new *words* for the next six months. * * * and * * *. The new sacred word is * * *—the reply * * *—the rejoinder * * *. The former word (now changed) was * * *—there is also * * *—* * *.[1] Things seem fast coming to a crisis—*ça ira!*

We talked over various matters of moment and movement. These I omit;—if they come to any thing, they will speak for themselves. After these, we spoke of Kosciusko.[2] Count R. G. told me that he has seen the Polish officers in the Italian war burst into tears on hearing his name.

Something must be up in Piedmont—all the letters and papers are stopped. Nobody knows anything, and the Germans are concentrating near Mantua. Of the decision of Leybach nothing is known. This state of things cannot last long. The ferment in men's minds at present cannot be conceived without seeing it.

---

[2] Dryden, *Aureng-Zebe*, Act IV, scene 1.

[1] Moore says (II, 422): "In the original MS. these watchwords are blotted over so as to be illegible".

[2] Tadeusz Koskiusko (1746–1817), hero of the Polish nationalist uprising against the Russians in 1794, had won fame as a general in the American Revolution, where he was of great assistance to Washington at New York and Yorktown. He was wounded and taken prisoner by the Russians, and spent his last years in exile.

For several days I have not written any thing except a few answers to letters. In momentary expectation of an explosion of some kind, it is not easy to settle down to the desk for the higher kinds of composition. I *could* do it, to be sure, for, last summer, I wrote my drama in the very bustle of Madame la Contessa G's divorce, and all its process of accompaniments. At the same time, I also had the news of the loss of an important lawsuit in England. But these were only private and personal business; the present is of a different nature.

I suppose it is this, but have some suspicion that it may be laziness, which prevents me from writing; especially as Rochefoucault says that "laziness often masters them all"[1]—speaking of the *passions*. If this were true, it could hardly be said that "idleness is the root of all evil," since this is supposed to spring from the passions only: ergo, that which masters all the passions (laziness, to wit) would in so much be a good. Who knows?

Midnight

I have been reading Grimm's Correspondence. He repeats frequently, in speaking of a poet, or of a man of genius in any department, even in music, (Gretry,[2] for instance), that he must have "une ame qui se tourmente, un esprit violent". How far this may be true, I know not; but if it were, I should be a poet "per excellenza;" for I have always had "une ame", which not only tormented itself but every body else in contact with it; and an "esprit violent", which has almost left me without any "esprit" at all. As to defining what a poet *should* be, it is not worth while, for what are *they* worth? what have they done?

Grimm, however, is an excellent critic and literary historian. His Correspondence forms the annals of the literary part of that age of France, with much of her politics, and still more of her "way of life". He is as valuable, and far more entertaining than Muratori[3] or Tiraboschi[4]—I had almost said, than Ginguené[5]—but there we should pause. However, 't is a great man in its line.

---

[1] *Reflexions Morales*, 274.

[2] Grimm, *Correspondance*, ed. Tourneaux, Vol. VIII, Septembre, 1768.

[3] Ludovico Antonio Muratori (1672–1750) published *Rerum Italicarum præcipui ab Anno 500*, 29 vols., fol. 1723–51, at Milan.

[4] Geronimo Tiraboschi (1731–1794) published his *Storia della Letteratura Italiana*, 13 vols, quarto, 1772–1782, at Modena.

[5] See Diary, Jan. 6, 1821, note 1.

Monsieur St. Lambert[6] has,

> "Et lorsqu'à ses regards la lumière est ravie,
> Il n'a plus, en mourant, à perdre que la vie."

This is, word for word, Thomson's

> "And dying, all we can resign is breath,"[7]

without the smallest acknowledgment from the Lorrainer of a poet. M. St. Lambert is dead as a man, and (for any thing I know to the contrary) damned, as a poet, by this time. However, his Seasons have good things, and, it may be, some of his own.

February 2d, 1821

I have been considering what can be the reason why I always wake, at a certain hour in the morning, and always in very bad spirits—I may say, in actual despair and despondency, in all respects—even of that which pleased me over night. In about an hour or two, this goes off, and I compose either to sleep again, or, at least, to quiet. In England, five years ago, I had the same kind of hypochondria, but accompanied with so violent a thirst that I have drank as many as fifteen bottles of soda-water in one night, after going to bed, and been still thirsty—calculating, however, some lost from the bursting out and effervescence and overflowing of the soda-water, in drawing the corks, or striking off the necks of the bottles from mere thirsty impatience. At present, I have *not* the thirst; but the depression of spirits is no less violent.

I read in Edgeworth's Memoirs of something similar (except that his thirst expended itself on *small beer*) in the case of Sir F. B. Delaval; —but then he was, at least, twenty years older. What is it?—liver? In England, Le Man (the apothecary) cured me of the thirst in three days, and it had lasted as many years. I suppose that it is all hypochondria.

What I feel most growing upon me are laziness, and a disrelish more powerful than indifference. If I rouse, it is into fury. I presume that I shall end (if not earlier by accident, or some such termination) like

---

6 François, Marquis de St. Lambert (1716–1803), soldier, courtier, and writer, was associated with Helvetius and contributed to the *Encyclopédie*. He published his *Saisons* in 1769. The passage quoted is from "L'Automne", Chant troisième.
7 Thomson, "Verses occasioned by the death of Mr. Aikman".

Swift—"dying at top." I confess I do not contemplate this with so much horror as he apparently did for some years before it happened. But Swift had hardly *begun life* at the very period (thirty-three) when I feel quite an *old sort* of feel.

Oh! there is an organ playing in the street—a waltz, too! I must leave off to listen. They are playing a waltz which I have heard ten thousand times at the balls in London, between 1812 and 1815. Music is a strange thing.

February 5th, 1821

At last, "the kiln's in a low."[1] The Germans are ordered to march, and Italy is, for the ten thousandth time to become a field of battle. Last night the news came.

This afternoon—Count P. G. came to me to consult upon divers matters. We rode out together. They have sent off to the C. for orders. To-morrow the decision ought to arrive, and then something will be done. Returned—dined—read—went out—talked over matters. Made a purchase of some arms for the new inrolled Americani, who are all on tiptoe to march. Gave order for some *harness* and portmanteaus necessary for the horses.

Read some of Bowles's dispute about Pope, with all the replies and rejoinders. Perceive that my name has been lugged into the controversy, but have not time to state what I know of the subject. On some "piping day of peace"[2] it is probable that I may resume it.

February 9th, 1821

Before dinner wrote a little; also, before I rode out, Count P. G. called upon me, to let me know the result of the meeting of the C[arbonar]i at F[aenza] and at B[ologna] * * returned late last night. Every thing was combined under the idea that the Barbarians would pass the Po on the 15th inst. Instead of this, from some previous information or otherwise, they have hastened their march and actually passed two days ago; so that all that can be done at present in Romagna is, to stand on the alert and wait for the advance of the Neapolitans. Every thing was ready, and the Neapolitans had sent on their own

[1] Scott, *Rob Roy*, Chapter 20: "The kiln's on fire—she's a' in a lowe." [Scottish: flame, blaze.]
[2] *Richard III*, Act 1, scene 1.

instructions and intentions, all calculated for the *tenth* and *eleventh*, on which days a general rising was to take place, under the supposition that the Barbarians could not advance before the 15th.

As it is, they have but fifty or sixty thousand troops, a number with which they might as well attempt to conquer the world as secure Italy in its present state. The artillery marches *last*, and alone, and there is an idea of an attempt to cut part of them off. All this will much depend upon the first steps of the Neapolitans. *Here*, the public spirit is excellent, provided it be kept up. This will be seen by the event.

It is probable that Italy will be delivered from the Barbarians if the Neapolitans will but stand firm, and are united among themselves. *Here* they appear so.

February 10th, 1821

Day passed as usual—nothing new. Barbarians still in march—not well equipped, and, of course, not well received on their route. There is some talk of a commotion at Paris.

Rode out between four and six—finished my letter to Murray on Bowles's pamphlets—added postscript. Passed the evening as usual—out till eleven—and subsequently at home.

February 11th, 1821

Wrote—had a copy taken of an extract from Petrarch's Letters, with reference to the conspiracy of the Doge, M[arino] Faliero,[1] containing the poet's opinion of the matter. Heard a heavy firing of cannon towards Comacchio—the Barbarians rejoicing for their principal pig's birthday, which is to-morrow—or Saint day—I forget which. Received a ticket for the first ball to-morrow. Shall not go to the first, but intend going to the second, as also to the Veglioni.

February 13th, 1821

To-day read a little in Louis B.'s Hollande,[1] but have written nothing since the completion of the letter on the Pope controversy.

[1] Included as Note B at the end of *Marino Faliero*.
[1] *Documents Historiques, et Réflexions sur le Gouvernement de la Hollande*, 3 vols, by Louis Buonaparte, ex-King of Holland, was published in Paris in 1820.

Politics are quite misty for the present. The Barbarians still upon their march. It is not easy to divine what the Italians will now do.

Was elected yesterday "Socio" of the Carnival ball society. This is the fifth carnival that I have passed. In the four former, I racketed a good deal. In the present, I have been as sober as Lady Grace herself.

February 14th, 1821

Much as usual. Wrote, before riding out, part of a scene of "Sardanapalus" The first act nearly finished. The rest of the day and evening as before—partly without, in conversazione—partly at home.

Heard the particulars of the late fray at Russi, a town not far from this. It is exactly the fact of Roméo and Giulietta—*not* Roméo, as the Barbarian writes it. Two families of Contadini (peasants) are at feud. At a ball, the younger part of the families forget their quarrel, and dance together. An old man of one of them enters, and reproves the young men for dancing with the females of the opposite family. The male relatives of the latter resent this. Both parties rush home and arm themselves. They meet directly, by moonlight, in the public way, and fight it out. Three are killed on the spot, and six wounded, most of them dangerously,—pretty well for two families, methinks—and all *fact*, of the last week. Another assassination has taken place at Cesenna,—in all about *forty* in Romagna within the last three months. These people retain much of the middle ages.

February 15th, 1821

Last night finished the first act of Sardanapalus. To-night, or tomorrow, I ought to answer letters.

February 16th, 1821

Last night Il Conte P. G. sent a man with a bag full of bayonets, some muskets, and some hundreds of cartridges to my house, without apprizing me, though I had seen him not half an hour before. About ten days ago, when there was to be a rising here, the Liberals and my brethren C[arbonar]i asked me to purchase some arms for a certain few of our ragamuffins. I did so immediately, and ordered ammunition, etc., and they were armed accordingly. Well—the rising is prevented

45

by the Barbarians marching a week sooner than appointed; and an *order* is issued, and in force, by the Government, "that all persons having arms concealed, &c. &c., shall be liable to," &c. &c.—and what do my friends, the patriots, do two days afterwards? Why, they throw back upon my hands, and into my house, these very arms (without a word of warning previously) with which I had furnished them at their own request, and at my own peril and expense.

It was lucky that Lega was at home to receive them. If any of the servants had (except Tita and F[letcher] and Lega) they would have betrayed it immediately. In the mean time, if they are denounced, or discovered, I shall be in a scrape.

At nine went out—at eleven returned. Beat the crow for stealing the falcon's victuals. Read "Tales of my Landlord"—wrote a letter—and mixed a moderate beaker of water with other ingredients.

February 18th, 1821

The news are that the Neapolitans have broken a bridge, and slain four pontifical carabiniers, whilk carabiniers wished to oppose. Besides the disrespect to neutrality, it is a pity that the first blood shed in this German quarrel should be Italian. However, the war seems begun in good earnest: for, if the Neapolitans kill the Pope's carabiniers, they will not be more delicate towards the Barbarians. If it be even so, in a short time "there will be news o' thae craws," as Mrs. Alison Wilson says of Jenny Blane's "unco cockernony" in the *Tales of my Landlord*.[1]

In turning over Grimm's Correspondence to-day, I found a thought of Tom Moore's in a song of Maupertuis[2] to a female Laplander.

> "Et tous les lieux
> Ou sont ses yeux,
> Font la Zone brûlante."

This is Moore's,

> "And those eyes make my climate, wherever I roam."

But I am sure that Moore never saw it; for this was published in Grimm's Correspondence in 1813, and I knew Moore's by heart in 1812. There is also another, but an antithetical coincidence—

[1] Scott, *Old Mortality*, Chap. 5.
[2] Pierre Louis Moreau de Maupertuis (1698–1759), quoted in Grimm's *Correspondance*, Ed. Tourneaux, Vol. VII, pp. 180, 181.

"Le soleil luit,
Des jours sans nuit
Bientôt il nous destine;
Mais ces longs jours
Seront trop courts,
Passés pres de Christine."

This is the *thought reversed*, of the last stanza of the ballad on Charlotte Lynes, given in Miss Seward's Memoirs of Darwin, which is pretty—I quote from memory of these last fifteen years.

"For my first night I'll go
To those regions of snow,
Where the sun for six months never shines;
And think, even then
He too soon came again,
To disturb me with fair Charlotte Lynes."[3]

To-day I have had no communication with my Carbonari cronies; but, in the mean time, my lower apartments are full of their bayonets, fusils, cartridges, and what not. I suppose that they consider me as a depôt, to be sacrificed, in case of accidents. It is no great matter, supposing that Italy could be liberated, who or what is sacrificed. It is a grand object—the very *poetry* of politics. Only think—a free Italy!!! Why, there has been nothing like it since the days of Augustus. I reckon the times of Caesar (Julius) free; because the commotions left every body a side to take, and the parties were pretty equal at the set out. But, afterwards, it was all praetorian and legionary business—and since!—we shall see, or, at least, some will see, what card will turn up. It is best to hope, even of the hopeless. The Dutch did more than these fellows have to do, in the Seventy Years' War.

February 19th, 1821

Came home solus—very high wind—lightning—moonshine—solitary stragglers muffled in cloaks—women in mask—white houses—clouds hurrying over the sky, like spilt milk blown out of the pail—altogether very poetical. It is still blowing hard—the tiles flying, and the house rocking—rain splashing—lightning flashing—quite a fine Swiss Alpine evening, and the sea roaring in the distance.

Visited—conversazione. All the women frightened by the squall:

[3] Seward's *Memoirs of Dr. Darwin*, 72–74.

they *won't* go to the masquerade because it lightens—the pious reason!

Still blowing away. A[lborghetti] has sent me some news to-day. The war approaches nearer and nearer. Oh those scoundrel sovereigns! Let us but see them beaten—let the Neapolitans but have the pluck of the Dutch of old, or the Spaniards of now, or of the German protestants, the Scotch presbyterians, the Swiss under Tell, or the Greeks under Themistocles—*all* small and solitary nations (except the Spaniards and German Lutherans), and there is yet a resurrection for Italy, and a hope for the world.

February 20th, 1821

The news of the day are, that the Neapolitans are full of energy. The public spirit *here* is certainly well kept up. The "Americani" (a patriotic society here, an under branch of the "Carbonari") give a dinner in *The Forest* in a few days, and have invited me, as one of the C[arbonar]i. It is to be in *the Forest* of Boccacio's and Dryden's "Huntsman's Ghost"; and, even if I had not the same political feelings, (to say nothing of my old convivial turn, which every now and then revives), I would go as a poet, or, at least, as a lover of poetry. I shall expect to see the spectre of "Ostasio degli Onesti"[1] (Dryden has turned him into Guido Cavalcanti—an essentially different person, as may be found in Dante) come "thundering for his prey" in the midst of the festival. At any rate, whether he does or no, I will get as tipsy and patriotic as possible.

Within these few days I have read, but not written.

February 21st, 1821

As usual, rode—visited, &c. Business begins to thicken. The Pope has printed a declaration against the patriots, who, he says, meditate a rising. The consequence of all this will be, that, in a fortnight, the whole country will be up. The proclamation is not yet published, but printed ready for distribution. * * [Alborghetti] sent me a copy privately—a sign that he does not know what to think. When he wants

---

[1] Byron has confused the names of the characters in Boccaccio's *Decameron* (5th day, 8th story). Nastagio degli Onesti was in love with the daughter of Paolo Traversari. The spectral horseman in the story is Guido degli Anastagi. Dryden told the story in his way in "Theodore and Honoria".

to be well with the patriots, he sends to me some civil message or other.

For my own part, it seems to me, that nothing but the most decided success of the Barbarians can prevent a general and immediate rise of the whole nation.

February 23d, 1281

Almost ditto with yesterday—rode, &c.—visited—wrote nothing—read Roman History.

Had a curious letter from a fellow, who informs me that the Barbarians are ill-disposed towards me. He is probably a spy, or an imposter. But be it so, even as he says. They cannot bestow their hostility on one who loathes and execrates them more than I do, or who will oppose their views with more zeal, when the opportunity offers.

February 24th, 1821

Rode, &c. as usual. The secret intelligence arrived this morning from the frontier to the C[arbonar]i is as bad as possible. The *plan* has missed—the Chiefs are betrayed, military, as well as civil—and the Neapolitans not only have *not* moved, but have declared to the P[apal] government, and to the Barbarians, that they know nothing of the matter!!!

Thus the world goes; and thus the Italians are always lost for lack of union among themselves. What is to be done *here*, between the two fires, and cut off from the N[orther]n frontier, is not decided. My opinion was,—better to rise than be taken in detail; but how it will be settled now, I cannot tell. Messengers are despatched to the delegates of the other cities to learn their resolutions.

I always had an idea that it would be *bungled*; but was willing to hope, and am so still. Whatever I can do by money, means, or person, I will venture freely for their freedom; and have so repeated to them (some of the Chiefs here) half an hour ago. I have two thousand five hundred scudi, better than five hundred pounds, in the house, which I offered to begin with.

February 25th, 1821

Came home—my head aches—plenty of news, but too tiresome to set down. I have neither read nor written, nor thought, but led a

49

purely animal life all day. I mean to try to write a page or two before I go to bed. But, as Squire Sullen says, "My head aches consumedly: Scrub, bring me a dram!"[1] Drank some Imola wine, and some punch.

Log-book continued

I have been a day without continuing the log, because I could not find a blank book. At length I recollected this.

Rode, &c.—wrote down an additional stanza for the 5th canto of D[on] J[uan] which I had composed in bed this morning.[1] Visited *l'Amica*. We are invited, on the night of the Veglione (next Domenica) with the Marchesa Clelia Cavalli and the Countess Spinelli Rasponi. I promised to go. Last night there was a row at the ball, of which I am a "socio". The Vice-legate had the imprudent insolence to introduce *three* of his servants in masque—*without tickets*, too! and in spite of remonstrances. The consequence was, that the young men of the ball took it up, and were near throwing the Vice-legate out of the window. His servants, seeing the scene, withdrew, and he after them. His reverence Monsignore ought to know, that these are not times for the predominance of priests over decorum. Two minutes more, two steps farther, and the whole city would have been in arms, and the government driven out of it.

Such is the spirit of the day, and these fellows appear not to perceive it. As far as the simple fact went, the young men were right, servants being prohibited always at these festivals.

Yesterday wrote two notes on the "Bowles and Pope" controversy and sent them off to Murray by the post. The old woman whom I relieved in the forest (she is ninety-four years of age) brought me two bunches of violets. "Nam vita gaudet mortua floribus."[2] I was much pleased with the present. An Englishwoman would have presented a pair of worsted stockings, at least, in the month of February. Both excellent things; but the former are more elegant. The present, at this season, reminds one of Gray's stanza, omitted from his elegy:

[1] Farquhar, *The Beaux' Strategem*, Act. V. scene 4.
[1] Stanza 158 beginning:

> "Thus in the East they are extremely strict,
> And wedlock and a padlock mean the same."

[2] Abraham Cowley, *Epitaphium vivi Auctoris.*

> "Here scatter'd oft, the *earliest* of the year,
>   By hands unseen, are showers of violets found;
> The red-breast loves to build and warble here,
>   And little footsteps lightly print the ground."

As fine a stanza as any in his elegy. I wonder that he could have the heart to omit it.[3]

Last night I suffered horribly—from an indigestion, I believe. I *never* sup—that is, never at home. But, last night, I was prevailed upon by the Countess Gamba's persuasion, and the strenuous example of her brother, to swallow, at supper, a quantity of boiled cockles, and to dilute them, *not* reluctantly, with some Imola wine. When I came home, apprehensive of the consequences, I swallowed three or four glasses of spirits, which men (the venders) call brandy, rum, or Hollands, but which Gods would entitle spirits of wine, coloured or sugared. All was pretty well till I got to bed, when I became somewhat swollen, and considerably vertiginous. I got out, and mixing some soda-powders, drank them off. This brought on temporary relief. I returned to bed; but grew sick and sorry once and again. Took more soda-water. At last I fell into a dreary sleep. Woke, and was ill all day, till I had galloped a few miles. Query—was it the cockles, or what I took to correct them, that caused the commotion? I think both. I remarked in my illness the complete inertion, inaction, and destruction of my chief mental faculties. I tried to rouse them, and yet could not—and this is the *Soul*!!! I should believe that it was married to the body, if they did not sympathise so much with each other. If the one rose, when the other fell, it would be a sign that they longed for the natural state of divorce. But as it is, they seem to draw together like post-horses.

Let us hope the best—it is the grand possession.

[TO CONTE GIUSEPPE ALBRIZZI] [*1821?*]

[In Countess Guiccioli's handwriting]

Egregio Sigr, Conte—Non potrei dirle quanto piacere m'abbiano recato la di Lei Lettera, e la di Lei Poesia; perchè mi fanno fede della memoria ch'ella conserva per me di dover sentire sommo diletto della lettura de' di Lei versi.—Solo mi duole che ella me n'abbia tenuto così lungo tempo privo; e però nel rendergliene le più distinte grazie, la

---

[3] Printed in some of the early editions.

prego a non volermi d'ora innanzi più ritardare un simile piacere, per un riguardo che a Lei non conviene punto, sebbene aggiunga pregio alle rare parti che l'adornano.—Ardisco anche dice che io non sono affatto in degno di ricevere codesto favore da Lei; non già per i sentimenti di stima che io ho espressi ne' miei ultimi scritti a di Lei riguarda; e che la sola di Lei cortesia poteva prendere in considerazione; i quali non sono che una debole espressione di ciò che io sento, e che dee[deve] sentire ognuno che la conosce—ma sebbene per la sincera Amicizia che io conservo per Lei—e colla quale ho il bene di dirmi—

devo[ti]ssimo obb[ligatissi]mo Servo ed Amico

L B

[TRANSLATION]   [1821?]

Dear Signor Conte—I cannot tell you how much pleasure your letter and your poetry have brought me; since they are evidence of the memory you preserve of me, and because I must have the greatest delight in reading your verses.—I only regret that you have so long deprived me of them; and on that account in giving you the kindest thanks, I beg of you not to withhold from me a similar pleasure for a consideration that does not apply to you at all, although it may add merit to the exceptional parts which it adorns.—I also dare say that I am not entirely unworthy of receiving this kindness from you; certainly not for the sentiments of esteem that I have expressed in my latest writings with regard to you[1]; and that only your kindness could have taken into consideration; which are just a feeble expression of what I feel, and which everyone must feel who knows you—but truly for the sincere friendship that I cherish for you—and with which I have the honour to declare myself

Your most devoted and obliged Servant and Friend

L B[2]

---

[1] This suggests that the letter is addressed to Count Giuseppe Albrizzi, to whom he had referred in a note to *Marino Faliero*. See May 25, 1821, to Hoppner, note 1.

[2] The autograph signature is in Byron's hand. The letter is translated by Ricki B. Herzfeld of the Carl H. Pforzheimer Library.

You say that the play[1] pleases "beyond your &c. &c."—You now
see the good of *not* puffing before hand—if you had [praised] it too
much—it would not have done half so well—(*if* it does well even
now) the best way is to say little before hand—& let them find their
way fairly.——

I prefer *"New York"* to the "Sketch Book"[1] but the Public *won't*—
the humour is far too good & too dry for them—it is like Hudibras in
prose.—He must have meant to quiz the three presidents or at least
two—Jefferson & *Madison*—one of them had a wooden leg like Peter
Stuyvesant.[2]—Why does a *note* in the Q[uarterl]y represent *Galileo* as
depreciating *Ariosto*?[3] on the contrary *Galileo* wrote the strongest &
best criticism ever composed against *tasso*—See Ginguiné & Serassi.[4]
—The note is from *Spence*.

Sculpture the noblest of the arts[1] because the noblest imitation of
Man's own nature with a view to perfection—being a higher resemblance of man so approaching in it's ideal to God who distantly made
him in his *own* image—that the Jehovah of the Jews forbade the wor-
ship of Images—because he was "a jealous God"—that is jealous of
man's embodied conception of deity.——

---

[1] *Marino Faliero.*
[1] Washington Irving's burlesque of the old Dutch settlers, *A History of New
York by Diedrich Knickerbocker*, appeared in 1809. His *Sketch-Book* was published
by Murray in 1819.
[2] Byron was misinformed. No American president had a wooden leg. Perhaps
he was thinking of Gouverneur Morris, of the illustrious New York family, who
had a leg amputated after a coach accident and thereafter used a wooden leg.
[3] *Quarterly Review*, Vol. XXIII, p. 408 (July, 1820) in a review of Joseph
Spence's *Anecdotes, Observations, and Characters of Books and Men.* . . .
[4] *Vita di Torquato Tasso*, by Pier Antonio Serassi, Roma, 1785; reprinted in
Bergamo, 1790. For Ginguené see Diary, Jan. 6, 1821, note 1.
[1] This fragment was possibly intended for Byron's first letter on Bowles's
"Strictures on the Life and Writings of Pope". In commenting on the phrase
"shapeless sculpture" in Gray's *Elegy*, he there says: "Of sculpture in general, it
may be observed, that it is more poetical than nature itself. . . ."

Your entering into my project for the Memoir is pleasant to me. But I doubt (contrary to my dear Mad Mac F * *,[1] whom I always loved, and always shall—not only because I really *did* feel attached to her *personally*, but because she and about a dozen others of that sex were all who stuck by me in the grand conflict of 1815 [sic])—but I doubt, I say, whether the Memoir could appear in my lifetime;—and, indeed, I had rather it did not; for a man always *looks dead* after his Life has appeared, and I should certes not survive the appearance of mine. The first part I cannot consent to alter, even although Mad[ame] de S[taël]'s opinion of B[enjamin] C[onstant], and my remarks upon Lady C.'s beauty[2] (which is surely great, and I suppose that I have said so—at least, I ought) should go down to our grandchildren in unsophisticated nakedness.

As to Madame de S[taël], I am by no means bound to be her beads-man—she was always more civil to me in person than during my absence. Our dear defunct friend, M[onk] L[ewis], who was too great a bore ever to lie, assured me upon his tiresome word of honour, that, at Florence, the said Madame de S[taël] was open-*mouthed* against me; and when asked, in *Switzerland*, *why* she changed her opinion, replied with laudable sincerity, that I had named her in a sonnet with Voltaire, Rousseau, &c. &c. and that she could not help it, through decency. Now, I have not forgotten this, but I have been generous,—as mine acquaintance, the late Captain Whitby, of the navy, used to say to his seamen (when "married to the gunner's daughter")—"two dozen and let you off easy." The "two dozen" were with the cat-o'-nine tails; the "let you off easy" was rather his own opinion than that of the patient.

My acquaintance with these terms and practices arises from my having been much conversant with ships of war and naval heroes in the years of my voyages in the Mediterranean. Whitby was in the gallant action off Lissa[3] in 1811. He was brave, but a disciplinarian. When he left his frigate, he left a *parrot*, which was taught by the

---

[1] Probably Madame de Flahault (née Mercer Elphinstone). See July 29, 1812, to Miss Mercer Elphinstone, note 1 (Vol. 2, p. 183.)

[2] Lady Charlemont, wife of the 2nd. Earl of Charlemont. Byron twice referred to her beauty in his diary of 1813 (Nov. 22 and Dec. 1; vol. 3, pp. 241, 228), and once in the second letter on Bowles.

[3] On March 13, 1811, a combined French and Italian squadron was defeated by the English squadron under Commodore Hoste. Whitby was in this action which took place off the island of Lissa on the Dalmatian coast.

crew the following sounds—(It must be remarked that Captain Whitby was the image of Fawcett[4] the actor, in voice, face, and figure, and that he squinted).

The Parrot *loquitur*.

"Whitby! Whitby! funny eye! funny eye! two dozen, and let you off easy. Oh you ——————!"

Now, if Madame de B. has a parrot, it had better be taught a French parody of the same sounds.

With regard to our purposed Journal, I will call it what you please, but it should be a newspaper, to make it *pay*. We can call it "The Harp," if you like—or any thing.

I feel exactly as you do about our "art,"[5] but it comes over me in a kind of rage every now and then, like * * * *, and then, if I don't write to empty my mind, I go mad. As to that regular, uninterpreted love of writing, which you describe in your friend, I do not understand it. I feel it as a torture, which I must get rid of, but never as a pleasure. On the contrary, I think composition a great pain.

I wish you to think seriously of the Journal scheme—for I am as serious as one can be, in this world, about any thing. As to matters here, they are high and mighty—but not for paper. It is much about the state of things betwixt Cain and Abel. There is, in fact, no law or government at all; and it is wonderful how well things go on without them. Excepting a few occasional murders, (every body killing whosoever he pleases, and being killed, in turn, by a friend, or relative, of the defunct), there is as quiet a society and as merry a Carnival as can be met with in a tour through Europe. There is nothing like habit in these things.

I shall remain here till May or June, and, unless "honour comes unlooked for,"[6] we may perhaps meet, in France or England, within the year.

Yours, &c.

Of course, I cannot explain to you existing circumstances, as they open all letters.

---

[4] John Fawcett (1768–1837) an actor who made his reputation in low comedy parts.

[5] Moore had written that he always felt about his art "as the French husband did when he found a man making love to his (the Frenchman's) wife:—'Comment, Monsieur,—sans y être obligé!' " (Moore, II, 434.)

[6] *Henry IV*, Part I, Act V, scene 3.

Will you set me right about your curst "Champs Elysées?"—are they "és" or "ées" for the adjective? I know nothing of French, being all Italian. Though I can read and understand French, I never attempt to speak it; for I hate it. From the second part of the Memoirs cut what you please.

[TO JOHN MURRAY]   *Ravenna—J[anuar]y 4th. 1821*

D[ea]r M[urra]y—I write to you in considerable surprize that since the first days of November—I have never had a line from you.— It is so incomprehensible—that I can only account for it—by supposing some accident.———I have written to you at least ten letters—to none of which I have had a word of answer—one of them was on yr own affairs—a proposal of Galignani—relative to your publications— which I referred to you (as was proper) for yr. own decision.——— Last week I sent (addressed to Mr. Kinnaird) two packets containing the 5th. Canto of D[on] J[uan]—I wish to know what you mean to do? anything or nothing.—Of the state of this country I can only say,— that besides the assassination of the Commandant on the 7th. (of which I gave you an account as I took him up, and he died in my house) that there have been *six* murders committed within twenty miles— three last night.—

yours very truly
[Scrawl]

P.S.—Have you gotten "the Hints" that I may alter parts & portions?—I just see by the papers of Galignani—that there is a new tragedy of great expectation by Barry Cornwall[1];—of what I have read of his works I liked the *dramatic* sketches—but thought his Sicilian Story—& Marcian Colonna in rhyme—quite spoilt by I know not what affectation of Wordsworth—and Hunt—and Moore—and Myself—all mixed up into a kind of Chaos.—I think him very likely to produce a good tragedy—if he keep to a natural style—and not play tricks to form Harlequinades for an audience.—As he (B[arry] C[ornwall] is not his *true* name) was a schoolfellow of mine I take more than common interest in his success—& shall be glad to hear of it speedily.—If I had been aware that he was in that line—I should have spoken of him in the preface to M[arino] F[aliero]—he will do a World's wonder if he produce a great tragedy.—I am however per-

---

[1] The pen name of Brian Waller Procter, who had been at Harrow with Byron.

suaded that this is not to be done by following the old dramatists—who are full of gross faults—pardoned only for the beauty of their language—but by writing naturally and *regularly*—& producing *regular* tragedies like the *Greeks*—but not in *imitation*—merely the outline of their conduct adapted to our own times and circumstances—and of course *no* chorus.—

You will laugh & say "why don't *you* do so?"—I have—you see tried a Sketch—in M[arino] F[aliero]—but many people think my talent *"essentially undramatic"*—and I am not at all clear that they are not right.—If M. F. don't fall—in the perusal—I shall perhaps try again—(but not for the Stage) and as I think that *love* is not the principal passion for tragedy—(& yet most of ours turns upon it)—you will not find me a popular writer.—Unless it is Love—*furious*—*criminal*—and *hapless*—it ought not to make a tragic subject—when it is melting & maudlin—it *does*—but it ought not to do—it is then for the Gallery—and second price boxes.——If you want to have a notion of what I am trying—take up a *translation* of any of the *Greek* tragedians. If I said the original—it would be an impudent presumption of mine—but the translations are so inferior to the originals that I think I may risk it.—Then Judge of the "simplicity of plot—&c."—and do not judge me by your mad old dramatists—which is like drinking Usquebaugh[2]—& then proving a fountain—yet after all I suppose that you do not mean that Spirits is a nobler element than a clear spring bubbling in the Sun—& this I take to be the difference between the Greeks & those turbid mountebanks—always excepting B. Jonson—who was a Scholar & a Classic.———Or take up a translation of Alfieri—& try the interest &c. of these my new attempts in the old line—by *him* in *English*.—And then tell me fairly your opinion.—But don't measure me by the [sic] YOUR OWN *old or new* tailor's yards.—Nothing so easy as intricate confusion of plot—and rant.——Mrs. Centlivre[3] in comedy has *ten times the bustle* of Congreve—but are they to [be] Compared? & yet she drove Congreve from the theatre.—

[TO DOUGLAS KINNAIRD]   *R[avenn]a J[anuar]y 4 o 1821*

My dear Douglas—Last week I sent to you *two packets* (for Murray) and a letter for you *yourself*.—It is now *two months* since I have had a

---

[2] Whisky.

[3] Mrs. Susanna Centlivre (1680?–1723) wrote 19 plays, the most popular of which, *The Busy Body* (1709) and *The Wonder* (1714), were greater stage successes in her day than Congreve's comedies.

line from Murray—never has he written since the second reading of the Queen's bill.—Now *this looks like shuffling*—it was his business to *write* at any rate—whatever he intends.——Pray—let me know something of him—& his—& you & yours—and anything of mine worth knowing.—I write in the greatest haste—with a *girl* in waiting —which I know will excuse me to you for the brevity of yrs.

[Scrawl]

P.S.—I have written to Murray——at least 10 times.—Can it be possible that either his letters—or mine have not arrived to their address?—Love to Cam &c. &c.

[TO JOHN MURRAY]   *Ravenna. January 6th. 1821*

On the "Braziers' Address[1] to be presented in *Armour* by the Company &c. &c." as stated in the Newspapers.

> It seems that the Braziers propose soon to pass
> An Address and to bear it themselves *all* in *brass*;
> A Superfluous Pageant, for by the Lord Harry!
> They'll *find* where they're going, much *more* than they carry.

or

> The Braziers it seems are determined to pass
> An Address and present it themselves All in brass,
>
> A Superfluous pageant,/trouble, for by the Lord Harry!
> They'll find, where they're going, much more than they carry.

Ra. Jy. 8th. 1821

Illustrious Sir—I enclose you a long note[2] for the 5th. Canto of Don Juan—you will find where it should be placed on referring to the MS.—which I sent to Mr. Kinnaird.—I had subscribed the authorities —Arrian—Plutarch—Hume &c. for the *correction* of Bacon—but thinking it pedantic to do so—have since erased them.——I have had

---

[1] After Queen Caroline, wife of George IV, was acquitted of the charge of adultery, in November, 1820, she was the subject of much popular acclaim. Various tradesmen's groups sent deputations and addresses to her. The most splendid was that of the brass-founders and braziers.

[2] This was an addition to his note to stanza 147 on Bacon's inaccuracies.

no letter from you since *one* dated 3d. of Novr.—You are a pretty fellow but I will be even with you some day.—

yours &c. &c.
BYRON

P.S.—The Enclosed *epigram* is *not* for publication, recollect.—

[TO JOHN MURRAY *(a)*]   R[avenn]a. J[anuar]y *11th. 1821*

D[ea]r M[urra]y—Put this—"I am obliged for this excellent translation of the old Chronicle to Mr. Cohen, to whom the reader will find himself indebted for a version which I could not myself (though after so many years intercourse with Italians) have given by any means so purely and so faithfully."[1] I have looked over "the Hints"[2]—(of which by the way—You have not sent the whole), and see little to alter,—I do not see yet any *name* which could be offended—at least of my friends.——As an advertisement or short preface say as follows— (Let me have the rest though first).

"However little this poem may resemble the annexed Latin—it has been submitted to one of the great rules of *Horace*—having been kept in the desk for more than *nine* years.[3]——It was composed at Athens in the Spring of 1811—and received some additions after the author's return to England in the same year.——"

I protest—and desire you to *protest* stoutly and *publicly*—(if it be necessary) against any attempt to bring the tragedy on *any* stage.—It was written solely for the reader.—It is too regular—and too simple and of too remote an interest for the Stage. I will not be exposed to the insolences of an audience—without a remonstance.—As thus——

"The Author—having heard that notwithstanding his request and remonstrance—it is the intention of one of the London Managers to attempt the introduction of the tragedy of M[arino] F[aliero] upon the Stage—does hereby protest publicly that such a proceeding is as totally against his wishes—as it will prove against the interest of the theatre.—That Composition was intended for the Closet only—as the reader will easily perceive.—By no kind of adaptation can it be made

---

[1] This note was appended to the translation by Francis Cohen (afterwards Sir Francis Palgrave) of Muratori's edition of Marino Sanuto's *Vite dei Dogi* in an appendix to *Marino Faliero*.

[2] "Hints from Horace" which was not published until 1831.

[3] Horace's advice to keep one's composition in the cupboard for nine years before giving it to the public. *Ars Poetica, 388.)*

fit for the present English Stage.——If the Courtesy of the Manager is not sufficient to withhold him from exercising his power over a published drama—which the Law has not sufficiently protected from such usurpation. . . ."[4]

[TO JOHN MURRAY (*b*)] *R[avenn]a J[anuar]y 11th. 1821*

Dear Murray—I have read with attention the enclosed[1] of which you have not sent me however the *whole* (which *pray* send) and have made the few corrections I shall make in what I have seen at least.— I will omit nothing and alter little;—the fact is (as I perceive)—that I wrote a great deal better in 1811—than I have ever done since.—I care not a sixpence whether the work is popular or not—*that* is *your* concern—and as I neither name price—nor care about terms—it can concern you little either—so that it pays it's expence of printing.—I leave all those matters to yr. magnanimity (which is something like Lady Byron's) which will decide for itself.—You have about I know not what quantity of my stuff on hand just now (a 5th Canto of Don Juan also by this time) and must cut according to yr. cloth.——Is not one of the Seals meant for my Cranium? and the other who or what is he?—

yrs. ever truly
BYRON

P.S.—What have you decided about Galignani?[2]—I think you might at least have acknowledged my letter—which would have been civil—also a letter on the late murders here—also pray do not omit to protest and impede (as far as possible) any Stage-playing with the tragedy.—I hope that the Histrions will see their own interest too well to attempt it.—See my other letter.

P.S.—You say—speaking of acting—"let me know your pleasure in this"—I reply that there is no pleasure in it—the play is *not for acting*—Kemble or Kean could *read* it—but where are they?—Do not let me be sacrificed in such a manner—depend upon it—it is some party-work to run down you and yr. favourite horse.——I know something of Harris and Elliston[3] personally—and if they are not Critics enough to

---

[4] The remainder of the letter is missing.

[1] The proof of *Hints from Horace.*

[2] See Nov. 4, 1820, to Murray (Vol. 7, p. 216)

[3] Harry Harris was manager of Covent Garden Theatre. Robert W. Elliston, the comedian, had taken over the management of Drury Lane Theatre in 1819.

see that it would not do, I think them Gentlemen enough to desist at my request—Why don't they bring out some of the thousands of meritorious & neglected men who cumber their shelves—instead of lugging me out of the library?—Will you excuse the severe postage—with which my late letters will have taxed you? "I had taken such strong resolutions against anything of that kind from seeing how much every body that *did* write for the Stage was obliged to subject themselves to the players and the town." Spence's Anecdotes, page 22.

[TO JOHN MURRAY (*c*)]   *[January 11? 1821]*

To Mr. Murray—Where is the *rest?*[1] here has been some of what Perry called (in 1815 at Drury Lane when Douglas K[innaird]—cut down the salaries) "your da*u*mned cutting and slashing"—but I won't have anything cut out except anything against those who may happen to be now my friends—such as Moore—Campbell—Scott—Jeffrey—Sir J. B. Burgess and the rest.——I must protest against the liberties which are so liberally taken by you all with my works in my absence ——I will allow none of you to *dock*;—except *Gifford.*——Will you have the goodness also to put all that regards *Pope* (in the prose letter to B[lackwood's] Editor sent last Spring to you) as a *note* under the name of *Pope* [where it?] first occurs in this Essay (which it does [begin?]) as that part of the letter was in fact distinct from the rest of it, it will do as well here. When you talk of altering and omitting you should remember that all the English *refers* to passages in the Latin—and that the merit in this kind of writing consists in the *adaptation*—*now*—to omit or alter much would destroy the closeness of the allusions —(and these are often very close as you see) and spoil the whole.——

yrs. truly
[Scrawl]

Is not the Seal of your second letter Walter Scott's bust?

[TO LADY BYRON]   *R[avenn]a January 11th. 1821*

I have just heard from Mr. Kinnaird that (through the juggling of Hanson) Mr. Bland (with the advice of Counsel) has refused to consent to the Irish loan on Mortgage, to Lord Blessington.———As

---

[1] The proof of *Hints from Horace*. The letter is written at the end of part of the galley proof of the "Hints".

you of course did not do this intentionally—I shall not upbraid you nor yours—though the connection has proved so unfortunate a one for us all, to the ruin of my fame—of my peace—and the hampering of my fortune.———I suppose that the trustees will not object to an English Security,—if it can be found—though the terms may necessarily be less advantageous.—I had, God knows, unpleasant things enough to contend with just now without this addition—I presume that you were aware that the Rochdale Cause also was lost last Summer—however it is appealed upon—but without great hopes on my part. The State of things *here*—you will have seen—if you have received my two letters of last month.—But the grand consolation is that all things must end—whether they mend or no.———

yrs ever
\ [Scrawl]

P.S.—I write to thank you for your consent about the futurities of Augusta's family.———I had set my heart upon getting out of these infernal funds—which are all false—and thought that the difficulties were at length over.—Yours has been a bitter connection to me in every sense—it would have been better for me never to have been born than to have ever seen you.—This sounds harsh—but is it not true? and recollect I do not mean that you were my *intentional* evil Genius—but an Instrument for my destruction—and you yourself have suffered too (poor thing) in the agency—as the lightning perishes in the instant with the Oak which it strikes.—

[TO JOHN HANSON]   *R[avenn]a January 11th. 1821*

Sir—By the intervention of yr. good offices—Lady B's trustee has declined to ratify the mortgage.—I shall content myself with observing—that knowing my wishes so well upon the subject, knowing also how frivolous the objection is in *fact*—whatever it may be in *law*—that whether as my friend—(and I have always shown myself the friend of yr. family—in circumstances even where others condemned you) you ought to be ashamed of yourself for having suggested the objection.—My object in writing to you at present—besides to reprove you for this piece of conduct is—to desire that Mr. Claughton may be made to pay up his money and that an English mortgage—(since it must be so) may be sought for.—I have the honour to be

yr. obedt. Servt.
BYRON

My dear Douglas—You must look out then for an English Mortgage;—it is very vexatious—but as there is no remedy—I know not
what to say.——Things have not gone luckily for me of late—but
I suppose that they will end—or mend, in time.——Lady Byron (as I
believe she once said to Somebody) thinks or thought that I looked
upon her as a *Curse* to me—she looks to be sure a little like it.—She
has ruined my reputation—destroyed my comfort—and hampered my
fortune—neither perhaps intentionally but of all this—she has been
the cause and the means.———I beg leave that you will protest publicly
in my name against any attempt to bring the tragedy on the Stage.—
It *never was written for the Stage*—I make it my particular request that
it be NOT brought forward on any theatre—And if it is—I beg that the
Public be fully advertized—that it is against my most positive wish—
& Consent.———It is too bad to do such things against the wishes of the
Writer.———I desire that Claughton may be prosecuted & made to
pay.—

yrs. ever & truly
BYRON

P.S.—Put a note in this note and forward it—& I will thank you.—
Read it first—is it sharp enough?—
[At top of letter] by this post I have written to Hanson. on 2d. thought
I enclose the note

Amor Mio +—Ecco la verità di ciò che io ti dissi pochi giorni fa—
come vengo sagrificato in tutte le maniere—senza sapere il *perche* o il
come.———La tragedia di così si parla—non è (e non era mai) nè
scritta nè adattata al teatro—ma non è però romantico il disegno—è
piuttosto—regolare—regolarissimo per l'unità del tempo—e man-
cando poco a quella del' sito.—Tu sai bene—se io poteva avere
intenzione di farla rappresentare—poiche fosse scritta al' tuo fianco—e
nei momenti per certo più *tragici* per me come *uomo*—che come
autore—perche *tu* fosti in affanno ed in pericolo.——In tanto—senti
dalla tua Gazzetta che sia nata una cabala—"un partito"—ed una
diavolezza—e senza che io ho preso la minima parte.—Se dice che
"l'autore ne fece la lettura!!!" *qui* forse—a Ravenna!—ed a Che [chi]?

forse a Fletcher!!! quel' illustre letterato! Ecco delle buffonate solenni. —non isto bene—mi duole la testa—ed un poco il Cuore.—Ti bacio 1000 volte

sempre tutto tuo
+B

[TRANSLATION]   *January 18th, 1821*

My Love +—Here is the truth of what I said to you a few days ago about how I am being misinterpreted in every way—without knowing *why* or *how*.——

The tragedy they are talking about—is not (and never was) either written for or adapted to the theatre—but the form is not romantic—it is rather regular—certainly regular as to the unity of time—and failing but slightly in that of place.—You well know—whether I ever intended to have it acted—for it was written by your side—and in moments certainly more tragic for me as a *man*—than as a writer— for *you* were in distress and danger.——In the meantime—I hear from your Gazette that a 'cabala' has been formed—a party—and a devil of a *row* and without my having taken the slightest part in it.— They say that *the author read it aloud*!!!—*here perhaps*—in *Ravenna*! and to whom? perhaps to Fletcher!!! that illustrious man of letters!

This is portentous fooling—I do not feel well—my head aches—and my heart a little.—

I kiss you a 1000 times. Always all yours

+B

[TO JOHN MURRAY]   *Ravenna—January 19th. 1821*

Dear Moray—Yours of ye. 29th Ultmo. hath arrived. I must really and seriously request that you will beg of Messrs Harris or Elliston— to let the Doge alone—it is *not* an acting play;— it will not serve *their* purpose—it will destroy *yours* (the Sale)—and it will *distress* me.—It is not courteous, it is hardly even gentlemanly to persist in this appropriation of a man's writings to their Mountebanks.——I have already sent you by last post—a short protest to the Public (against this proceeding); in *case* that *they* persist, which I trust that they will not—you must then publish it in the Newspapers.—I shall not let them off with that only, if they go on—but make a longer appeal on that subject—and state what I think the injustice of their mode of behaviour.——It is hard that I should have all the buffoons in Britain—to deal with—*pirates* who *will* publish—and *players* who *will* act—when there are thousands of worthy and able men who can neither get bookseller nor manager for love nor money.——You never answered me a word about *Galignani*—if *you* mean to use the two *documents*—*do* if *not*—*burn* them—I do not choose to leave them in any one's possession—suppose someone found them—without the letters—what would they *think?*—why—that *I* had been doing the *opposite* of what I have *done*—to wit—referred the whole thing to *you*— an act of civility at least—which required saying—"I have received your letter."——I thought that you might have some hold upon those publications by this means—to *me*—it can be no interest one way or the other.——

The *third* Canto of D. J. *is dull*—but you must really put up with it—if the two first—and the two following are tolerable—what can you object?—particularly as I neither dispute with you on it—as a matter of criticism—or a matter of business. Besides what am I to understand? you and D[ougla]s Kinnaird—& others—write to me that the *two first* published Cantos are among the *best* that I ever wrote—and are reckoned so—Mrs. Leigh writes that they are thought *"execrable"* (bitter word *that* for an author—Eh Murray?) as a *composition* even—and that she had heard so much against them—that she would [*never?*] *read them*, & never has.——Be that as it may—I can't alter.—That is not my forte.—If you publish the three new ones without ostentation—they may perhaps succeed.——Pray publish the Dante and the *Pulci*—(the *Prophecy of Dante* I mean)—I look upon the *Pulci* as my grand performance.——The remainder of "the Hints" where be they?—Now bring them all out about the same time —otherwise "the *variety*" you wot of—will be less obvious.——I am in bad humour—some obstructions in business—with the damned trustees—who object to an advantageous loan which I was to furnish to a Nobleman on Mortgage—because his property is in *Ireland*— have shown me how a man is treated in his absence.—Oh—if I do come back—I will make some of those who little dream of it—*spin*—or they or I shall go down.——The news here is—that Col. Brown[1] (the Witness-buyer) has been stabbed—at Milan—but *not* mortally.—I wonder that any body should dirty their daggers in him.—They should have beaten him with Sandbags—an old Spanish fashion.——I sent

---

[1] Colonel Brown was employed to gather evidence in Italy against Queen Caroline.

you a line or two on the Braziers' Company last week—*not* for publication.

yrs. [Scrawl]

The lines were even worthy

"Of Turdsworth the great Metaquizzical poet
   A man of great merit amongst those who know it
Of whose works, as I told Moore last autumn at Mestri*
   I owe all I know to my passion for *Pastry*.

Mestri and *Fusina* are the ferry trajects to Venice—I believe however that it was at Fusina that Moore and I embarked in 1819 when Thomas came to Venice—like Coleridge's Spring "slowly up this way."[1] *Omit* the dedication to Goethe.

[TO JOHN MURRAY (*a*)]   *Ravenna. January 20th. 1821*

Dear Murray—If Harris or Elliston persist[1]—after the remonstrance which I requested you and Mr. Kinnaird to make on my behalf—& which I hope will be sufficient—but—*if*—I say—they *do persist*—then I pray you to *present in person* the enclosed letter to the Lord Chamberlain—I have said—*in person*—otherwise—I shall have neither answer nor knowledge that it has reached it's address—owing to "the insolence of office"[2]. I wish you would speak to Lord Holland—and to all my friends and yours to interest themselves in preventing this cursed attempt at representation.——God help me—at this distance—I am treated like a corpse or a fool—by the few people whom I thought that I could rely upon;—and I *was* a fool—to think any better of them than of the rest of mankind.—Pray write—

yrs. ever
BYRON

P.S.—I have nothing more at heart—(that is in literature) than to prevent this drama from going upon the Stage;—in short—rather than

---

[1] *Christabel*, Part I.
[1] Elliston did persist. Murray published *Marino Faliero* on April 21, 1821, and on April 25 Elliston put the play on the stage at Drury Lane, after much cutting of the lines. Despite Murray's efforts to get an injunction from the Lord Chamberlain, it was performed seven times, without great success, but it was not such a failure as Byron had feared.
[2] *Hamlet*, Act III, scene 1.

permit it—it must be *suppressed altogether*—and only *forty copies struck off privately* for presents to my friends.———What damned fools those speculating buffoons must be *not* to see that it is unfit for their Fair—or their booth.——

[TO JOHN MURRAY (*b*)]   *January 20th. 1821*

D[ea]r M[urra]y—I did not think to have troubled you with the plague and postage of a *double letter*—this time—but I have just read in an *Italian paper* "That Ld. B. has a tragedy coming out" &c. &c.—and that the Courier and Morning Chronicle &c. &c. are pulling one another to pieces about it and him &c.——Now—I do reiterate—and desire that every thing may be done to prevent it from coming out in *any theatre* for *which* it never was designed—and on which (in the present state of the stage in London) it could never succeed,—I have sent you my appeal by last post—which you *must publish* in *case* of *need* —and I require you even in *your own* name (if my honour is dear to you) to declare that such representation would be contrary to my *wish and to my judgement.*—if you do not wish to drive me mad altogether—you will hit upon some way to prevent this.——

                                                              yrs. [Scrawl]

P.S.—I cannot conceive how Harris or Elliston can be so insane as to think of acting M[arino] F[aliero]—they might as well act the Prometheus of Æschylus—I speak of course humbly—and with the greatest sense of the distance of time and merit between the two performances—but merely to show the absurdity of the attempt.——The Italian paper speaks of a "party against it". To be sure there would be a party—can you imagine that after having never flattered man—nor beast—nor opinion—nor politics—there would not be a party against a man who is also a *popular* writer—at least a successful—why *all parties* would be a party against.——

[TO THOMAS MOORE]   *Ravenna, January 22d, 1821*

Pray get well. I do not like your complaint. So, let me have a line to say you are up and doing again. To-day I am thirty-three years of age.

> Through life's road, so dim and dirty,
> I have dragged to three-and-thirty.
> What *have* these years left to me?
> Nothing—except thirty-three.

Have you heard that the "Braziers' Company" have, or mean to present an address at Brandenburgh House,[1] "in armour," and with all possible variety and splendour of brazen apparel?

> The Braziers, it seems, are preparing to pass
> An address, and present it themselves all in brass—
> A superfluous pageant—for, by the Lord Harry,
> They'll find where they're going much more than they carry.

There's an Ode for you, is it not?—worthy

> Of * * * * * [Turdsworth], the grand metaquizzical poet,
> A man of vast merit, though few people know it;
> The perusal of whom (as I told *you* at Mestri)
> I owe, in great part, to my passion for pastry.

Mestri and Fusina are the "trajects, or common ferries," to Venice; but it was from Fusina that you and I embarked, though "the wicked necessity of rhyming"[2] has made me press Mestri into the voyage.

So, you have had a book dedicated to you? I am glad of it, and shall be very happy to see the volume.

I am in a peck of troubles about a tragedy of mine, which is fit only for the (* * * *) closet, and which it seems that the managers, assuming a *right* over published poetry, are determined to enact, whether I will or no, with their own alterations by Mr. Dibdin,[3] I presume. I have written to Murray, to the Lord Chamberlain, and to others, to interfere and preserve me from such an exhibition. I want neither the impertinence of their hisses, nor the insolence of their applause. I write only for the *reader*, and care for nothing but the *silent* approbation of those who close one's book with good humour and quiet contentment.

Now, if you would also write to our friend Perry, to beg of him to mediate with Harris and Elliston to *forbear* this intent, you will greatly oblige me. The play is quite unfit for the stage, as a single

---

[1] The residence of Queen Caroline in Fulham.

[2] Milton, Preface to *Paradise Lost*, "the troublesome and modern bondage of Riming".

[3] Thomas Dibdin had been active as playwright and adapter at Drury Lane while Byron was on the sub-committee of management in 1815, but he left Drury Lane and opened the Surrey Theatre at Easter, 1821. It was his intention to represent *Marino Faliero* at the opening, but he was warned by Murray that he would be prevented by an injunction.

glance will show them, and, I hope, *has* shown them; and, if it were ever so fit, I will never have any thing to do willingly with the theatres.

Yours ever, in haste, &c.

[TO JOHN MURRAY] *Ravenna J[anuar]y 27th. 1821*

Dear Moray—I *have* mentioned Mr. Cohen in a letter to you last week—from which the passage should be extracted—and prefixed to his translation.—You will also have received two or three letters upon the subject of the *Managers*—in one enclosed an epistle for the Lord Chamberlain—(in case of the worst) and I even prohibited the *publication* of the Tragedy—limiting it to a few copies for my private friends.—But this would be useless—after going so far—so you *may publish*—as we intended—only—(if the Managers attempt to act) pray present my letter to the Ld. Chamberlain—and publish my appeal in the papers—adding that it has all along been against my wishes—that it should be represented.——I differ from you about the *Dante*[1]—which I think should be published *with* the tragedy.—But do as you please—you must be the best judge of your own craft.—I agree with you about the *title*.——The play may be good or bad—but I flatter myself that it is original as a picture of *that* kind of passion—which to my mind is so natural—that I am convinced that I should have done precisely what the Doge did on those provocations.——

I am glad of Foscolo's approbation.—I wish you would send me the remainder of "the Hints"—you only sent about half of them. As to the other volume—you should publish them about the same period—or else *what* becomes of the *"variety"* which you talk so much of?——Excuse haste—I believe I mentioned to you that—I forget what It was—but no matter.——Thanks for your compliments of the year—I hope that it will be pleasanter than the last—I speak with reference to *England* only as far as regards myself—*where* I had every kind of disappointment—lost an important lawsuit;—and the trustees of that evil Genius of a woman Ly. B. (who was born for my desolation) refusing to allow of an advantageous loan to be made from my property to Lord Blessington &c. &c. by way of closing the four seasons. —These and a hundred other such things made a year of bitter business for me in England—luckily things were a little pleasanter for me *here*—else I would have taken the liberty of Hannibal's ring.[2]——

---

[1] *The Prophecy of Dante* was published with *Marino Faliero* on April 21, 1821.

[2] That is, have taken poison, as did Hannibal to avoid surrender into the hands of the Romans.

Pray thank Gifford—for all his goodnesses—the winter is as cold here—as Parry's polarities[3]—I must now take a canter in the forest—my horses are waiting—

yrs. ever & truly
[Scrawl]

P.S.—It is exceedingly strange that you have never acknowledged the receipt of *Galignani's letters* which I enclosed to you three months ago—what the devil does that mean?

[TO RICHARD BELGRAVE HOPPNER]   *Ravenna.—January 28th. 1821*

My dear Hoppner—I have not heard from you for a long time—and now I must trouble you—as usual.——Messrs. Siri—and Willhalm have given up business.—They had three cases of mine.—I desired them to consign these cases to Missiaglia.——There were 4 Telescopes—a case of watches—and a tin case of English Gunpowder—containing about five pounds of the same—which I have had for *five years.*——Siri & Willhalm *own* to all three—and the telescopes and watches they have consigned to M.—of the other (though they mention it in a letter of last week) they *now* say nothing—and M[issiaglia] pretends that it is not to be found.——Will you make enquiry? it is of importance to me—because I can find no other such in these countries—and can be of none to the Government because it is in so small a quantity.—If it has in fact been seized by those fellows—I will present a slight memorial to the Governor of Venice—which (though it may not get me back my three or four pounds of powder—) will at least tell him some truths—upon things in general—as I shall use some pretty strong terms in expressing myself.——I shall feel very much obliged by your making this enquiry.——Of course upon other topics I can say nothing at present—except that your Dutch friends will have their hands full—one of these days—probably.——Pray let me know how you are—

I am yrs. very truly
BYRON

My best respects to Madame Hoppner—could not you and I—contrive to meet somewhere this Spring———I should be solus.—

[3] Sir William Edward Parry (1790–1855) published in 1821 his *Journal of a Voyage for the Discovery of a North-West Passage from the Atlantic to the Pacific, performed in the years 1819–20, in H. M. Ships Hecla and Griper.*

P.S.—I sent you all the romances and light reading which Murray has forwarded—except the Monastery—which you told me that you had already seen.—I wish the *things* which were at Siri & W[illhalm]'s to *remain* with Missiaglia and *not* to be sent here at least for the present. Pray do what you can about the p[owde]r for me—it is hard that the rascals should seize the poor little miserable Canister—after the money I spent in relieving their wretched population at Venice.— I did not trouble you with the things—because I thought that they would bore you.—I never got the *translation* of the German *translator* —but it don't signify—as you said it was not worth while. They are printing some things of mine in England—and if any parcel comes from London addressed to me at Venice—pray take any work of mine out you like—and keep it—as well as any other books you choose.—— They are always addressed to Missiaglia.——

[TO PELLEGRINO GHIGI?]   *Ravenna. Febbraio 1821*

[In Lega Zambelli's hand—signed by Byron]
    Dal Sig.e Pellegrino Ghigi mi sono state pagate Lire cinquanta Sterline per altrettanta somma da esso ricevuta a quitanza del biglietto del Banco di firma Ransom di Londra postante la data 18 Gennaio 1820 col No. 439 giratogli sotto questo giorno.—La presente io [or si?] rilascia per dupplicato e per garanzia del sud[dett]o Sig.e Ghigi.—

                                                    BYRON

[Translation]   *Ravenna. February 1821*
    Signor Pellegrino Ghigi has paid me fifty English pounds for the same amount received by him on receipt of the note from Ransom's Bank of London, dated 18 January 1820 with the number 439 endorsed there under this date.—The present note is issued in duplicate, and as a guarantee of the above mentioned Signor Ghigi[1]——

                                                    BYRON

[TO DOUGLAS KINNAIRD]   *Ravenna—February 1st. 1821*

    Dear Douglas/—Murray's offer is not a liberal one—nor in proportion to what he has offered for Ld. W[aldegrave]'s trash of memoirs[1]

    [1] Translated by Ricki B. Herzfeld of the Carl H. Pforzheimer Library.
    [1] James, 2nd. Earl Waldegrave (1716–1763) was once Governor of George III while he was Prince of Wales. His *Memoirs* were published in 1821.

—Lord Orford's[2] may & must be better—he was a truly clever fellow.—
Besides it was my intention to deal with Mr. M[urray] for the *whole*—
—& not in parts.——Murray certainly has shuffled a little with me
of late;—when Galignani wrote to offer me in an indirect manner to
purchase to [the?] *Copy-right in France* of my works I *enclosed his letters
with the instruments signed*—to Murray—desiring him to *make use of
them for himself only*—as I thought it fair that *he* should have the
advantage.—He never wrote for *three months* even to acknowledge—
far less to thank me—but after repeated letters of mine—he at last
owns that he had the letters—and offered the *instruments* to Galignani
—for "a reasonable sum."——In this he only did as I meant him to do
but it was not very liberal to say nothing about it—till it was wrung
from him.—I can name no sum for the *whole* of the poems—I have been
five years out of England—things may be altered—the Sale of books—
different—my writing less popular—what can I say? you must be in
the way of judging better than I can by a little enquiry—or by consulting with our mutual friends.——Had it been five years ago—
(when I was in my zenith) I certainly would not have taken three
thousand guineas—for the *whole* of the M.S.S. now in his hands—and
I speak of the very lowest—but still I will not swerve from any agreement *you* may make with him—with *me* he always avoids the subject—
and always has done whenever he could.——

With Mr. Hanson I shall henceforward be *two*—I sent my answer
to him enclosed to *you*—the other day—and I beg you to advise him
that from henceforward there is an end of all *personal* friendship
between him and me—and that the sooner we close our professional
connection also the better.——Of course I desire a mortgage—but
this their last piece of rascality makes me despair.—You may give my
compliments to Mr. Bland[3] and tell him that I have no *personal* pique
against him—for I do not even know him—but if—the funds ever fail
—and I lose my property in them—it is through him & his formalities
—and by all that is dear to man—I will *blow his brains out*—and take
what fortune may afterwards send me.——I am perfectly serious—&
pray tell him so—for as I have said so will I do.—I address this to Pall
Mall—anticipating yr. return.

yrs. ever & most truly
BYRON

[2] Robert Walpole, first Earl of Orford (1676–1745). His *Memoirs of the Last
Nine Years of the Reign of George II* was published by Murray in 1821.
[3] Thomas Davison Bland, a close friend of the Noels, was one of the trustees of
Lady Byron's marriage settlement.

P.S.—I had heard through your brother the other day—something of what you tell me about the boy—but you know by experience that I never interfere in any matters with the women or children of my friends—it is the only quiet course.—

P.S.—I wrote to desire you to interfere to oppose any representation of "The Doge"—and have written ditto to Mr. Murray.——

[TO DOUGLAS KINNAIRD]   R[avenn]a F[ebruar]y 2d. 1821

Dear Douglas—Read the enclosed letter to Murray—put a wafer in it—and either present—or forward it as you please.——On reading your letter again—I do not know—(if the landed interest be so low) whether we should not rather sell out and *purchase*—rather than lend on mortgage—what think you? if a bargain offered.—My mother's estate of Gight was sold to the former Lord Aberdeen many years ago—before I was born I believe—I have always preferred my mother's family—for it's royalty—and if I could buy it back—I would consent even at a reduction of income.—It is in Scotland.— What think you of this or some such?——Write to yrs ever

BYRON

P.S.—The "High minded Moray" offers a thousand pounds for the tragedy and for the prophecy!!![1] why he gave as many guineas for Larry—and Rogers's Jacky[2]—as much for the Siege of C[orinth] and for Parisina.——I must either be fallen as a writer or he as a bookseller—if this be his way of accounting.—*You* can easily ascertain which.——I shall be quite satisfied with what *you* and Hobhouse think fair & reasonable.——I sent you the 5th. Canto of D.J. on the 30th. of Decr. last year.—Half year's fee received by yesterday's post.

[TO JOHN MURRAY]   Ravenna. Feb[ruar]y 2d. 1821

Dear Moray—Your letter of excuses has arrived.—I receive the letter but do not admit the excuses except in courtesy—as when a man treads on your toes and begs your pardon—the pardon is granted— but the joint aches—especially if there is a corn upon it.—However I shall scold you presently.——In the last speech of "the Doge" there

---

[1] *Marino Faliero* and *The Prophecy of Dante.*
[2] Byron's *Lara* was published by Murray in 1814 in a volume with Rogers's *Jacqueline.*

73

occurs (I think, from memory) the phrase—"*And thou who makest and unmakest Suns*" Change this to "And thou *who kindlest and who quenchest Suns*"—that is to say—if the verse runs equally well—and Mr. Gifford thinks the expression improved.——Pray—have the bounty to attend to this—you are grown quite a minister of State—mind—if some of these days—you are not thrown out.—God will not be always a Tory—though Johnson says the first Whig was the Devil.——

You have learnt one secret from Mr. Galignani's (somewhat tardily acknowledged) correspondence.—This is—that an *English* Author may dispose of his exclusive copy-right in *France*—a fact of some consequence (in *time of peace*) in the case of a popular writer.—Now I will tell you what *you* shall do—and take no advantage of you—though you were scurvy enough never to acknowledge my letter for three months.——Offer Galignani the *refusal* of the copy-right in France—if he refuses—approve any bookseller in France you please—and I will sign any assignment you please—and it shall never cost you a Sou on *my* account.——Recollect that *I* will have nothing to do with it—except as far as it may secure the copyright to yourself.——I will have no bargain but with English publishers—and I desire no interest out of that country.—Now that's fair and open and a little handsomer than your *dodging* silence—to see what would come of it.—You are an excellent fellow—mio Caro Moray—but there is still a little leaven of Fleet-street about you now and then—a crumb of the old loaf.——You have no right to act suspiciously with me for I have given you no reason—I shall always be frank with you—as for instance.—Whenever you talk with the votaries of Apollo authentically—it should be in guineas not pounds—to poets as well as physicians—and bidders at Auctions.——I shall say no more at this present save that I am

yrs. very truly
BYRON

P.S.—If you venture as you say—to Ravenna this year—through guns, which (like the Irishman's) "shoot round a corner" I will exercise the rites of hospitality while you live—and bury you handsomely (though not in holy-ground) if you get "shot or slashed in a creagh or Splore"[1] which are rather frequent here of late among the native parties.—But perhaps your visit may be anticipated, for Lady Medea's trustees—and my Attorneo—do so thwart all business of

[1] *Waverley*, Chapter 18.

74

mine ⟨that I shall be⟩ in despite of Mr. K[innair]d and myself—that I
may probably come to your country—in which case write to her
Ladyship—the duplicate of the epistle the King of France wrote to
Prince John.[2]——She and her Scoundrels shall find it so.——

[TO RICHARD BELGRAVE HOPPNER]   *Ravenna. February 10th. 1821*

My dear Hoppner—I have only time to write you a word or two by
this post to request you to withdraw my telescopes and watches from
Mr. Missiaglia—and give them a corner in yr. garret.—The rascally
cowardice of the powder business has decided me ⟨rather⟩ to throw
them into the Canal (if you won't be troubled with them) rather than
leave them in the hands of such base mountebanks.——I thought
better of Missiaglia—I did not believe him a *modern* Venetian—at
least to *such* a degree.—*He* is written to—by Lega—by *this post* to
assign the things to you—that is—if you choose to take so much
trouble with them.—There are 4. telescopes—and a dozen *Turkish*
watches meant for presents on a Journey through my old friends'
countries.———And pray—tell Missiaglia directly *from me*—that
whatever esteem or credit I held him in is completely neutralized—by
his paltry behaviour.—Had he been fined—I would have paid a dozen
fines over and over—and that he knows.—But he is a shabby—pol-
troon—and Siri a rascal,—What right have they to dispose of another's
property without consulting him? Had it been *fairly lost*—I should not
have cared one sixpence—it was natural & to be overlooked—but
to throw it away—the devil damn them all to the lowest maid of their
own kitchen.————
     If any books &c. come—pray—select and retain—what seems good
unto you—& yours.—

                                        Yrs. in haste & ever
                                                    BYRON

P.S.—My respects to Mrs. H. I *have* the "best opinion" of her
country women,—and at my time of life (three and thirty 22d January
1821) that is to say after the life ⟨of⟩ I have led—a "*good*" opinion is
the only rational one which a man should entertain of the whole
sex——up to *thirty*—the worst possible opinion a man can have of
them in *general*—the better for himself—afterwards it is a matter of no

[2] "So soon as Philip heard of the King's delivery from captivity, he wrote to his
confederate John, in these terms: '*Take care of yourself: the Devil is broke loose.*'"
(Hume's *History of England*, 1770, Vol. II, p. 32.)

importance to *them* nor to him either, *what opinion* he entertains;—his day is over, or at least should be.————You see how sober I am become.————Allegra is well—but not well disposed—her disposition is perverse to a degree.—I am going to place her in a Convent for education.——

I shall write again soon.————

[TO DOUGLAS KINNAIRD]   *Ravenna. February 12th. 1821*

Dear Douglas—By the enclosed paragraph you will perceive Mr. Murray's opinion of his own offer for the drama and P[ulci]—I do not understand this—he offered me a thousand guineas per canto—for as many cantos of D.J. as I chose to send him.—I let him *off* this bargain of *my own* accord—because I saw that he had taken fright that the new Canto was not written according to [his] own notions.—*How* he could [affect to?] offer a *thousand guineas* for every canto of a poem so decried and proscribed as D. J. and then tell me that he could not make more of the F[aliero] and P[ulci]—at "any rate of speculation" I neither understand nor believe.—He is in the wrong about one or the other. I have written to you on the subject before.—I have sent him by this post—some notes—and a letter upon Bowles's [sic] and Pope.[1] I also wrote to you upon Hanson—and enclosing a letter.——I am

yrs. ever & truly
BYRON

P.S.—I am so completely reduced to despair about the last juggling —that I have no scheme to form except that I am fully resolved to blow Bland's brains out—if the funds fail—and I am in consequence ruined by it.—Pray—tell him so—I do not say it by way of menace—it is my fixed quiet—settled determination.———

[TO JOHN MURRAY]   *R[avenn]a F[ebruar]y 12th. 1821*

D[ea]r S[i]r—You are requested to take particular care that the enclosed note is printed with the drama.—Foscolo or Hobhouse will

---

[1] William Lisle Bowles had edited Pope's works in ten volumes in 1806, and in his editing he had criticized Pope's character as a man and as a poet. A controversy had started in 1819 between Bowles and Thomas Campbell and others over the character of Pope in which Byron joined in his *Letter to * * * * * * * * * * [John Murray], on the Rev. W. L. Bowles' Strictures on the Life and Writings of Pope*. Murray published it as a pamphlet in 1821. Bowles replied with two letters and Byron with another, which he withheld, however, because of a conciliatory letter from Bowles. The letters and details of the controversy are given by Prothero (*LJ*, V, Appendix III).

correct the Italian—but do not *you* delay—every one of yr. cursed proofs—is a two months' delay—which you only employ to gain time, because you think it a bad [spec]ulation.—

yrs.
BYRON

P.S.—If the thing fails in the publication—you are *not pinned* even to your own terms—merely print and publish *what* I desire you—and if you don't succeed—I will abate whatever you please.——⟨If the alteration of two lines in anything I have written⟩ I care nothing about that—but I wish what I desire to be printed to be so.——I have never had the ⟨additional⟩ remaining sheets of the "Hints from H[orac]e". ——In the letter on Bowles—after the words "the long walls of Palestrina and Malamocco" add "*i Murazzi*" which is their Venetian title. ——[On cover] Mr. M. is requested to acknowledge the receipt of this by return of post.

[TO JOHN MURRAY] *Ravenna—Feb[brai]o 16o 1821*

Dear Moray—In the month of March will arrive from Barcelona— *Signor Curioni*[1] engaged for the Opera.—He is an acquaintance of mine—and a gentlemanly young man—high in his profession.—I must request your personal kindness and patronage in his favour.——Pray introduce him to such of the theatrical people—Editors of Papers— and others, as may be useful to him in his profession publicly and privately.—He is accompanied by the Signora Arpalice Taruscelli[2]—a Venetian lady of great beauty and celebrity and a particular friend of mine—your natural gallantry will I am sure induce you to pay her proper attention.—Tell Israeli—that as he is fond of *literary* anecdotes —she can tell him some of your acquaintance abroad.—I presume that he speaks Italian.—Do not neglect this request, but do them and me this favour in their behalf.——I shall write to some others to aid you in assisting them with your countenance.

I agree to your request of leaving in abeyance the terms for the three D. J.s till you can ascertain the effect of publication.—If I refuse to alter—you have a claim to so much courtesy in return.—I had let you off your proposal about the price of the Cantos, last year (the 3d. & 4th. always to reckon as *one* only—which they originally were) and

---

1 Alberico Curioni, an Italian tenor, sang operatic parts in London from 1821 to 1832.
2 See May 19, 1818, to Hobhouse. (Vol. 6, p. 40.)

I do not call upon you to renew it.—You have therefore no occasion to fight so shy of such subjects as I am not conscious of having given you occasion.——The 5th. is so far from being the last of D. J. that it is hardly the beginning.—I meant to take him the tour of Europe—with a proper mixture of siege—battle—and adventure—and to make him finish as *Anacharsis Cloots*[3]—in the French revolution.—To how many cantos this may extend—I know not—nor whether (even if I live) I shall complete it—but this was my notion.—I meant to have made him a Cavalier Servente in Italy and a cause for a divorce in England—and a Sentimental "Werther-faced man"[4] in Germany—so as to show the different ridicules of the society in each of those countries—— and to have displayed him gradually gaté and blasé as he grew older—as is natural.—But I had not quite fixed whether to make him end in Hell—or in an unhappy marriage,—not knowing which would be the severest.—The Spanish tradition says Hell—but it is probably only an Allegory of the other state.——You are now in possession of my notions on the subject.—

You say "the Doge" will not be popular—did I ever write for *popularity*?——I defy you to show a work of mine (except a tale or two) of a popular style or complexion.—It appears to me that there is room for a different style of the drama—neither a servile following of the old drama—which is a grossly erronious one—nor yet *too French*—like those who succeeded the older writers.—It appears to me that good English—and a severer approach to the rules—might combine something not dishonourable to our literature.——I have also attempted to make a play without love.——And there are neither rings—nor mistakes—nor starts—nor outrageous ranting villains—nor melodrame—in it.—All this will prevent it's popularity, but does not persuade me that it is *therefore* faulty.—Whatever faults it has will arise from deficiency in the conduct—rather than in the conception—which is simple and severe.—So—*you epigrammatize* upon *my epigram.*——I will *pay you* for *that*—mind if I don't—some day.—I never let anyone off in the long run—(*who first begins*)—remember *Sam*—and see if I don't do you as good a turn.—You unnatural publisher!—what—quiz your own authors!—You are a paper Cannibal.—

[3] Jean Baptiste (Anacharsis) Clootz was a Prussian baron who became involved in the French Revolution. He described himself before the National Convention as "l'orateur du genre humain". He later came under the suspicion of Robespierre and was executed in 1794.

[4] Byron borrowed the phrase from Letter 5 of Moore's *Fudge Family in Paris* (1818): "A fine, sallow, sublime, sort of Werther-faced man".

In the letter on Bowles—(which I sent by Tuesday's post) after the words *"attempts had been made"* (alluding to the republication of "English Bards")—add the words *"in Ireland"* for I believe that Cawthorn did not begin his attempts till after I had left England the second time.—Pray attend to this.—Let me know what you & your Synod think of the letter on Bowles.——I did not think the second *Seal* so bad—surely it is far better than the Saracen's head with which you have sealed your *last letter*—the larger in *profile* was surely much better than that.—[So] Foscolo says he will get you a [*seal*] *cut* better in Italy—he means a *throat*—that is the only thing they do dexterously. —The Arts—all but Canova's and Morghen's[5]—and Ovid's[6];—(I don't *mean poetry*) are as low as need be—look at the Seal which I gave to Wm. Bankes—and own it.—How came George Bankes[7] to quote English Bards in the House of Commons? all the World keep flinging that poem in my face.——Belzoni[8] *is* a grand traveller and his English is very prettily broken.——As for News—the Barbarians are marching on Naples——and if they lose a single battle, all Italy will be up.—It will be like the Spanish war if they have any bottom.—— *"Letters opened!"* to be sure they are—and that's the reason why I always put in my opinion of the German Austrian Scoundrels;—there is not an Italian who loathes them more than I do—and whatever I could do to scour Italy and the earth of their infamous oppression— would be done "con amore".—

yrs. ever & truly
BYRON

Recollect that the *Hints* must be printed with the *Latin* otherwise there is no sense.—

[5] Raphael Morghen (1758–1835) was a famous Italian engraver who settled in Florence.

[6] Ovid's *Ars Amatoria.*

[7] George Bankes, M.P. for Corfe Castle, in an address at the opening of Parliament on January 23, 1821, said that "the new springs of knowledge were endeavoured to be poisoned at their source "which reminded him of "the lines of the poet, when he expressed the keen pangs of the bird, wounded by the arrow feathered from his own wing". He then quoted two lines from *English Bards and Scotch Reviewers:*

> "Keen were his pangs, but keener far to feel
> He nursed the pinion which impelled the steel."

[8] Giovanni Battista Belzoni (1778–1823), an Italian explorer, insisted on writing in English the account of his travels, though his knowledge of the language was imperfect. Murray published in 1820 his *Narrative of the Operations and Recent Discoveries within the Pyramids, Temples, Tombs, and Excavations in Egypt and Nubia.*

Dear Sir,—In the 44th. page vol 1st. of Turner's travels[1] (which you lately sent me) it is stated that "Lord Byron—when he expressed such confidence of it's practicability seems to have forgotten that Leander swam both ways with and against the tide, whereas *he* (Ld. B.) only performed the easiest part of the task by swimming *with* it from Europe to Asia."[2]—I certainly could not have forgotten what is known to every Schoolboy—that Leander crossed in the Night and returned towards the morning.—My object was to ascertain that the Hellespont could be crossed *at all* by swimming—and in this—Mr. Ekenhead & myself both succeeded—the one in an hour and ten minutes—the other in one hour & five minutes. The *tide* was *not* in our favour—on the contrary the great difficulty was to bear up against the current—which so far from helping us to the Asiatic side—set us down right towards the Archipelago.—Neither Mr. Ekenhead, myself—nor I will venture to add—any person on board the frigate from Captain (now Admiral) Bathurst downwards—had any notion of the difference of the current on the Asiatic side, of which Mr. Turner speaks.—I never heard of it till this moment—or I would have taken the other course. Lieutenant Ekenhead's sole motive—and mine also, for setting out from the European side was—that the little Cape above Sestos was a more prominent starting place—and the frigate which lay below close under the Asiatic castle—formed a better point of view for us to swim towards—and in fact we landed immediately below it.——

Mr. Turner says—"Whatever is thrown into the Stream on this part of the European bank, *must* arrive at the Asiatic shore."—This is so far from being the case—that it *must* arrive in the Archipelago—if left to the Current—although a strong wind in the Asiatic direction might have such an effect occasionally.——Mr. Turner attempted the passage from the Asiatic side and failed.—"After five and twenty minutes in which he did not advance a hundred yards he gave it up from complete exhaustion."—This is very possible—and might have occurred to him just as readily on the European side.———He should have set out a couple of miles higher—and would then have come out

---

[1] *Journal of a Tour in the Levant*, by William Turner, 3 vols., published by Murray in 1820. Turner, a diplomatist, was attached to the Embassy in Constantinople.

[2] See Byron's account of his feat in his letter to Henry Drury, May 3, 1810. (Vol. 1, p. 237.)

below the European castle.—I particularly stated—and Mr. Hobhouse has done so also—that we were obliged to make the real passage of one mile—extend to between *three* and *four*—owing to the force of the stream.———I can assure Mr. Turner that his Success would have given me great pleasure—as it would have added one more instance—to the proof of the practicability.—It is not quite fair in him to infer—that—because *he* failed—Leander could not succeed.—There are still four instances on record—a Neapolitan—a young Jew—Mr. Ekenhead—& myself—the two last done in the presence of hundreds of *English* Witnesses.———With regard to the difference of the *current*—I perceived none—it is favourable to the Swimmer on neither side—but may be stemmed by plunging into the Sea—a considerable way above the opposite point of the coast which the Swimmer wishes to make, but still bearing up against it; it is very strong but—if you *calculate* well you may reach land. My own experience & that of others bids me pronounce the passage of Leander perfectly practicable;—any young man in good health—and tolerable skill in swimming might succeed in it from *either* side.——

I was three hours in swimming across the Tagus—which is much more hazardous, *being two hours* longer than the passage of the Hellespont.—Of what may be done in swimming I will mention one more instance.—In 1818—The Chevalier Mengaldo (a Gentleman of Bassano) a good Swimmer wished to swim ⟨with an English Gentleman⟩ with my friend Mr. Alexander Scott and myself. As he seemed particularly anxious on the subject we indulged him.—We all three started from the Island of the Lido and swam to Venice.—At the entrance of the Grand Canal—Scott and I were a good way ahead—and we saw no more of our foreign friend—which however was of no consequence—as there was a Gondola to hold his cloathes and pick him up.—Scott swam on till past the Rialto—where he got out—less from fatigue than from *chill*—having been *four hours* in the water—without rest or stay—except what is to be obtained by floating on one's back—this being the *condition* of our performance.—I continued my course on to Santa Chiara—comprizing the whole of the Grand Canal (beside the distance from the Lido) and got out where the Laguna once more opens to Fusina.—I had been in the water by my watch without help or rest—and never touching ground or boat *four hours* and *twenty* minutes.—To this Match and during the greater part of its performance Mr. Hoppner the Consul General was witness—and it is well known to many others.—Mr. Turner can easily verify the fact—if he thinks it worth while—by referring to Mr. Hoppner.—

81

The distance we could not *accurately* ascertain—it was of course considerable.——

I crossed the *Hellespont* in *one* hour and ten minutes only.—I am now ten years older in time and twenty in constitution—than I was when I passed the Dardanelles—and yet two years ago—I was capable of swimming four hours and twenty minutes—and I am sure that I could have continued two hours longer though I had on a pair of trowsers—an accoutrement which by no means assists the performance. My two companions were also *four* hours in the water.——Mengaldo might be about thirty years of age—Scott about six and twenty.—— With this experience in swimming at different periods of life—not only upon the *Spot*—but elsewhere—of various persons, what is there to make me doubt that Leander's exploit was perfectly practicable?— If three individuals did more than the passage of the Hellespont why should he have done less? But Mr. Turner failed—and naturally seeking a plausible reason for his failure—lays the blame on the *Asiatic* side of the Strait.——To me the cause is evident.—He tried to swim *directly* across—instead of going higher up to take the vantage. —He might as well have tried to fly over Mount Athos.——That a young Greek of the heroic times—in love—and with his limbs in full vigour might have *succeeded* in such an attempt is neither wonderful nor doubtful.—Whether he *attempted* it or *not* is another question— because he might have had a small *boat* to save him the trouble.—— I am

yrs. very truly
BYRON

P.S.—Mr. Turner says that the swimming from Europe to Asia— was "the *easiest* part of the task"—I doubt whether Leander found it so—as it was the return—however he had several hours between the intervals. The argument of Mr. T. "that higher up or lower down the strait widens so considerably that he would save little labour by his starting" is only good for indifferent swimmers—a man of any practice or skill—will always consider the distance far less than the strength of the stream.—If Ekenhead & myself had thought of crossing at the *narrowest point* instead of going up to the Cape above it we should have been swept down to Tenedos.——The Strait is however not extremely wide—even where it broadens above and below the forts.—As the frigate was stationed some time in the Dardenelles waiting for the firman—I bathed often in the strait subsequently to our traject—and generally on the Asiatic side without

perceiving the greater strength of the opposing Stream by which
the diplomatic traveller palliates his own failure.———An amusement
in the small bay which opens immediately below the Asiatic fort was
to *dive* for the LAND tortoises which we flung in on purpose—as they
amphibiously crawled along the bottom.—*This* does not argue any
greater violence of current than on the European shore. With regard
to the modest insinuation that we chose the European side as "easier"
—I appeal to Mr. Hobhouse and Admiral Bathurst if it be true or no?
(poor Ekenhead being since dead)—had we been aware of any such
difference of Current as is asserted—we would at least have proved
it—and were not likely to have given it up in the twenty five minutes
of Mr. T.'s own experiment. The secret of all this is—that Mr. Turner
failed and that we succeeded—and he is consequently disappointed—
and seems not unwilling to overshadow whatever little merit there
might be in our Success.———why did he not try the European side?
—If he had succeeded there after failing on the Asiatic his plea would
have been more graceful and gracious.—Mr. T. may find what fault
he pleases with my poetry—or my politics—but I recommend him to
leave aquatic reflections—till he is able to swim "five and twenty
minutes" without being *"exhausted"* though I believe he is the first
modern Tory who ever swam *"against* the Stream" for half the time.
———3

[TO JOHN CAM HOBHOUSE]   *Ravenna. F[ebruar]y 22d. 1821*

My dear Hobhouse—Why the devil don't you write? are you out
of humour?—and why?—I am not—and shall therefore favour you
with one epistle and two requests.—The first is to make a short
note to a letter I have written to Murray for publication (in any
Magazine or in the Examiner) on the remarks of a diplomatic puppy
called Turner—who having *failed* in swimming the Hellespont—says
that Ekenhead & I succeeded because the *Current* was in our *favour*!!—
from the *European* side—was it so? were we not obliged to *swim up*
against it to pass at all?———My next request is that you will be
personally polite—and request Douglas K[innaird] to be so—to Mr.
Curioni (an Opera Singer) & Madame Taruscelli—a Venetian fair
(the same that Kinnaird wanted to be introduced to and was refused)

---

3 This letter was published in the *Monthly Magazine* for April, 1821, and in the
Traveller for April 3, 1821. Turner's reply was not published until after Byron's
death. See Moore, II, 451, 817–819.

who will arrive in London early in March from Barcelona for the Opera.——I am sure that you would like the Lady's society vastly—and oblige her by yours; she is an old friend of mine—and very pretty.——She has written to me the enclosed epistle—which will explain her.—Now an't I a good fellow?——I am not like those Venetian fellows who—when their own liaisons are over with a piece—would prevent all others from partaking of the public property—as they did by Kinnaird—and *would* have done by me—but I introduced myself—being piqued by their "Dog in a Manger" behaviour.——As to politics I enclose you the Pope's proclamation———of course I cannot write at length—all letters being opened.—The Germans are within hail of the Neapolitans by this time.——They will get their Gruel.—They marched ten days sooner than expected—which prevented a general rising.—But they are in a situation that if they do not win their first battle—they will have all Italy upon them.—They are damned rascals and deserve it.—It is however hard upon the poor Pope—in his old age to have all this row in his neighbourhood.—

yrs. ever & truly
B

[TO THOMAS MOORE]   *Ravenna, February 22d, 1821*

As I wish the soul of the late Antoine Galignani to rest in peace (you will have read his death, published by himself, in his own newspaper), you are requested particularly to inform his children and heirs, that of their "*Literary Gazette,*" to which I subscribed more than *two* months ago, I have only received one *number,* notwithstanding I have written to them repeatedly. If they have no regard for me, a subscriber, they ought to have some for their deceased parent, who is undoubtedly no better off in his present residence for this total want of attention. If not, let me have my francs. They were paid by Missiaglia, the *W*enetian bookseller. You may also hint to them that when a gentleman writes a letter, it is usual to send an answer. If not, I shall make them "a speech," which will comprise an eulogy on the deceased.

We are here full of war, and within two days of the seat of it, expecting intelligence momently. We shall now see if our Italian friends are good for any thing but "a shooting round a corner," like the Irishman's gun. Excuse haste,—I write with my spurs putting on. My horses are at the door, and an Italian Count waiting to accompany me in my ride.

Yours, &c.

P.S.—Pray, amongst my letters, did you get one detailing the death of the commandant here? He was killed near my door, and died in my house.

BOWLES AND CAMPBELL

To the air of "*How now, Madame Flirt,*" in the Beggars' Opera.

BOWLES.   Why, how now, saucy Tom,
                    If you thus must ramble,
            I will publish some
                    Remarks on Mr. Campbell.

                    Answer.

CAMPBELL.   Why, how now, Billy Bowles?
                        Sure the priest is maudlin!
(*To the public*)   How can you, damn your souls!
                        Listen to his twaddling?

[TO JOHN MURRAY]   *Ravenna. February 26th. 1821*

Dear Moray—Over the *second Note*[1] viz—the one on Lady M. Montague—I leave you a complete discretionary power of *omission altogether* or curtailment, as you please—since it may be scarcely chaste enough for the Canting prudery of the day.—The *first* note on a different subject you had better append to the letters.——Let me know what your Utican Senate[2] say, and acknowledge all the packets.

                                            yrs. ever
                                            BYRON

Write to *Moore* and ask him for my lines to *him* beginning with

            "My Boat is at the shore["]

they have been published incorrectly—*you* may publish them.——
I have written *twice* to Thorwaldsen without any answer!!—Tell

[1] This note, intended as an addition to Byron's first letter to Murray on the Bowles-Pope controversy was withheld by Murray and was first published by Prothero (*LJ*, V, 565–566.) The note concerns Pope's relationship with Mary Wortley Montagu.

[2] Byron often used references to Pope's attack on Addison and his little coterie to rib Murray and his advisers. Cf. the Epistle to Dr. Arbuthnot (lines 209–210):

            "Like Cato, give his little Senate laws,
              And sit attentive to his own applause."

Cato Uticensis made his last stand against Caesar in Utica in North Africa.

Hobhouse so—he was *paid* four years ago—you must address some English at Rome upon the subject—I know none there myself.

Ode on the 2d. January 1821

Upon this day I married & full sore
Repent that marriage but my father's more.

—
or
—

Upon this day I married and deplore
That marriage deeply but my father's more.
[Scrawl]

On the same day to *Medea*

This day of all our days has done
The most for me and you
T is just *six* years since we were *one*—
And *five* since we were two.

[TO DOUGLAS KINNAIRD]   *Ravenna. F[ebruary] 26th. 1821*

My dear Douglas—You will have seen or soon will see—a greater number of yr. circular billets than usual from my quarter—and that you may not suppose me more extravagant than usual I will let you know the reason.—In the present confusion—and approaching convulsion of all these Countries—Mr. Ghigi—(my banker here) has taken a fancy to your notes—and is continually giving me *cash* for them—which Cash is still in my strong box—and not more of it spent than usual. I believe that Ghigi is speculating upon grain &c. on account of the war—or that he finds your notes *better paper* than the Country bills of exchange:—this is all I know—& the reason of this apparent extravagance of mine.

I have a favour to ask you.—Curioni the Opera Singer will arrive in England from Barcelona in March—he is accompanied by the Signora Arpalice Taruscelli of Venice—a very pretty woman—and an old ⟨fr⟩ acquaintance of mine.—They have written to me for letters.—Will you call upon them? and introduce them to such of the theatrical people and Editors—Perry[1] &c. as may be useful to them? You may perhaps *not* have to repent of it—for She is very pretty—and no less gallant—and grateful for any attention.—You will find them out by

---

[1] James Perry, editor of *The Morning Chronicle*, had been an actor in his youth.

enquiring at the Opera house.—I have lately written to you on various matters.—On politics I can say nothing—but you will hear strange things soon probably—The Confusion is as great as it can well be—I am going to put my daughter into a convent—& for myself—I shall take what Fortune is pleased to send;—you may imagine what sort of scene Italy is likely to present in a row.—

If you can do anything by way of Sale purchase or mortgage to lay my money out on while the funds are high—let me know—Hanson's rascality throws me into despair.—You will have received my message *for* him—which I beg of you to repeat, I am anxious to have done with him.—Could we not purchase—or find an English mortgage? In the course of time land must get up again—& now might be the time to buy.—As I want no *mansion house* nor ornamental grounds—nothing but *rental* land—what think you? I shall be guided by your opinion in all such matters—but if the funds fail I will blow Bland's brains out.—

yrs. ever & truly
[Scrawl]

P.S.—I answered you about Murray.

[TO JOHN MURRAY]   *Ravenna—March 1st. 1821*

D[ea]r Moray—After the Stanza near the close of Canto 5th. which ends with

"Has quite the contrary effect on Vice"[1]

Insert the following

———

> Thus in the East they are extremely strict
> And *Wedlock* and a *Padlock* mean the same,
> Excepting only when the former's picked
> It never can be replaced in proper frame,
> Spoilt, as a pipe of Claret is when pricked—
> But then their own Polygamy's to blame,
> Why don't they knead two virtuous souls for life,
> Into that moral Centaur, Man and Wife?[2]

[1] *Don Juan*, Canto V, stanza 157.
[2] To Byron's annoyance, Murray omitted this stanza in his first printing of the Canto.

I have received the remainder of the *Hints without* the *Latin*—and *without* the *Note* upon *Pope* from the Letter to the E[dinburgh] B[lackwood's] M[agazine].——Instead of this you send the *lines* on *Jeffrey*[3]—though you knew so positively that they were to be omitted —that I *left the direction that they should be cancelled appended to my power of Attorney* to you previously to leaving England—and in case of my demise before the publication of the "Hints".—Of course they must be omitted—and I feel vexed that they were sent.—Has the whole English text been sent regularly continued from the part broken off in the first proofs?—And Pray request Mr. Hobhouse to adjust the *Latin* to the English—the imitation is so close—that I am unwilling to deprive it of it's principal merit, it's closeness.——I look upon it and my Pulci as by far the best things of my doing—*you* will not think so— and *get* frightened for fear I shall charge accordingly—but I know that they will *not* be popular—so don't be afraid—publish them together.
———

The enclosed letter will make you laugh.—Pray answer it for me & *secretly*—not to mortify him.—Tell Mr. Balfour that I never wrote for a *prize* in my life—and that the very thought of it would make me write worse than the worst Scribbler.—As for the twenty pounds he wants to gain—[you may] *send* them to him for me—and *deduct* them in reckoning with Mr. Kinnaird.—*Deduct also your own bill for books and powders &c. &c.* which must be considerable.——Give my love to Sir W. Scott—& tell him to write more novels;—pray send out Waverley and the Guy M[annering]—and the Antiquary—It is five years since I have had a copy——I have read all the others forty times.——Have you received all my packets—on Pope, letters, &c. &c. &c.? I write in great haste.

yrs. ever [Scrawl]

P.S.—I have had a long letter from Hodgson who it seems has also taken up Pope—and adds "the liberties I have taken with *your* poetry in this pamphlet are no more than I might have ventured in those delightful days &c. ["]—that may very well be—but if he has said anything I don't like—I'll Archbishop of Granada him.[4]—I am in a polemical humour.

---

[3] *Hints from Horace*, lines 589–626. For variants in the manuscripts, see *Poetry*, I, 429. The poem was not published until after Byron's death, in 1831.

[4] The Archbishop dismissed Gil Blas for his candour in criticising his sermons and wished him prosperity, "avec un peu plus de goût."

Ravenna, Marza [Marzo?] 1mo, 1821

I have received your message, through my sister's letter, about English security, &c. &c. It is considerate, (and true, even,) that *such* is to be found—but not that I shall find it. Mr. ∗ ∗ [Hanson], for his own views and purposes, will thwart all such attempts till he has accomplished his own, viz. to make me lend my fortune to some client of his choosing.

At this distance—after this absence, and with my utter ignorance of affairs and business—with my temper and impatience, I have neither the means nor the mind to resist ∗ ∗ ∗ ∗ Thinking of the funds as I do, and wishing to secure a reversion to my sister and her children, I should jump at most expedients.

What I told you is come to pass—the Neapolitan war is declared. Your funds will fall, and I shall be in consequence ruined. That's nothing—but my blood relations will be so. You and your child are provided for. Live and prosper—I wish so much to both. Live and prosper—you have the means. I think but of my real kin and kindred, who may be the victims of this accursed bubble.

You neither know nor dream of the consequences of this war. It is a war of *men* with monarchs, and will spread like a spark on the dry, rank grass of the vegetable desert. What it is with you and your English, you do not know, for ye sleep. What it is with us here, I know, for it is before, and around, and within us.

Judge of my detestation of England and of all that it inherits, when I avoid returning to your country at a time when not only my pecuniary interests, but, it may be, even my personal security, require it. I can say no more, for all letters are opened. A short time will decide upon what is to be done here, and then you will learn it without being more troubled with me or my correspondence. Whatever happens, an individual is little, so the cause is forwarded.

I have no more to say to you on the score of affairs, or on any other subject.

[TO JOHN MURRAY]   *March 2d. 1821*

D[ea]r Murray—This was the beginning of a letter which I meant for Perry—but stopt short—hoping you would be able to prevent the theatres.—Of course you need not send it—but it explains to you my feelings on the subject—you say that "there is nothing to fear let them do what they please" that is to say that *you* would see me *damned with great tranquility—you are a fine fellow—*

Dear Sir—I have received a strange piece of news which cannot be more disagreeable to your Public than it is to me.—My Letters and the Gazettes do me the honour to say that it is the intention of some of the London Managers to bring forward on the Stage the poem of "Marino Faliero &c."—which was never intended for such an exhibition—and I trust will never undergo it.——It is certainly unfit for it.——I have never written but for the solitary *reader*—and require no experiments for applause beyond his silent approbation.——Since such an attempt to drag me forth as a Gladiator in the Theatrical Arena—is a violation of all the courtesies of Literature—I trust that the impartial part of the Press will step between me and this pollution. —I say pollution—because every violation of a *right* is such—and I claim my right as an author to prevent what I have written from being turned into a Stage-play.—I have too much respect for the Public to permit this of my own free will.—Had I sought their favour it would have been by a Pantomine.——I have said that I write only for the readers—Beyond this I cannot consent to any publication—or to the abuse of any publication of mine to the purpose of Histrionism.—The applause of an audience would give me no pleasure—their disapprobation might however give me pain.—The wager is therefore not equal.—You may perhaps say—"how can this be?—if their disapprobation gives pain—their praise might afford pleasure?"—By no means.—The kick of an Ass, or the Sting of a Wasp may be painful to those who would find nothing agreeable in the Braying of the one— or in the Buzzing of the other.——This may not seem a courteous comparison—but I have no other ready—and it comes naturally.——

[TO JOHN MURRAY]   *R[avenn]a. March 9th. 1821*

Illustrious Moray—You are requested with the "advice of friends" to continue to patch the enclosed "Addenda" into my letter to you on the Subject of Bill Bowles's Pope &c.——I think that it may be inoculated into the body of the letter with a little care—Consult—& engraft it.——I enclose you the proposition of a Mr. [Fe]arman[1] one of yr. brethren—there is a civil gentleman for you.

yrs. truly
[Scrawl]

[1] Fearman, a publisher of 170 New Bond Street, offered to publish Cantos 3, 4, and 5 of *Don Juan*. Murray was hesitating about the publication.

Dear Douglas/—If the funds should continue to rise as you say—make the proposal to Lady B['s] trustee &c. to *sell out at all events*—and either invest the money in the *fives*—or in the hands of trustworthy bankers—till you can light upon security.—I *would willingly go without a year's interest* of the principal—to be once *fairly* out of the funds altogether—and so the *principal* is safe for the present—what need the trustees fear?——In that case—send me out a *power* (for *signature*) to enable you to sell—with proper directions.—Press this upon the others—all you can say—nor has—nor will have any effect upon me till I am out of the funds,—their idea haunts me & will drive me to some desperate thing for which you will all be sorry.——I am glad that you like the "Memoir"—As to the "meaning" we are obliged to it so often in the course of our lives—that it is not to be wondered at occasionally in relating the same, it is the more natural.

You ask me why I don't go to Paris?—Ask the trustees?——But independent of that consideration—though I read & comprehend French with far more ease & pleasure than Italian—(which is a heavy language to read in *prose*) yet my foreign speech is Italian—and my way of life very little adapted to the eternal French vivaciousness—& gregarious loquacity.—As to the impression which you say that I should make—at *three* and *twenty* it might perhaps have fascinated me—at three & thirty it is indifferent.——It is also incomprehensible to me how it can be as Moore & you both say—for surely my habits of thought & writing must cut a queer figure in a prose translation—which is the only medium through which they know them.——Besides I am in some measure familiarized & domesticated in Italy,—where I put my daughter the other day in a Convent for education.[1]——

You say nothing of Canto 5th.—whence I infer that it has not your imperial approbation.—Never mind.—Tell Hobhouse that I wrote to him a fortnight ago.——Of politics I *could* say a good deal—& must therefore be silent—for all letters are opened now, &—though I care not about myself—I might perhaps compromise others.—They *missed* here only by *five* days.—Understand you?——I have had a civil proposal from a Mr. Fearman bookseller 170 New Bond Street to treat for the "Don Juan"—pray give him a *civil* answer for me and say "that *supposing* that I were the author of that poem—Mr. Murray

---

[1] Byron put Allegra in the Convent school of San Giovanni Battista at Bagnacavallo on March 1, 1821.

would have naturally the refusal.["]—F[earman] wrote under the idea that I had not treated with Murray.—It is not my intention to come to England at present—perhaps I may take a run over *after* the *Coronation*—because I have a little affair to settle which has been on my mind some time.—But in case of settling it—& surviving the settlement—I should wish to return to Italy.—Till Lady N[oel] goes home—how could the *fee* suffice?—

yrs. ever
[Scrawl]

Mr. Murray has requested to publish the *Juans*—before he settles—and I have acceded to this.—He must also publish the Italian translation from the Morgante and the Hints from Horace. Have you seen my letter on Bowles's Pope?

[TO JOHN MURRAY]   *R[avenn]a M[arz]o 12 o 1821*

D[ea]r M[urra]y—Insert where they may seem apt—the *inclosed addenda* to the *Letter on Bowles* &c.; they will come into the body of the letter if you consult any of your Utica where to place them.—If there is too much—or too harsh—or not intelligible &c. let me know—and I will alter or omit the portion pointed out.——

[Scrawl]

P.S.—Please to acknowledge all *packets* containing matters of print—by return of post—letters of mere convenance may wait your bibliopolar pleasure & leisure.——

[TO JOHN MURRAY]   *Ravenna. Marzo [13–16?] 1821*

Dear Moray—In my packet of the 12th Instant—in the last sheet (*not* the *half* sheet)—last page—*omit* the sentence which (defining or attempting to define what and who are gentlemanly) begins—"I should say at least in life—that most military men have it & few naval—that several men of rank have it—& few lawyers &c. &c."[1]——I say—omit the whole of that Sentence—because like the "Cosmogony or Creation of the World" in "the Vicar of Wakefield"—it is not much to the purpose.—In the Sentence above too—almost at the top of the same page—After the words "that there ever was or can be an Aristocracy of poets"—add—& insert—these words——"I do not mean that they should write in the Style of the Song by a person of Quality—or *parle Euphuism*—but there is a *Nobility* of thought and

---

[1] The note was not added to the first letter on Bowles.

expression to be found no less in Shakespeare—Pope—and Burns—
than in Dante and Alfieri—&c. &c." & so on.——Or if you please—
perhaps you had better omit the whole of the latter digression on the
vulgar poets—and insert only as far as the end of the Sentence upon
Pope's Homer—where I prefer it to Cowper's—and quote Dr. Clarke
in favour of it's accuracy.——Upon all these points—take an opinion
—take the Sense (or nonsense) of your learned visitants—and act
thereby—I am very tractable—in PROSE.——

Whether I have made out the case for Pope—I know not—but I am
very sure that I have been zealous in the attempt.—If it comes to the
proofs—we shall beat the Blackguards—I will show more *imagery* in
twenty lines of Pope than in any equal length of quotation in English
poesy—& that in places where they least expect it,—for instance—in
his lines on *Sporus*—now—do just *read* them over——the subject is of
no consequence—(whether it be *Satire* or Epic) we are talking of
poetry and *imagery*—from *Nature and Art.*—Now—mark—the images
separately & arithmetically.—

1 The thing of *Silk*
2 *Curd* of *Ass's* Milk
3 The *Butterfly*—
4 The *Wheel*—
5 Bug with gilded wings.—
6 *Painted* Child of dirt.—
7 ⟨The⟩ Whose *Buzz* ⟨the witty &c.⟩
8 Well-bred *Spaniels*—
9 *Shallow streams run dimpling*
10 *Florid impotence.*—
11 *Prompter*——*Puppet squeaks*—
12 *The Ear of Eve.*—
13 *Familiar toad*—
14 *Half-froth—half-venom, spits* himself abroad.—
15 *Fop* at the *toilet*—
16 *Flatterer* at the *board*—
17 *Amphibious thing*—
18 Now *trips* a *lady*
19 Now *struts* a *Lord.*—
20 A *Cherub's face*—
20[21] A *reptile* all the rest.—
22 ⟨Eve's tempter⟩ The *Rabbins*—
23 Pride that *licks the dust.*

"Beauty that shocks you—parts that none will trust—
Wit that can creep—and *Pride* that *licks* the *dust*."

Now is there a line of all the passage without the most *forcible* imagery?
—(for his purpose)—look at the *variety* at the *poetry*—of the passage
——at the *imagination*——there is hardly a line ⟨of all that passage⟩
—from which a *painting* might not be made—and *is*.—But this is
nothing in comparison with his higher passages in the Essay on Man—
& many of his other poems—serious & comic. There never was such
an unjust outcry in this world—as that which these Scoundrels are
trying against Pope.——In the letter to you upon Bowles &c.—insert
these which follow (*under* the place as a Note—where I am speaking of
Dyer's Gronger Hill—and the use of *artificial* imagery in illustrating
Nature)—"Corneille's celebrated lines on Fortune—

> "Et comme Elle a l'éclat du *Verre*
> Elle en a la fragilité."[2]

are a further instance of the noble use which may be made of artificial
imagery, & quite equal to any taken from Nature.["]³

Ask Mr. Gifford—if in the 5th act of "the Doge" you could not
contrive (where the Sentence of the *Veil* is past) to insert the following
lines in M[arino] F[aliero]'s answer.——

> But let it be so.—It will be in vain.
> The Veil which blackens o'er the blighted name
> And hides—or seems to hide—these lineaments—
> Shall draw more Gazers than the thousand portraits
> Which glitter round it in their painted trappings—
> *Your* delegated Slaves—the people's tyrants.—[4]

Which will be best?—

> *painted* trappings
> or
> pictured—purple—
> or
> pictured trappings—
> or
> painted purple—

2 *Polyeucte*, Act. IV, scene 2.
3 The note was not added.
4 *Marino Faliero*, Act V, scene 1, line 501 ff.

Perpend—and let me know.——I have not had any letter—from you —which I am anxious for;—to know whether you have received my letters—and packets—the letter on Bowles's Pope &c. &c. Let me hear from you.—

yrs. truly
[Scrawl]

P.S.—Upon *public* matters—here—I say little.—You will hear soon enough of a general row throughout Italy.—There never was a more foolish step than the Expedition to N[aples]—by these fellows.
——

P.S.—I wish you to propose to *Holmes*[5] the miniature painter to come out to me this spring.—I will pay his expences—and any sum in reason.——I wish him to take my daughter's picture—(who is in a convent) and the Countess G[uiccioli]'s—and the head of a peasant Girl—which latter would make a study for Raphael.—It is a complete *peasant* face—but an *Italian* peasant's—and quite in the Raphael Fornarina style.——Her figure is tall, but rather large—and not at all comparable to her face—which is really superb.—She is not seventeen and I am anxious to have her likeness while it lasts.—Madame G[uiccioli] is also very handsome—but it is quite in a different style— completely blonde and fair—very uncommon in Italy—yet not an *English* fairness but more like a Swede or a Norwegian. Her figure too—particularly the bust is uncommonly good.——It must be *Holmes*—I like him because he takes such inveterate likenesses.—There is a war here but a solitary traveller with little baggage—& nothing to do with politics has nothing to [fear?]. Pack him up in the diligence. —Don't forget.——

[TO DOUGLAS KINNAIRD]   *R[avenn]a March 23d. 1821*

My Dear Douglas/—I shall consent to nothing of the kind.—Our good friends must have the goodness to "bide a wee".—One of these events must occur.—Lady Noel—will die or Lady B[yron]—or myself. —In the first case they will be paid out of the incoming—in the second my property will be so far liberated (the offspring being a daughter) as to leave a surplus to cover more than any outstanding present debts;—in the third—my executors will of course see their claims

[5] James Holmes had painted several miniatures of Byron in England, but he declined the invitation to come to Italy.

liquidated.——But as to my parting at this present with a thousand guineas—I wonder if you take me for an Atheist—to make me so unchristian a proposition.——It is true that I have reduced my expences in *that* line—but I have had others to encounter.—On getting to dry land—I have had to buy carriages—& some new horses—and to furnish my house—for here you find only walls *no furnished* apartments —it is not the Custom.—Besides—though I do not subscribe to liquidate the sum of two thousand pounds for a man of twenty thousand a year—nor write me down a contribution to the English radical societies—yet wherever I find a poor man suffering for his opinions— and there are many such in this country—I always let him have a shilling out of a guinea.—You speak with some facetiousness of the *Huns* &c.——wait till the play is played out.—Whatever happens— no tyrant nor tyranny—nor barbarian Army shall ever make me change my tone—or thoughts or actions—or alter anything but my temper. ——I say so *now*—as I said so then—now that they are at their— butcher-work—as before when they were merely preparing for it.——

As to Murray—I presume that you forwarded my letters———I acquiesce in what you say about the arrangement with him[1]—but not at all in the appropriation of the fee.—Let me see it in circulars and then I will tell you whether I will pay them away or no.——You must have a very bad opinion of my principles to hint at such a thing.— If you pay any thing—pay them the interest—provided it is not above a hundred & fifty pounds.—You persuaded me to give those bonds— & now you see the consequence.—It would have been better to have stood a suit at [law].—At the worst—Rochdale will always in any case bring enough to cover the bonds—and they may seize and sell it for anything I care.—I have had more trouble than profit with it.— As to Lady Noel—what you say of her declining health—would be very well to any one else—but the way to be immortal (I mean *not* to die at all) is to have me for your heir.—I recommend you to put me in your will—& you will see that (as long as *I* live at least)—you will never even catch cold.——I have written to you twice or thrice lately —and so on.—I could give you some curious and interesting details on things here—but they open all letters—and I have no wish to gratify any curiosity—except that of my friends & gossips.—Some day or other when we meet (if we meet) I will make your hair stand on end—& Hobhouse's wig (does he wear one still) start from its frame—& leave him under *bare poles*.—There is one thing which I wish

---

[1] Murray eventually paid £1000 for the copyright of *Marino Faliero*.

particularly to propose to you patriots—& yet it can't be—without this letter went in a balloon—and as Incledon says *"thaut's* impossible"[2]—Let me hear from you—and as good news as you can send in that agreeable soft conciliatory style of yrs.[3]

[Scrawl]

[TO RICHARD BELGRAVE HOPPNER (*a*)] [*April 3? 1821*]

D[ea]r Hoppner—The moral part of this letter upon the *Italians* &c. comes with an excellent grace from the writer now living with a *man* & his *wife*—and having planted a child in the N[aples] *Foundling* &c.[1] —with regard to the rest of the letter—*you* know as well as any one how far it is or is not correct—

[TO RICHARD BELGRAVE HOPPNER (*b*)] *Ravenna, April 3d. 1821*

My dear Hoppner—Thanks for the translation. I have sent you some books which I do not know whether you have read or not—you need not return them in any case.—I enclose you also a letter from Pisa[1]—on the usual subject—*not* to trouble you as "umpire" as the person desires—but to enable you to judge whether I do or do not deserve such a piece of objurgation. I have neither spared trouble nor expence in the care of the child—and as she was now four years old complete—and quite above the control of the Servants—& as it was not fit that she should remain with them longer in any case—and as a *man* living without any woman at the head of his house—cannot much attend to a nursery, ⟨as is necessary⟩—I had no resource but to place her for a time (at a high pension too) in the convent of Bagna-Cavalli (twelve miles off) where the air is good and where she will at least have her learning advanced—& her morals and religion inculcated.— I had also another reason—things were and are in such a state here— that I had no reason to look upon my personal safety as particularly insurable—and I thought the infant best out of harm's way, for the

---

[2] See Vol. 5, p. 182.

[3] Part of this letter was published by Prothero under the date February 25, 1822, together with parts of a letter of January 23, 1822. (*LJ*, VI, 24–27.) Prothero's source was *The Keepsake* in which a number of garbled letters of Kinnaird appeared in 1830.

[1] This is written on a letter of Claire Clairmont to Byron, dated March 24, 1821, protesting the placing of Allegra in the convent. It seems to indicate that at this point Byron was inclined to believe Elise's story, relayed to him by Hoppner, that Claire had a child by Shelley, which they placed in a foundling hospital in Naples.

[1] From Claire Clairmont.

present.——You *know* (perhaps more than I do) that to allow the Child to be with her mother—& with *them* & their principles—would be ⟨like⟩ absolute insanity—if not worse—that even her health would not be attended to properly—to say nothing of the Indecorum.—It is also fit that I should add that I by no means intended nor intend to give a *natural* Child an *English* Education, because with the disadvantages of her birth her after settlement would be doubly difficult.—Abroad—with a fair foreign education—and a portion of five or six thousand pounds—she might and may marry very respectably—in England such a dowry would be a pittance—while ⟨out of it⟩ elsewhere it is a fortune.——It is besides my wish that She should be a R[oma]n *Catholic*—which I look upon as the best religion as it is assuredly the oldest of the various branches of Christianity.———I have no[t?] explained my notions as to the *place* where she now is—it is the best I could find for the present—but I have no prejudices in its favour.—Of "the promise made at Geneva" of which this person speaks I have no recollection—nor can I conceive it possible to have been entered into—when the child was yet unborn—& might never have been born at all.——You recollect also (*entre nous* for I have not mentioned it as you will perceive by the letter) the pretty story you told me of what occurred at Naples—which I see no reason to doubt in the main points—though Elise might not relate all accurately.—[2] My best respects to Mrs. Hoppner—and to our acquaintances.——I do not speak of politics because it seems a hopeless subject—as long as these scoundrels are to be permitted to bully States out of their independence.—believe me

yrs. ever & truly
BYRON

P.S.—There is a report here of a change in France—but with what truth is not yet known.

[TO GIOVANNI BATTISTA MISSIAGLIA] *Ravenna. 13 Aprile 1821*

[Added to letter in Italian by Lega Zambelli]

Dear Sir—Collina[1] is a damned rascal who has cheated me of several scudi.—In case this opinion may be of service to you in yr. future dealings with him—I send it.—

yrs. very truly
BN

[2] See previous letter to Hoppner.
[1] Unidentified.

[TO JOHN MURRAY]   *Ravenna. April 21st. 1821*

Illustrious Moray—I enclose you another letter on *"Bowles"*.—
But I premise that it is not like the former—and I am not at all [sure]
how *much*—if *any* of it—should be published. Upon this point you can
consult with Mr. Gifford—and think *twice* before you publish it at
all.[1]—Pray send me some more pounds weight of Soda powders—I
drink them in Summer by dozens.

                                                        yrs. truly
                                                        B

P.S.—You may make my subscription to Mr. Scott's widow[2] &c.
thirty instead of the proposed *ten* pounds—but do not put down *my*
name—put down N. B. only—The reason is, that I have mentioned him
in the enclosed pamphlet—it would look indelicate.—I would give
more——but my disappointments of last year—about Rochdale—
and the transfer from the funds—render me more economical for the
present.—

P.S. 2d.—by next post I will send you the threatening Italian trash
alluded to in the enclosed letter—You can make a note of it for the
page alluding to the subject—I had not room for it in this cover—nor
time. [On cover]: Mr. M. is requested to acknowledge the receipt of
this packet by return of post—by way of Calais—as quickest.

[TO JOHN CAM HOBHOUSE]   *Ravenna—April 26th. 1821*

Dear Hobhouse/—You know by this time with all Europe—the
precious treachery and desertion of the Neapolitans. I was taken in
like many others by their demonstrations—& have probably been
more ashamed of them than they are of themselves.—I can write
nothing by the post—but if ever we meet I will tell you a thing or

---

[1] Byron's second letter on Bowles was not published until 1835.
[2] John Scott (1783–1821) had been a schoolfellow of Byron at Aberdeen. He
was editor successively of several periodicals. From 1815 to 1819 he lived abroad
and visited Byron in Venice. In 1819 he became the first editor of the new *London
Magazine*. In 1821 his attacks on *Blackwood's Magazine* led to a quarrel with
Lockhart, and a duel with J. H. Christie, which resulted in Scott's death on
February 16, 1821. Byron mentioned him in his second letter on Bowles (See *LJ*,
V, 576.)

two—of no great importance—perhaps—but which will serve you to laugh at.—I can't laugh yet—the thing is a little too serious;—if the Scoundrels had only compromised themselves—it would matter little —but they were busy every where—and all for this! The rest of the Italians execrate them as you will do, & all honest men of all nations. ——Poland and Ireland were Sparta and Spart*acus* compared to these villains.—But there is no room to be sufficiently bilious—nor bile enough to spit upon them.——

I have had a letter from the Dougal.—And one from you some weeks ago —I can give you no news in return that would interest you and indeed what can interest one after such a business?——I hear "Rogers cuts *you*"—because I called him "Venerable"—the next time I will state his age without the respectable epithet annexed to it— which in fact he does not deserve.—However he is Seventy three[1] and I can prove it by the register.——We see by the papers that you dine and return thanks as usual.—Fletcher says that "he supposes you have got Bergami's place by this time".[2]—His literal words I assure you— and not a clinch of mine.—With regard to your objections to my chastising that Scoundrel Brougham—it will be time enough to answer them (and Douglas also) if ever we meet again—which is not very certain. When you take away an honourable motive for returning to England why should I return?—To be abused & belied—and to live like a beggar with an Income which in any other country would suffice for all the decencies of a Gentleman.——Pray write when it suits you, I did not write because there was nothing to say—that could be said—without being pried into in this country of tyrants and Spies and foreign barbarians, let loose upon it again. From Murray I have had no news to signify except some literary intelligence about myself and other Scribblers.—I know nothing of the fortune of my publications —and can wait.——I hope that you and yours prosper.—

ever yrs. most affecty.
Bn

[1] Rogers was actually only 58 at the time, having been born in 1763, but most contemporary accounts indicate that he looked much older. His cadaverous appearance was the subject of many jests. Byron had written (in the Bowles letter) that he met Bowles "in the house of our venerable host", Rogers, "the last Argonaut of classic English poetry, and the Nestor of our inferior race of living poets.".

[2] Bergami was the Italian courier of Queen Caroline with whom she was accused of having an adulterous relationship while she was abroad. Hobhouse had been a defender of the Queen during her trial.

My dear Douglas—"The Mystery is resolved" as Mrs. Malaprop says.—You were not taken in—but I was.—However I cannot laugh at the joke for sundry reasons— some of them personal.—if ever we meet—I can tell you a few things which may perhaps amuse you for a moment.—In the mean time I have been disappointed—& you are amused without me.—So that there is no loss to you at least.—I have received your letters—all very kind and sensible—nobody like you for business.—But I cannot part with more of the produce than the 150— for the present.—As for Claughton—why don't he pay? I wrote to desire that he might be proceeded with weeks ago.—I hear from Mrs. L[eigh] that Lady N[oel] *has been* "dangerously ill"—but it should seem by *her* letter that She is now getting dangerously well again.— Your letter seems more dubious.—Your approval of *the B[owle]s Letter* is gratifying——I shall be glad to hear as much on the part of the General reader.———I did not mean you to be *"passive"* with Murray—on the contrary—I shall thank you to be *active*—for I will not treat with him except through *you* or Hobhouse.—*Judge* for yourself— according to the appearances of the impression made by the M. S. S. on their publication—or consult any honest men who understand such matters—and I will abide by your decision.—Murray complains to me that you are *brusque* with him—for that matter—so you are at times with most people—and I see no reason for any exception in his favour. ———I gave in about the D[on] Juans—because you all seemed to think them heavy;—you [see?] I am tractable—but if you had taken the other line—I should have been as acquiescent in your decision.—— I do not know how far your new Opera Acquaintances[1] may answer your expectations—but any civility to them will be an addition to the many you have conferred on your *trusting* client—and affectionate friend—

                                                                        B

P.S.—What's that you say about *"Yolk of Egg for the hair"*? The receipt—the receipt immediately.—Does the Letter take? Love to Hobhouse.—Why should Rogers take the "Venerable" ill?—He was sixty three years eleven months and fourteen days old when I first knew him ten years ago—come next November.—I meant but a compliment—as for his age I have seen the certificate from Bow Church dated "1747—October 10th—Baptized Samuel Son of Peter Rogers Scrivener Furnival's Inn".——He and Dryden—and Chaucer—are

[1] See Feb. 16, 1821, to Murray.

the oldest upon record who have written so well at that advanced period.—His age is a credit to him.——I wonder what you mean.——Don't forget the recipe.——

Dear Moray—I sent you by last *postis* a large packet—which will *not* do for publication (I suspect) being as the Apprentices say—"damned *low*".—I put off also for a week or two sending the Italian Scrawl which will form a Note to it.—The reason is that letters being opened I wish to "bide a wee".——Well have you published the trag[edy]? and does the letter take?[1]——Is it true—what Shelley writes me that poor John Keats died at Rome of the Quarterly Review? I am very sorry for it—though I think he took the wrong line as a poet—and was spoilt by Cockneyfying and Surburbing—and versifying Tooke's Pantheon and Lempriere's Dictionary.——I know by experience that a savage review is Hemlock to a sucking author—and the one on me—(which produced the English Bards &c.) knocked me down—but I got up again.—Instead of bursting a blood-vessel—I drank three bottles of Claret—and began an answer—finding that there was nothing in the Article for which I could lawfully knock Jeffrey on the head in an honourable way.—However I would not be the person who wrote the homicidal article—for all the honour & glory in the World,—though I by no means approve of that School of Scribbling—which it treats upon.——

You see the Italians here made a sad business of it.—All owing to treachery and disunion amongst themselves.—It has given me great vexation.—The Execrations heaped upon the Neapolitans by the other Italians are quite in unison with those of the rest of Europe.——Mrs. Leigh writes that Lady *No-ill* is getting *well* again.—See what it is to have luck in this world.—I hear that Rogers is not pleased with being called "venerable"—a pretty fellow—if I had thought that he would have been so absurd—I should have spoken of him as defunct—as he really is.—Why betwixt the years he really lived—and those he has been dead—Rogers has been upon the Earth seventy three years and upwards as I have proved in a postscript of my letter by this post to Mr. Kinnaird.——Let me hear from you—and send me some Soda-powders for the Summer dilution.—Write soon.—

yours ever & truly
B

[1] The first letter on Bowles.

P.S.—Your latest packet of books is on its way here but not arrived. Kenilworth excellent.—Thanks for the pocket-books of which I have made presents—to those ladies who like cuts—and landscapes and all that; I have got an Italian book or two which I should like to send you if I had an opportunity.——I am not at present in the very highest health. Spring probably—so I have lowered my diet—and taken to Epsom Salts. As you say my *"prose"* is good—why don't you treat with *Moore* for the reversion of the Memoirs—*conditionally*—*recollect*—not to be published before decease.—*He* has the permission to dispose of them and I advised him to do so.—

[TO PERCY BYSSHE SHELLEY]   *Ravenna, April 26th, 1821*

The child continues doing well, and the accounts are regular and favourable. It is gratifying to me that you and Mrs. Shelley do not disapprove of the step which I have taken, which is merely temporary.

I am very sorry to hear what you say of Keats—is it *actually* true? I did not think criticism had been so killing. Though I differ from you essentially in your estimate of his performances, I so much abhor all unnecessary pain, that I would rather he had been seated on the highest peak of Parnassus than have perished in such a manner. Poor fellow! though with such inordinate self-love he would probably have not been very happy. I read the review of "Endymion" in the Quarterly. It was severe,—but surely not so severe as many reviews in that and other journals upon others.

I recollect the effect on me of the Edinburgh on my first poem; it was rage, and resistance, and redress—but not despondency nor despair. I grant that those are not amiable feelings; but, in this world of bustle and broil, and especially in the career of writing, a man should calculate upon his powers of *resistance* before he goes into the arena.

> "Expect not life from pain nor danger free,
> Nor deem the doom of man reversed for thee."[1]

You know my opinion of *that second-hand* school of poetry. You also know my high opinion of your own poetry,—because it is of *no* school. I read Cenci—but, besides that I think the *subject* essentially *un*-dramatic, I am not an admirer of our old dramatists *as models*. I deny that the English have hitherto had a drama at all. Your Cenci, however, was a work of power, and poetry. As to *my* drama, pray revenge yourself upon it, by being as free as I have been with yours.

[1] Johnson's *Vanity of Human Wishes*, lines 155–156.

I have not yet got your Prometheus,[2] which I long to see. I have heard nothing of mine, and do not know that it is yet published. I have published a pamphlet on the Pope controversy, which you will not like. Had I known that Keats was dead—or that he was alive and so sensitive—I should have omitted some remarks upon his poetry, to which I was provoked by his *attack* upon *Pope*,[3] and my disapprobation of *his own* style of writing.

You want me to undertake a great Poem—I have not the inclination nor the power. As I grow older, the indifference—*not* to life, for we love it by instinct—but to the stimuli of life, increases. Besides, this late failure of the Italians has latterly disappointed me for many reasons,—some public, some personal. My respects to Mrs. S.

Yours ever,
B

P.S.—Could not you and I contrive to meet this summer? Could not you take a run *alone?*

[TO THOMAS MOORE]   *Ravenna, April 28th, 1821*

You cannot have been more disappointed than myself, nor so much deceived. I have been so at some personal risk also, which is not yet done away with. However, no time nor circumstances shall alter my tone nor my feelings of indignation against tyranny triumphant. The present business has been as much a work of treachery as of cowardice, —though both may have done their part. If ever you and I meet again, I will have a talk with you upon the subject. At present, for obvious reasons, I can write but little, as all letters are opened. In *mine* they shall always find *my* sentiments, but nothing that can lead to the oppression of others.

You will please to recollect that the Neapolitans are nowhere now more execrated than in Italy, and not blame a whole people for the vices of a province. That would be like condemning Great Britain because they plunder wrecks in Cornwall.

And now let us be literary;—a sad falling off, but it is always a consolation. If "Othello's occupation be gone," let us take to the next

---

[2] Shelley's *Cenci* was published at Leghorn in 1818; his *Prometheus Unbound* in London in 1820.

[3] Keats attacked the school of Pope in *Sleep and Poetry*, lines 193–206.

best; and, if we cannot contribute to make mankind more free and wise, we may amuse ourselves and those who like it. What are you writing? I have been scribbling at intervals, and Murray will be publishing about now.

Lady Noel has, as you say, been dangerously ill; but it may console you to learn that she is dangerously well again.

I have written a sheet or two more of Memoranda for you; and I kept a little Journal for about a month or two, till I had filled the paper-book. I then left it off, as things grew busy and, afterwards, too gloomy to set down without a painful feeling. This I should be glad to send you, if I had an opportunity; but a volume, however small, don't go well by such posts as exist in this Inquisition of a country.

I have no news. As a very pretty woman said to me a few nights ago, with the tears in her eyes, as she sat at the harpsichord, "Alas! the Italians must now return to making operas." I fear *that* and maccaroni are their forte, and "motley their only wear."[1] However, there are some high spirits among them still. Pray write.

And believe me &c.

[TO ?]   *[May ? 1821]*

These lines are by Moore & in his very best vein.[1]—You must distinguish however between these Lazzaroni of Neapolitans—and the other Italians—who now execrate and despise them with the rest of Europe.——Galignani was afraid to publish & only dared to print them.—

["MY DICTIONARY" (*journal*)][1]   *Ravenna May 1st. 1821*

Amongst various journals—memoranda—diaries &c. which I have kept in the course of my living—I began one about three months ago—& carried it on till I had filled one paper-book (thinnish) and two sheets or so of another.—I then left off partly—because I thought we

---

[1] *As You Like It*, Act II, scene 7.

[1] This note by Byron was attached to a printed poem by Moore on the Neapolitan surrender to the Austrians. See May 3, 1821, to Moore, note 1.

[1] Byron began this journal in May and probably left off because of the turmoil connected with the exile of the Gambas. He resumed it on October 15 as "Detached Thoughts" and continued it intermittently until May 18, 1822.

should have some business here—and I had furbished up my arms—&
got my apparatus ready for taking a turn with the Patriots—having
my drawers full of their proclamations—oaths—& resolutions—& my
lower rooms of their hidden weapons of most calibres——& partly
because I had filled my paper-book.—But the Neapolitans have
betrayed themselves & all the World—& those who would have given
their blood for Italy can now only give her their tears.—

Some day or other—if dust holds together—I have been enough in
the Secret (at least in this part of the country) to cast perhaps some
little *light* upon the atrocious treachery which has replunged Italy
into Barbarism.—At present I have neither the time nor the temper.—
However—the *real* Italians are *not* to blame—merely the Scoundrels at
the *Heel of the Boot*—which the *Hun* now wears & will trample them
to ashes with for their Servility.—I have risked myself with the others
here and how far I may or may not be compromised is a problem at this
moment [;] some of them like "Craigengelt" would "tell all—& more
than all to save themselves"[2] but come what may the cause was a
glorious one—though it reads at present as if the Greeks had run
away from Xerxes.——Happy the few who have only to reproach
themselves with believing that these rascals were less "rascaille" than
they proved.——*Here* in Romagna—the efforts were necessarily
limited to preparations and good intentions—until the Germans were
fairly engaged in *equal* warfare—as we are upon their very frontiers
without a single fort—or hill nearer than San Marino.—Whether
"Hell will be paved with" those "good intentions"—I know not—but
there will probably be good store of Neapolitans to walk upon the
pavement—whatever may be it's composition.—Slabs of lava from
their mountain—with the bodies of their own damned Souls for cement
would be the fittest causeway for Satan's "Corso".——But what shall
I write?—another Journal?—I think not.—Anything that comes uppermost—and call it "my Dictionary."—

My Dictionary

Augustus.—I have often been puzzled with his character.—Was he a
great Man? Assuredly.—But not one of *my* great men—I have always
looked upon Sylla as the greatest Character in History—for laying
down his power at the moment when it was

"too great to keep or to resign"

and thus despising them all.—As to the retention of his power by

[2] In Scott's *The Bride of Lammermoor*.

Augustus—the thing was already settled.—If he had given it up—the Commonwealth was gone—the republic was long past all resuscitation.—Had Brutus & Cassius gained the battle of Philippi—it would not have restored the republic—it's days ended with the Gracchi—the rest was a mere struggle of parties—you might as well cure a Consumption, restore a broken egg—as revive a state so long a prey to every uppermost Soldier as Rome had long been.——As for despotism—if Augustus could have been sure that all his Successors would have been like himself—(I mean *not* as *Octavius*—but Augustus) or Napoleon would have insured the world that *none* of his Successors would have been like himself—the antient—or modern World might have gone on like the Empire of China—in a state of lethargic prosperity.—Suppose for instance—that instead of Tiberius & Caligula—Augustus had been immediately succeeded by Nerva—Trajan—the Antonines—or even by Titus & his father—what a difference in our estimate of himself? so far from gaining by the *contrast* I think that one half of our dislike arises from his having been heired by Tiberius—and one half of Julius Caesar's fame—from his having had his empire consolidated by Augustus.—Suppose that there had been *no Octavius* & Tiberius had "jumped the life"[3] between and at once succeeded Julius?——And yet it is difficult to say whether hereditary right—or popular choice produce the worse Sovereigns—The Roman Consuls make a goodly show—but then they only reigned for a *year*—& were under a sort of personal obligation to distinguish themselves.—It is still more difficult to say which form of Government is the *worst*—all are so bad.—As for democracy it is the worst of the whole—for *what is* (*in fact*) democracy? an Aristocracy of Blackguards.—

Aberdeen—Old and New or the Auldtoun & Newtoun

For several years of my earliest childhood I was in that City—but have never revisited it since I was ten years old.—I was sent at five years old or earlier to a School kept by a Mr. *Bowers*—who was called "*Bodsy* Bowers" by reason of his dapperness.—It was a School for both sexes—I learned little there—except to repeat by rote the first lesson of Monosyllables—"God made man—let us love him" by hearing it often repeated—without acquiring a letter.—Whenever proof was made of my progress at home—I repeated these words with the most rapid fluency, but on turning over a new leaf—I continued to repeat them—so that the narrow boundaries of my first

[3] *Macbeth*, Act 1, scene 7.

year's accomplishments were detected—my ears boxed—(which they did not deserve—seeing that it was by *ear* only that I had acquired my letters)—and my intellects consigned to a new preceptor.—He was a very decent—clever—little Clergyman—named Ross—afterwards Minister of one of the kirks (*East* I think) [;] under *him*—I made an astonishing progress—and I recollect to this day his mild manners & good-natured painstaking.—The moment I could read—my grand passion was *history*—and why I know not—but I was particularly taken with the battle near the Lake Regillus in the Roman History— put into my hands the first.——Four years ago when standing on the heights of Tusculum—& looking down upon the little round Lake that was once Regillus & which dots the immense expanse below—I remembered my young enthusiasm & my old instructor.——After- wards I had a very serious—saturnine—but kind young man named Paterson for a Tutor—he was the son of my Shoemaker—but a good Scholar as is common with the Scotch.—He was a rigid Presbyterian also.—With him I began Latin in Ruddiman's Grammar—& con- tinued till I went to the "Grammar School" (*Scotice "Schule"*— *Aberdonice "Squeel"*) where I threaded all the Classes to the *fourth*— when I was re-called to England (where I had been hatched) by the demise of my Uncle.—I acquired this handwriting which I can hardly read myself under the fair copies of Mr. Duncan of the same city.— I don't think that he would plume himself upon my progress.— However I wrote much better then than I have ever done since;— haste and agitation of one kind or another have quite spoilt as pretty a scrawl as ever scratched over a frank.—The Grammar School might consist of a hundred & fifty of all ages under age.—It was divided into five Classes—taught by four masters—the Chief—teaching the fifth & fourth himself—as in England the fifth, sixth forms, and Monitors are heard by the Head Masters.——

[TO THOMAS MOORE]   *Ravenna, May 3d, 1821*

Though I wrote to you on the 28th ultimo, I must acknowledge yours of this day, with the lines.[1] They are sublime, as well as beautiful, and in your very best mood and manner. They are also but too true. However,

---

[1] Moore wrote these lines beginning "Aye, down to the dust with them, slaves as they are" on hearing of the surrender of the Neapolitans, without a blow, to the Austrians. The verses were published in the *Traveller* for April 9, 1821.

do not confound the scoundrels at the *heel* of the boot with their betters at the top of it. I assure you that there are some loftier spirits.[2]

Nothing, however, can be better than your poem, or more deserved by the Lazzaroni. They are now abhorred and disclaimed nowhere more than here. We will talk over these things (if we meet) some day, and I will recount my own adventures, some of which have been a little hazardous, perhaps.

So, you have got the Letter on Bowles? I do not recollect to have said any thing of *you* that could offend,—certainly, nothing intentionally. As for * * [Rogers?], I meant him a compliment. I wrote the whole off-hand, without copy or correction, and expecting then every day to be called into the field. What have I said of you? I am sure I forget. It must be something of regret for your approbation of Bowles.[3] And did you *not* approve, as he says? Would I had known that before! I would have given him some more gruel. My intention was to make fun of all these fellows; but how I succeed, I don't know.

As to Pope, I have always regarded him as the greatest name in our poetry. Depend upon it, the rest are barbarians. He is a Greek Temple, with a Gothic Cathedral on one hand, and a Turkish Mosque and all sorts of fantastic pagodas and conventicles about him. You may call Shakespeare and Milton pyramids, if you please, but I prefer the Temple of Theseus or the Parthenon to a mountain of burnt brickwork.

The Murray has written to me but once, the day of its publication, when it seemed prosperous. But I have heard of late from England but rarely. Of Murray's other publications (of mine), I know nothing, —nor whether he *has* published. He was to have done so a month ago. I wish you would do something,—or that we were together.

> Ever yours and affectionately,
> B

[TO JOHN MURRAY]   *Ravenna, May 8th, 1821*

Dear Moray,—Pray publish these additional notes.[1] It is of importance to the question in dispute, and even, if you can, print it on a separate page and distribute it to the purchasers of the former copies.

I have had no letters from you for this month past. *Acknowledge this*

[2] Byron is comparing the cowardice of the Neapolitans with the bravery of the Carbonari in the Romagna. But their revolution was also abortive and bungled.

[3] In his first letter on Bowles, Byron had written of Moore's supposed approval of Bowles's "invariable principles" of poetry: "Moore (*et tu, Brute*) also approves.". Moore protested that he agreed with neither Byron nor Bowles completely.

[1] An addition to the first letter on Bowles.

by post; as this note is worth the whole pamphlet as an *example* of what we are to prove against the Anti-christian anti-popists.

Yours,
BYRON

P.S.—I copy the following postscripts from Moore's latest letter to me of April 14th. "Since I wrote the above, Lady E. F. sent me your letter, and I have run through it. *How the devil could Bowles say that I agreed with his twaddling, and (still more strange) how could you believe him?*" There! what do you think of this? You may show this to the initiated, but *not* publish it in print—yet at least—till I have M.'s permission.

Get and send me, if possible, Tom Tyers's amusing tracts upon Pope and Addison.[2] I had a copy in 1812 which was, I know not how, lost, and I could not obtain another. It is a scarce book, but has run through three editions I think. It is in the Boswell style, but more rapid; very curious, and indeed necessary if you think of a new life of Pope. Why don't Gifford undertake a Life and edition? It is more necessary than that of Ben Jonson. Nobody can do it but Gifford, both from his qualities and turn of mind.

I have not sent you the Italian Scrap promised in my last letters, but will in a few posts.

Do you recollect the air of "How now, Madame Flirt?" in the *Beggar's Opera*?[3]

BOWLES.

"Why how now, Saucy Tom,
   If you thus must ramble,
I will publish some
   Remarks on Thomas Campbell.—

Saucy Tom."

CAMPBELL.

"Why how now, Billy Bowles,
   Sure the parson's maudlin.
How can you (damn your souls)   [To the public
   Listen to his twaddling?

Billy Bowles!"

  [2] Thomas Tyers (1726–1787) wrote *An Historical Rhapsody on Mr. Pope* (1781) and *An Historical Essay on Mr. Addison* (1782).
  [3] *Beggar's Opera*, Act. II, scene 2.

Thorwaldsen sent off the bust to be shipped from Leghorn last week. As it is addressed to your house and care you may be looking out for it, though I know not the probable time of the voyage in this Season of the year, which is one of light airs and breezes and calms in the Mediterranean.

May 10th. 1821

Dear Murray—I have just got your packet.—I am obliged to Mr. Bowles—& Mr. B. is obliged to me—for having restored him to good humour.—He is to write—& you to publish what you please—*motto* and subject—I desire nothing but fair play for all parties.—Of course, after the new tone of Mr. B.—you will *not* publish my *defence of Gilchrist*[1]—it would be brutal to do so—after his urbanity—for it is rather too rough like his own attack upon G.—You may tell him what I say there of *his Missionary*[2] (it is praised as it deserves) however— and if there are any passages *not personal* to Bowles—& yet bearing upon the question—you may add them to the reprint (if it is reprinted) of my 1st. letter to you.—Upon this consult Gifford—& above all don't let anything be added which can *personally* affect Mr. B.—In the enclosed notes—of course what I say of the *democracy* of poetry cannot apply to Mr. Bowles—but to the Cockney and Water washing-tub Schools.—Now what are we to think of Bowles's story—and Moore's!!!—they are at issue—is it not odd? I have copied M's postscript literally in my letter of the 8th.———The anecdote of Mr. B. is as follows—& of course *not* for the public.—

After dinner at Ld. Lansdowne's they were talking one evening as Sir Robert Walpole used to talk always.—Bowles said that after all *love* was the only thing worthy the risk of damnation.—"When I was a very young man (said he) a friend of mine would take me to Paris.—I was not very eager to go till he said that Paris contained the *finest women in the world—and the kindest.*—We then set off.—It was deep winter—I was dying of all kinds of cold and inconvenience—but still thought no more of it—when I heard perpetually that there were the finest women in the world to be had at Paris.—When we got to Paris —I sallied forth the first evening—and thinking that it was only to ask

---

[1] Octavius Graham Gilchrist (1779–1823) had published several volumes of poetry. He became involved in the Pope controversy when he reviewed *Spence's Anecdotes* in the *London Magazine* and was attacked by Bowles. Byron came to Gilchrist's defence in his second letter on Bowles, but suppressed it when Bowles made a mild reply to his first letter.

[2] *The Missionary of the Andes*, a poem by Bowles, was published in 1815.

111

and have—I accosted several with the tenderest politeness—but whether my French or my figure displeased them—I know not—I had short answers or none at all.—I returned—disconsolate—but having dined—my love revived—whatever my hope might.—At last wound up to a pitch of amatory desperation, I rushed forth determined to bring the question to a point with the first fair one of whatever quality I met with.———I had not gone far before I met with a lady-like modest-looking female—whom I accosted as follows—'Madame—voulez vous *foutre*?' she replied '*Si vous plaît Monsieur*' in the softest accents—I did so, caught a rousing p[ox]—was laid up for two months—& returned perfectly persuaded that there were the finest women in the world at Paris."——

This is "the tale as told to me"[3] by Moore—and at least as good a story as Cibber's of Pope.———You may tell it again to Mr. B—upon whom it reflects rather credit than otherwise for the humour of it.——I hope and trust that Elliston *won't* be permitted to act the drama?—Surely *he* might have the grace to wait for Kean's return before he attempted it—though *even then I* should be as much against the attempt as ever.———I have got a small packet of books but neither *Walde-grave—Orford*[4]—nor Scott's Novels among them.———Some *Soda powders pray?*—Why don't you *republish* Hodgson's C[hilde] Harold's Monitor—and latino-mastix?[5]—they are excellent—think of this—they are all for *Pope.*—

yrs truly
B

Ravenna May 11th. 1821

My dear Hoppner/—If I had but known yr. notion about Switzerland before—I should have adopted it at once.—As it is—I shall let the child remain in her Convent—where she seems healthy & happy—for the present—but I shall feel much obliged if you will enquire when you are in the Cantons—about the usual & better modes of education there for females—and let me know the result of your opinions.—It is some consolation that both Mr. & Mrs. Shelley—have written to

---

[3] cf. Scott, *The Lay of the Last Minstrel*: "I say the tale as was told to me."
[4] See Feb. 1, 1821, to Kinnaird, notes 1 and 2.
[5] Francis Hodgson published in 1818 two poems mildly critical of the tendency of Byron's poetry. One was *Childe Harold's Monitor, or Lines occasioned by the Last Canto of Childe Harold, including Hints to other Contemporaries.* The other was *Saeculo Mastix, or the Lash of the Age we live in.* But since Hodgson defended Pope Byron thought the poems deserved republication.

approve entirely my placing the child with the Nuns for the present.
——No one but the amiable Claire disapproves of it in the natural
circumstances—in the interim.—As to what might be said by people—
as she amiably puts it—I can refer to my whole conduct—as having
neither spared care—kindness—nor expence—since the child was
sent to me.—The people may say what they please—I must content
myself with not deserving (in this instance) that they should speak ill.
—The place is a *Country* town—in a good air—where there is a large
establishment for education—& many children some of considerable
rank placed in it.—As a *country* town—it is less liable to objections of
every kind.—It has always appeared to me that the moral defect in
Italy does *not* proceed from a *Conventual* education—because—to my
certain knowledge they come out of their convents innocent even to
ignorance of moral evil—but to the state of Society into which they are
directly plunged on coming out of it.——It is like educating an infant
on a mountain top—and then taking him to the Sea—& throwing him
into it, & desiring him to swim.——The evil however—though still
too general is partly wearing away—as the women are more permitted
to marry from attachment.—This is I believe the case also in France.—
And after all—what is the higher society of England?—according to
my own experience & to all that I have seen & heard—(and I have
lived there in the very highest—& what is called the *best*) no way of
life can be more corrupt.——In Italy however it is—or rather *was*
more *systematized*—but *now* they themselves are ashamed of *regular*
Serventismo.——In England the only homage which they pay to
Virtue—is hypocrisy.——I speak of course of the *tone* of high life—
the middle ranks may be very virtuous.——I have not got any copy—
(nor have yet had) of the letter on Bowles—of course I should be
delighted to send it to you.—How is Mrs. H? well again I hope.—Let
me know when you set out—I regret that I cannot meet you in the
Bernese Alps this summer—as I once hoped and intended.—With my
best respects to Madame—I am

ever & most truly yr. obliged Sert.
[Scrawl]

P.S.—I gave to a Musician*er* a letter for you some time ago—has
he presented himself?—Perhaps you could introduce him to the
Ingrams[1] and other dilettanti.—He is simple and unassuming—two

---

[1] English friends of Hoppner whom Byron later met again in Genoa.

strange things in his profession—and he fiddles like Orpheus himself—
or Amphion—tis a pity that he can't make Venice dance away from
the brutal tyrant who tramples upon it.—

[TO FRANCIS HODGSON]   *Ravenna. May 12th. 1821*

Dear Hodgson,—At length your two poems have been sent. I have
read them over (with the notes) with great pleasure. I receive your
compliments kindly and your censures temperately, which I suppose is
all that can be expected among poets. Your poem is, however, excellent, & if not popular only proves that there is a *fortune* in *fame* as in
every thing else in this world. Much, too, depends upon a publisher, &
much upon luck; and the number of writers is such,—that as the mind
of a reader can only contain a certain quantum of poetry & poet's
glories, ⟨they are⟩ he is sometimes saturated, & allows many good
dishes to go away from table untouched (as happens at grand dinners),
& this not from fastidiousness but fullness.

You will have seen by my pamphlet on Bowles that our opinions
are not very different. Indeed, my Modesty would naturally *look* at
least bashfully on being termed the "first of living minstrels"[1] (by a
brother of the art) if both our estimates of "living minstrels" in
general did not leaven the praise to a sober compliment. It is something
like the priority in a retreat. There is but one of your "tests" which
is not infallible: Translation. There are three or four *French* translations, and several German and Italian which I have seen. Moore
wrote to me from Paris months ago that "the French had caught the
contagion of Byronism to the highest pitch" and has written since to
say that nothing was ever like their "entusymusy" (you remember
Braham) on the subject, even through the "slaver of a prose translation:" these are his words. The Paris translation[2] is also very inferior
to the Geneva one, which is very fair, although in prose also. So you
see that your test of "translateable or not" is not so sound as could be
wished. It is no pleasure, however, you may suppose, to be criticised
through such a translation, or indeed through any. I give up "Beppo,"
though ⟨I suppose⟩ you know that it is no more than an imitation of
Pulci & of a style common & esteemed in Italy. I have just published a
drama, which is at least good English—I presume—for Gifford lays
great stress on the purity of its diction.

[1] Near the beginning of *Childe Harold's Monitor* Hodgson had referred to "The
first of living minstrels—Harold, thee!"

[2] The French translation was probably the *Oeuvres Complètes de Lord Byron*,
Traduites de l'Anglais Par MM. A.-P. et E. -D. S [Amédée Pichot et Eusèbe de
Salle]. Vols. I-VIII were issued in 1821. Two more volumes followed in 1822.

I have been latterly employed a good deal more on politics than on anything else, but the Neapolitan treachery and desertion have spoilt all our hopes here, as well as our preparations. The whole country was ready. Of course I should not have sate still with my hands in my breeches' pockets. In fact they were full; that is to say, the hands. I cannot explain further now, for obvious reasons, as all letters of all people are opened. Some day or other we may have a talk over that and other matters. In the mean time there did not want a great deal of my having to finish like Lara.[3]

Are you doing nothing? I have scribbled a good deal in the early part of last year, most of which scrawls will now be published, & part is, I believe actually printed. Do you mean to sit still about Pope? If you do, it will be the first time. I have got such a headache from a cold & swelled face, that I must take a gallop into the forest and jumble it into torpor. My horses are waiting. So good-bye to you.

yours ever,
BYRON

Two hours after the "Ave Maria", the Italian date of twilight

Dear Hodgson,—I have taken my ⟨gallop⟩ canter, and am better of my headache. I have also dined, & turned over yr. notes. In answer to yr. note of page 90, I must remark from *Aristotle* and *Rymer*, that the *hero* of tragedy and (I add meo periculo) a *tragic* poem must be *guilty*, to excite *"terror and pity,"* the end of tragic poetry. But hear not *me*, but my betters. "The pity which the poet is to labour for is *for* the criminal—not for those or him he has murdered—as who have been the occasion of the Tragedy. The terror is likewise in the punishment of the said criminal, who, if he be represented too great an offender, will *not be pitied*; if altogether *innocent* his punishment will be unjust. In the Greek tragedy Innocence is unhappy often, and the Offender escapes."[4] I must also ask you is *Achilles* a *good* character? or is even *Aeneas* anything but a successful ⟨rascal⟩ *runaway*? It is for *Turnus* men feel and not for the Trojan. Who is the hero of "Paradise lost"? Why Satan,—and *Macbeth*, and *Richard*, & *Othello* and *Pierre*, and *Lothario*, & *Zanga*?[5] If you talk so I shall "cut you up like a gourd," as the Mamelukes say. But never mind, go on with it.

---

[3] Lara, in Byron's poem of that name, died of wounds received in battle.

[4] "Dryden's Life" in Johnson's *Lives of the Poets*.

[5] In Young's tragedy *The Revenge*. Byron recited a soliloquy of Zanga at a Harrow Speech Day.

Dear Murray/—A Milan paper states that the play has been re-presented & universally condemned.—As remonstrance has been vain—complaint would be useless.—I presume however for yr. own sake (if not for mine) that you and my other friends will have at least published my different protests against it's being brought upon the stage at all—and have shown that Elliston (in spite of the writer) *forced* it upon the theatre.[1]—It would be nonsense to say that this has not vexed me a good deal,—but I am not dejected—and I shall not take the usual resource of blaming the public (which was in the right) or my friends for not preventing what they could not help—nor I neither—a *forced* representation by a Speculating Manager.—It is a pity that you did not show them it's *unfitness* for ye stage before the play was *published*—& exact a promise from the managers not to act it. —In case of their refusal—we would not have published it at all.— But this is too late.

yrs [Scrawl]

P.S.—I enclose Mr. Bowles's letters—thank him in my name for their candour & kindness.—Also a letter for Hodgson—which pray forward.—The Milan paper states that "*I brought forward* the play!!!" —This is pleasanter still.—But don't let yourself be worried about it, and if (as is likely) the folly of Elliston—checks the sale—I am ready to make any deduction—or the entire cancel of your agreement.— You will of course *not* publish my defence of Gilchrist—as after Bowles's good humour upon the subject—it would be too savage.— Let me hear from you the particulars, for as yet I have only the simple fact.—If you knew *what* I have had to go through here—on account of the failure of these rascally Neapolitans—you would be amused.—— But it is now apparently over.—They seemed disposed to throw the whole project and plans of these parts upon [me chiefly].———[2]

[TO THOMAS MOORE]   *May 14th, 1821*

If any part of the letter to Bowles has (unintentionally, as far as I remember the contents) vexed you,[1] you are fully avenged; for I see by an Italian paper that, notwithstanding all my remonstrances through all my friends (and yourself among the rest), the managers persisted

---

[1] See Jan. 20, 1821, to Murray, note 1.
[2] Byron had been a confidant and encourager of the revolutionary Carbonari and had allowed them to use his house as an arsenal. See his diary for Feb. 16, 1821.
[1] See May 3, 1821, to Moore, note 3.

in attempting the tragedy, and that it has been "unanimously hissed!!" This is the consolatory phrase of the Milan paper (which detests me cordially and abuses me, on all occasions, as a Liberal), with the addition, that *I* "brought the play out" of my own good will.

All this is vexatious enough, and seems a sort of dramatic Calvinism —predestined damnation, without a sinner's own fault. I took all the pains poor mortal could to prevent this inevitable catastrophe—partly by appeals of all kinds up to the Lord Chamberlain, and partly to the fellows themselves. But, as remonstrance was vain, complaint is useless. I do not understand it—for Murray's letter of the 24th, and all his preceding ones, gave me the strongest hopes that there would be no representation. As yet, I know nothing but the fact, which I presume to be true, as the date is Paris, and the 30th. They must have been in a *hell* of a hurry for this damnation, since I did not even know that it was published; and, without its being first published, the histrions could not have got hold of it. Any one might have seen, at a glance, that it was utterly impracticable for the stage; and this little accident will by no means enhance its merit in the closet.

Well, patience is a virtue, and, I suppose, practice will make it perfect. Since last year (spring, that is) I have lost a lawsuit, of great importance, on Rochdale collieries—have occasioned a divorce—have had my poesy disparaged by Murray and the critics—my fortune refused to be placed on an advantageous settlement (in Ireland) by the trustees—my life threatened last month (they put about a paper here to excite an attempt at my assassination, on account of politics, and a notion which the priests disseminated that I was in a league against the Germans)—and, finally, my mother-in-law recovered last fortnight, and my play was damned last week! These are like "the eight-and-twenty misfortunes of Harlequin."[2] But they must be borne. If I give in, it shall be after keeping up a spirit at least. I should not have cared so much about it, if our southern neighbours had not bungled us all out of freedom for these five hundred years to come.

Did you know John Keats? They say that he was killed by a review of him in the Quarterly—if he be dead, which I really don't know. I don't understand that *yielding* sensitiveness. What I feel (as at this present) is an immense rage for eight-and-forty hours, and then, as usual—unless this time it should last longer. I must get on horseback to quiet me.

Yours, &c.

---

[2] *Le disgratie d'Arlecchino* [*Harlequin's Misfortunes*, London, 1726.]

Francis I. wrote, after the battle of Pavia, "All is lost except our honour." A hissed author may reverse it—"*Nothing* is lost, except our honour." But the horses are waiting, and the paper full. I wrote last week to you.

[TO RICHARD BELGRAVE HOPPNER]   *Ravenna. May 17th. 1821*

My dear Hoppner/—You will have seen a paragraph in the Italian papers stating that "Ld. B had exposed his t[ragedy] of M[arino] F[aliero] &c. & that it was universally hissed."—You will also have seen in Galignani (what is confirmed by my letters from London) that this is *twice* false—for in the first place—*I opposed* the representation at all—& in the *next*—it was *not* hissed—but is continued to be acted—in spite of Author—publisher—& the Lord Chancellor's injunction. Now I wish *you* to obtain a statement of this short & simple truth in the Venetian & Milan papers—as a contradiction to their former lie.—I say *you*—because your consular dignity will attain this justice—which out of their hatred for *me* (as a *liberal*) they would not concede to an unofficial Individual.—Will you take this trouble? I think two words from you to those in power will do it—because I require nothing but the statement of what we both know to be the fact—& that a *fact* in no way political.——Am I presuming too much upon your good nature?—I suppose that I have no other resource—and to whom can an Englishman apply in a case of ignorant insult like this—(where no *personal* redress is to be had) but to the person resident most nearly connected with his own government?——I wrote to you last week—and am now in all haste—

yours ever & most truly
BYRON

P.S.—Humble Reverences to Madame—pray favour me with a line in answer.——If the play had been condemned—the Injunction would be *superfluous* against the continuance of the representation.—

[TO JOHN MURRAY]   *Ravenna—May 19th. 1821*

Dear Murray/—Enclosed is a letter of Valpy's[1] which it is for you to answer.—I have nothing further to do with the mode of publication.—

---

[1] Probably Abraham John Valpy (1787–1854) editor and publisher particularly of classical works. Since the reference here and in a later letter (Aug. 10, 1821, to Murray) seems to be to some publishing proposal, it is possible that he wanted to publish Byron's translation of Pulci.

By the papers of Thursday—& two letters from Mr. K[innair]d I perceive that the Italian Gazettes had lied most *Italically*—& that the drama had *not* been hissed—& that my friends *had* interfered to prevent the representation.———So it seems they continue to act it—in spite of us all.—For this we must "trouble them at '*Size*'"———let it by all means be brought to a plea—I am determined to try the right—& will *meet* the expences.———The reason of the Lombard Lie—was that the Austrians who keep up an Inquisition throughout Italy and a *list* of *names* of all who think or speak of any thing but in favour of their despotism—have for five years past abused me in every form in the Gazettes of Milan &c.———I wrote to you a week ago upon the subject.———Now—I should be glad to know what compensation Mr. Elliston could make me—not only for dragging my writings on the stage in *five* days—but for being the cause that I was kept for *four* days—(from Sunday to Thursday morning the only post days) in the *belief* that the *tragedy* had been acted & "unanimously hissed" and with the addition—that "*I* had brought it upon the stage"—and consequently that none of my friends had attended to my request to the contrary.———Suppose that I had burst a blood vessel like John Keats, or blown [out] my brains in a fit of rage—neither of which would have been unlikely a few years ago.———At present I am luckily calmer than I used to be—& yet I would not pass those four days over again—for—I know not what.—

I wrote to you to keep up yr. spirits.—for reproach is useless always & irritating—but my feelings were very much hurt—to be dragged like a Gladiator to the fate of a Gladiator—by that "*Retiarius*"[2] Mr. Elliston———As to his defence—& offers of compensation—what is all this to the purpose? It is like Louis the 14th. who insisted upon buying at any price Algernon Sydney's horse—& on refusal—on taking it by force.—Sydney shot his horse.[3]—I could not shoot my tragedy—but I would have flung it into the fire rather than have had it represented.—I have now written nearly *three* acts of another[4] (intending to complete it in five) and am more anxious than

---

[2] A gladiator furnished with a net, with which he strove to entangle his adversary. It was a term which Byron probably found in Suetonius (*Caligula*, 30).

[3] An apocryphal story told of Louis XIV and Algernon Sydney, according to which Louis coveted a horse of Sydney, who refused to sell it. When the King sent an order to seize it, Sydney shot it, "saying that his horse was born a free creature, had served a free man, and should not be mastered by a king of slaves." (Ewald, *Life and Times of Algernon Sydney*, Vol. II, p. 17.)

[4] *Sardanapalus*.

ever to be preserved from such a breach of all literary courtesy—& gentlemanly consideration.——If we succeed—well;—if not—previous to any future publication—we will request a *promise* not to be acted —which I would even pay for—(as money is their object)—or I will not publish—which however you will probably not much regret.———The Chancellor has behaved nobly.[5]—You have also conducted yourself in the most satisfactory manner—and I have no fault to find with anybody but the Stage-players, & their proprietor.—I was always so civil to Elliston personally—that he ought to have been the last to attempt to injure me.——

There is a most rattling thunder-storm pelting away at this present writing—so that I write neither by day nor by candle nor torch light— but by *lightning*-light——the flashes are as brilliant as the most Gaseous glow of the Gaslight company.—My chimney-board has just been thrown down by a gust of wind.—I thought it was the "bold Thunder" and the "brisk Lightning"[6] in person—*three* of us would be too many.—There it goes—*flash* again—but

> "I tax not you ye elements with unkindness
> I never gave ye *franks* nor *called* upon you"[7]

as I had done by & upon Mr. Elliston.———Why do not you write— you should have at least sent me a line of particulars—I know nothing yet—but by Galignani & the honourable Douglas.——Hobhouse has been paying back Mr. Canning's assault.[8]—He was right—for Canning had been like Addison "trying to *cuff* down *new-fledged*

---

[5] Murray had written to Byron on March 20, 1821 (*Memoir*, Vol. I, pp. 420–421): "Hobhouse spoke to Lord Grey about the impropriety of allowing a play, not intended for performance, to be acted on the stage. Earl Grey spoke to the Lord Chancellor, who said he would grant an injunction."

[6] Buckingham, *The Rehearsal*, Act I.

[7] *King Lear*, Act III, scene 2:
"I tax you, ye elements, with unkindness,
I never gave you kingdom, called you children . . ."

[8] Hobhouse had said that Parliament was becoming a Fool's Paradise "where the beams of truth have not penetrated, and where error and obstinacy seem to have placed their last footsteps". And he spoke of the necessity of "restoring it [the House] to its original character, and of making it a control *for* the people, rather than a control upon the people". On March 16, 1821, Canning threw out a remark that Hobhouse took as a personal affront: "I have never known a demagogue" he said, "who, when elected to a seat in this house, did not in the course of six months shrink to his proper dimensions." Hobhouse took his time to reply, but on April 17, he launched an extended attack on the kind of "smart sixth-form boy" who thrived and never found his level in an unreformed Parliament.

merit."[9] Hobhouse has in him "something dangerous"[10] if not let alone.—Well—& how does our Pope Controversy go on—& the pamphlet?—It is impossible to write any news the Austrian scoundrels rummage all letters.—

yrs. [Scrawl]

P.S.—I could not [*sic*] have sent you a good deal of Gossip—& some *real* information were it not—that all letters pass through the Barbarians' inspection—and I have no wish to inform *them* of anything but my utter abhorrence of them & theirs.———They have only conquered by treachery however.—Send me some Soda-powders—some of "Acton's Corn-rubbers"—and W. Scott's romances.—And do pray write—when there is anything to interest—you are always silent.—

[TO JOHN CAM HOBHOUSE]   *Ravenna. May 20th. 1821*

My dear Hobhouse/—Galignani gave with great accuracy your defence—& offence—for "this defence offensive comes by cause."[1] against Mr. Canning—which is as pretty a piece of invective—as one would wish to read on a Summer's day.[2]———You served him right—because he had attempted like Addison "to cuff down new-fledged merit".—Besides [to] talk of "a demagogue's dimensions" to a Gentleman of the middle stature—was downright "scurrilous".—But you have not spared him—like the Boatswain on boarding the French vessel (don't you remember Bathurst's story?) "no no you b–gg–r *you* fired first." It is a piece of eloquence,—& the style much more easy than your usual prose (in *writing* that is) and I begin to think that your real strength lies in vituperation.—How did he look under it?—He has not attempted any rejoinder—but I suppose that you will be both at it for the remainder of yr. lives.—It must have had

[9] Otway's *Venice Preserved*, Act II, scene 2: "We cuff down new-fledged virtues. . . ."

[10] *Hamlet*, Act V, scene 1.

[1] Byron's adaptation of a passage in *Hamlet*, Act. II, scene 2: "for this effect defective comes by cause."

[2] Speaking on Lambton's motion on reform of Parliament, Hobhouse made an eloquent reply to the objection that the House would be inundated with demogogues, denouncing "the regular adventurers, the downright trading politicians", who filled the House under the "Rotten Borough" system. (See *Recollections of a Long Life*, II, 145 ff.)

a great effect. I am glad that you quoted Pope too—that's always right,—though you might as well have left out the further quotation from Sir Car Scrope[3]—a vulgar lampooner of the most licentious gang of Charles the Second's reign.——

You will be well acquainted with the row about the ryghte merry & conceitede tragedy of your humble Servant.—But you do not know that for *four* days I believed it damned—owing to a paragraph from an Italian French paper.—which added that *I had brought* it on the stage!—The next post set me at ease on that point—by papers & letters—explaining the whole thing—but making me wonder that either the town or the Chancellor permitted the buffoons to go on acting it.—I bore the belief with philosophy as my letter to Murray written during the interval will show.—But this very circumstance is an additional one against the Managers—for what can compensate for four such days to a man who had so anxiously avoided the exhibition? —Ten years ago I should have gone crazy—at present I lived on as usual.—I will have the question brought to a pleading however—just to see how the right really stands.—It is thus far of import to all writers, for the future.—

Douglas has written—but neither you nor Moray—nor anybody else.—I cannot write news because the letters are all opened.— However I suppose you know what is no news—that the Neapolitans were bought & sold.—The *Spy* is *here* (in Ravenna) who carried the letters between Frimont & Carascosa[4]—and complains publicly of being ill-paid for his pains.—Perhaps he may be *better* paid if he don't take care.—It is a savage sort of neighbourhood.——Our Greek acquaintances are making a fight for it—which must be a dilemma for the Allies—who can neither take their part (as liberals) nor help longing for a leg or a wing & bit of the heart—of Turkey.—Will you tell Douglas that as he had agreed (& I also) upon *that* price with M[*urray*] that of course I abide by it—but he should recollect that I have been entirely guided by *himself* (Douglas) & *you*—in your opinion of what I ought to ask or receive.—From my absence & ignorance of how things stand in literature in England—It is impossible for me to know how to act otherwise. I do not even know how the Bowles pamphlet has sold—nor the drama—nor anything else.—

[3] Sir Carr Scrope, 1st Baronet (1649–1680) became a versifier and man of fashion and a companion of Charles II.

[4] Marshall Frimont commanded the Austrian troops sent to quell the Neapolitan rebels. Pepe and Carrascosa were the Neapolitans who surrendered to the Austrians on March 7, 1821.

Lady Noel is dangerously *well* again I hear.—Mrs. Leigh's news who never sends any thing agreeable of herself or anybody else.

yours ever

Fletcher's respects, & expects that you & Canning will *fight*, but *hopes not*.—

[TO THOMAS MOORE] *Ravenna, May 20th, 1821*

Since I wrote to you last week I have received English letters and papers, by which I perceive that what I took for an Italian *truth* is, after all, a French lie of the Gazette de France. It contains two ultra-falsehoods in as many lines. In the first place, Lord B. did *not* bring forward his play, but opposed the same; and, secondly, it was *not* condemned, but is continued to be acted, in despite of publisher, author, Lord Chancellor, and (for aught I know to the contrary) of audience, up to the first of May, at least—the latest date of my letters. You will oblige me, then, by causing Mr. Gazette of France to contradict himself, which, I suppose, he is used to. I never answer a foreign *criticism*; but this is a mere matter of *fact*, and not of *opinions*. I presume that you have English and French interest enough to do this for me—though to be sure, as it is nothing but the *truth* which we wish to state, the insertion may be more difficult.

As I have written to you often lately at some length, I won't bore you further now, than by begging you to comply with my request; and I presume the "esprit du corps" (is it "du" or "de"? for this is more than I know) will sufficiently urge you, as one of *"ours"*, to set this affair in its real aspect. Believe me always yours ever and most affectionately,

BYRON

[TO RICHARD BELGRAVE HOPPNER] *R[avenn]a May 21st. 1821*

My dear Hoppner—I return to the subject of Saturday (I wrote by that day's post), because the Milan Gazette again repeats the same thing in the same words only with a different date and an additional word. I ask you to interfere because otherwise they will do an absent & obnoxious individual no justice. If the play had been hissed, let them repeat it till they are tired; but at least state, as all our papers have done, *how & why* it was *dragged* upon the stage against my positive orders.

I merely wish the *matter* of *fact*; as to criticism, that is *opinion* & of course open to all men. I have had Galignani's English papers (which you will have seen) sent to Milan. I enclose you two letters from Douglas Kinnaird which will show you what to think,—unless he has egregiously mis-stated. A few words from you to the uppermost of the [illegible] party at Milan & Venice will be enough. I require nothing but the statement of the *facts* as you will have read them.

Yours ever & most truly,
BYRON

[TO COUNT GIUSEPPE ALBORGHETTI]   *Ravenna May 25th. 1821*

Dear Sir—I enclose you the copy for one or two slight alterations and also the petition of the Signor Giant [the Neapolitan's name was Giuseppe Gigante][1]—The document itself confirms what I have said—

If you would have the goodness to have copied out the enclosed sheet of paper the *answer* to the Cardinal I will sign it with pleasure—

Yours very truly
B

[TO RICHARD BELGRAVE HOPPNER]   *Ravenna. May 25th. 1821*

My dear Hoppner/—It seemed proper that I should mention in the notes—the persons esteemed for a certain character in this our city[1]— either for literature or otherwise—and the more so—because the Doge's denunciation was—however true—so—bitter—as to appear like a *personal* feeling.—This it really was not—but it seemed one in conformity with the dramatic character of M[arino] F[aliero] and yet *true* for I have quoted the French Historian Daru[2] and others—(not trusting entirely to my own opinions) as well as the famous Alamanni.

---

[1] Byron had entrusted his address to the Neapolitan insurgents (see [Oct. ? 1820] to the Neapolitans) to Gigante who, when he was later arrested, swallowed some of the documents he was carrying, perhaps including Byron's letter. The Cardinal had sent, through Alborghetti, a letter requiring answers to questions about Byron's relations with Gigante.

[1] In a note to *Marino Faliero* (Act V, scene 3, line 54) Byron had listed some of the "honourable exceptions" to the "present decay and degeneracy of Venice under the Barbarians".

[2] Byron quoted a passage from Daru's *Histoire de la République de Venise* on, "Venetian Society and Manners" in an appendix to *Marino Faliero*.

—I did not consult my own *personal* feelings for or against the individuals *praised*—as some of them are *not* of my acquaintance—but merely their estimation in their place of birth—or residence.——As to the Albrizzi I do not know what they think of her *now* but you know that she was flattered by them formerly. I was also anxious to evince that I had no resentment against her—on account of our little discrepancy. You can hardly say less than "accomplished" of a young man who speaks & writes half a dozen languages[3]—and his mother has written *books*—and really in present Italy it is so high a merit to spell with precision—that I cannot help respecting a woman who writes at all.———Of their recent *Ultraism* I was not aware—recollect it is now two years—(except a couple of Autumn months—which I passed in the house with a fever) since I have been in Venice as a resident.—— I am very sorry to hear it,—but knew nothing of it till now.——

I am very much pleased with what you say of Switzerland—and will ponder upon it;—I would rather she married there than here for that matter.—For fortune I shall make all that I can spare—(if I live and she is correct in her conduct) & if I die before she is settled—I have left her by will five thousand pounds—which is a fair provision *out* of England, for a natural child.—I shall encrease it all I can—if circumstances permit me—but of course—(like all other human things) this is very uncertain.—You will oblige me very much by interfering to have the FACTS of the play-acting stated—I care nothing for their criticism, but the matter of fact—I have written *four* acts of another tragedy—so you see they *can't* bully me.—as those Scoundrels appear to be organizing a system of abuse against me;—because I am in their "*list*"—you know I suppose that they actually keep a *list* of all individuals in Italy—who dislike them—It must be numerous.—Their Suspicions and actual alarms—about my conduct & personal intentions —in the late row were truly ludicrous—though not to bore you—I touched upon them lightly—they believed—& still believe here—or affect to believe it—that the whole plan & project of rising was settled by me—& the *means* furnished &c. &c.—All this was more fomented by the Barbarian agents—who are numerous here—(one of them was stabbed yesterday by the way but not dangerously).—And although when the Commandant was shot here before my door in Decr.—I took him into my house where he had every assistance—till he died on Fletcher's bed—and although not one of them dared receive him into

---

[3] In his note on the Venetians Byron had called Giuseppe Albrizzi "the accomplished son of an accomplished mother".

their houses but myself;—they leaving him to perish in the Night in the Streets—when I ran down (armed of course) and carried him from the spot where he was lying—with Tita to help me (and a soldier or two who were scared out of their wits)——they put up a paper about three months ago—denouncing me as the chief of the Liberals—& stirring up persons to assassinate me.—But this shall never silence nor bully my opinions.——All this came from the German Barbarians.—

[TO JOHN MURRAY]   R[avenn]a May 25th. 1821

Mr. Moray/—Since I wrote the enclosed a week ago—& for some weeks before—I have not had a line from you.—Now I should like to know upon what principle of common or *un*common feeling—you leave me without any information but what I can derive from garbled gazettes in English—& abusive ones in Italian (the Germans hating me as a *Coal-heaver*)[1] while all this kick up has been going on about the play?—You SHABBY fellow!!—Were it not for the letters from D[ouglas] K[innaird] I should have ·been as ignorant as you are negligent.—I send you an Elegy as follows—

> Behold the blessing of a lucky lot!
> My play *is damned*—and Lady Noel *not*.

So—I hear Bowles has been abusing Hobhouse[2]—if that's the case he has broken the truce like Morillo's successor[3]—and I will cut him out as Cochrane did the Esmeralda.[4]——Since I wrote the enclosed packet—I have completed (but not copied out) four acts of a new tragedy.—When I have finished the fifth—I will copy it out.——It is on the subject of "Sardanapalus"—the last king of the Assyrians.——The words *Queen*—& *pavilion* occur—but it is not an allusion to his Britannic Majesty—as you may tremulously (for the admiralty custom)[5] imagine—This you will one day see (if I finish it) as I have

[1] *i.e..* Carbonaro.

[2] Hobhouse had contributed fourteen lines on Bowles's *Pope* to the first edition of *English Bards and Scotch Reviewers*. In later editions Byron substituted lines of his own. Bowles attacked Hobhouse in the second of his *Two Letters to the Right Honourable Lord Byron* (pp. 103–104).

[3] The Spanish General Pablo Morillo (1778-1837) fought at the battle of Trafalgar and at Bailen, and later at Cartagena and elsewhere in South America.

[4] Lord Cochrane, then in command of the Chilean navy, cut out the Spanish frigate *Esmeralda* from under the batteries of Callao on Nov. 5, 1820.

[5] Murray was publisher to the Admiralty.

made Sardanapalus *brave* (though voluptuous as history represents him)—and also as *amiable* as my poor powers could render him.—So that it could neither be truth nor satire on any living monarch.—I have strictly preserved all the unities hitherto—& mean to continue them in the fifth if possible—but *not for the Stage*.——yrs. in haste & hatred—you scrubby correspondent—

[Scrawl]

[TO JOHN MURRAY]   *Ravenna. May 28th. 1821*

Dear Moray/—Since my last of ye 26th. or 25th. I have dashed off my fifth act of ye tragedy called "Sardanapalus".—But now comes ye copying over which may prove heavy work—heavy to ye writer as to the reader.—I have written to you at least 6 times sans answer—which proves you to be a—bookseller.——I pray you to send me a copy of *"Wrangham's"* reformation of *"Langhorne's Plutarch"*[1]—I have the Greek which is somewhat small of print—and the Italian which is too heavy in style—and as false as a Neapolitan patriot proclamation.—I pray you also to send me a life published some years ago of the *Magician Apollonius* of T[yana].[2]—It is in English, & I think edited or written by what "Martin Marprelate" calls *"a bouncing priest"*.—I shall trouble you no further with this sheet than ye postage.

yrs. &c.

ℬ

P.S.—Since I wrote this I determined to inclose it (as a half sheet) for Mr. K[innaird]—who will have the goodness to forward it.— Besides it saves sealing wax.—

[TO DOUGLAS KINNAIRD]   *Ravenna, May 28th. 1821*

My dear Douglas—A line merely to acknowledge more letters than I have present time to answer. They were extremely consoling, for I have had no other news, except gross abuse in the Italian papers

---

[1] A new edition of the Rev. John Langhorne's translation of Plutarch's *Lives* (1770) was edited by the Rev. Francis Wrangham in 1810.

[2] The *Life* of Apollonius of Tyana was translated from the Greek of Philostratus by the Rev. Edward Berwick in 1810.

of me, and of my drama. Such as that it was "unanimously hissed," &c., without a word of the author's opposition, the Chancellor's injunction, or the manager's villainy.

My other comfort has been an "Elegy on the recovery of Lady Noel." I dreamt it.

> "Behold the blessings of a lucky lot
> *My play is damned*, and *Lady Noel* not."

I have not yet received your conversion of Murray's bill into circulars, but presume it to be upon the way.

I have also written another play in *five acts* (*not for the stage recollect always*), but it is to be copied out, a task for me heavy as for the reader.

Remember me to Hob. and all the *Mob Aristocracy*.

                                                          Yours.

P.S.—I believe you to be right about M., but what is to be done? Both you and *Hobhouse* discouraged me into accepting his terms, and being accepted they must be observed.

[TO JOHN MURRAY]   *R[avenn]a May 31st. 1821*

Dear Moray/—You say you have written often—I have only received yrs. of the eleventh—which is very short.—By this post—in *five* packets I sent you the tragedy of Sardanapalus—which is written in a rough hand—perhaps Mrs Leigh can help you to decypher it.—You will please to acknowledge it by *return* of post.—You will remark that the *Unities* are all *strictly* observed.—The Scene passes in the same *Hall* always.—The time—a *Summer's night* about nine hours—or less, though It begins before Sunset—and ends after Sunrise.——In the third act—when Sardanapalus calls for a *mirror* to look at himself in his armour—recollect—to quote the Latin passage from *Juvenal* upon *Otho*[1]—(a similar character who did the same thing) Gifford will help you to it.—The trait is perhaps too familiar—but it is historical—(of *Otho* at least) & natural in an effeminate character.——Preface &c. &c. will be sent when I know of the arrival.——For the historical account I refer you to Diodorus Siculus—from which you must have

---

[1] Juvenal, *Satire* II, lines 99–103. The note, quoting the passage, was not included in any edition of *Sardanapalus* until 1832.

128

the *chapters* of the Story translated[2]—as an explanation—and a *note* to the drama.—You write so seldom & so shortly—that you can hardly expect from me more than I receive—

yrs. truly &c.

B

P.S.—Remember me to Gifford—and say that I doubt that the M. S. S. will puzzle him to decypher it.—The Characters are quite different from any I have hitherto attempted to delineate.——You must have it *copied out* directly—as you best can——& *printed off* in *proofs* (more than one) as I have retained no copy in my hands.——With regard to the publication—I can only protest as heretofore against it's being acted—it being expressly written *not* for the theatre.——

[TO DOUGLAS KINNAIRD] *R*[*avenn*]*a May 31st. 1821*

Dear Douglas/—Yours with the Egg receipt—& Circulars has just arrived.—I have to acknowledge many recent *kind* letters—*doubly* so—because I was quite in the dark—& unable to understand the transaction with the theatres till yr. explanation.—By this post I enclose in *five* packets—*five* acts of a new tragedy addressed to Mr. Murray.——Will you take a look at them? and desire him to acknowledge the *arrival* by return of post.——I differ from you about Mr. Elliston—who has used me not at all well.——In this play—I have observed the *unities* (*all three*) strictly—the whole action passes in the *same hall* of the palace of Sardanapalus.——Now the funds are up again—can't we find—land to place the money on?——I *had* agreed with Murray—on his assuring me that on the *"utmost possible* speculation" it *could* clear no more.——Of the merits of what I now send him I cannot judge.—The characters are of a totally different nature from any hitherto drawn by me in writing.—I am very glad of yr. civility to the Italian Singer & his appendage.[1]—Will you make my remembrances to them—& say that I hope they like *London*.——*Try her*—you will find her a good one to go—and she is—or was uncommonly *firm* of *flesh*—a *rarity* in Italian & Southern women after twenty.——She is

---

[2] Byron claimed as his source *The Historical Library of Diodorus the Sicilian*, made English by G. Booth (1700), but he also drew from the account of Mitford in his *History of Greece*.

[1] Signor Curioni and Arpalice Taruscelli. See May 19, 1818, to Hobhouse (Vol. 6, p. 40), and Feb. 16, 1821, to Murray.

also sufficiently expert in all the motions—like the rest of her country-women—and though a little too full in her person—is certainly a desirable woman.——Give my remembrances to Hobhouse—who wrote to me complaining of *Bowles*—but how could I help it?—was I to suppose that B[owles] would only *now* notice what has been published these eleven years & more?—I revealed no secret—*his* part was proclaimed in the preface to the second edition.—Besides—does he allow such things to ruffle him much?—He should see the abuse of *me* in the *Italian* papers—(under the Germans) & which cannot be remedied as they are under the protection—& pay of the Germans. They consider me too as a grand promoter & upholder of *Coal-heaving* ——and as such there is a small suspicion—that they tried to have me assassinated.—At least *papers* were stuck up—denouncing me as a *Chief* about three months ago—in the thick of the row—and trying to have me attacked.——Will you favour me with an answer [to] this—as soon as you have seen Murray that I may know if the packets have arrived.—

yrs. ever & most truly
B

[TO RICHARD BELGRAVE HOPPNER] *Ravenna, May 31st, 1821*

I enclose you another letter, which will only confirm what I have said to you.

About Allegra—I will take some decisive step in the course of the year; at present, she is so happy where she is, that perhaps she had better have her *alphabet* imparted in her convent.

What you say of the *Dante* is the first I have heard of it—all seeming to be merged in the *row* about the tragedy. Continue it!—Alas! what could Dante himself *now* prophesy about Italy? I am glad you like it, however, but doubt that you will be singular in your opinion. My *new* tragedy is completed.

The B[enzoni] is *right*,—I ought to have mentioned her *humour* and *amiability*, but I thought at her *sixty*, beauty would be most agreeable or least likely.[1] However, it shall be rectified in a new edition; and if any of the parties have either looks or qualities which they wish to be

---

[1] In a note to *Marino Faliero* Byron referred to the Countess Marina Benzoni as "the celebrated beauty, the heroine of 'La Biondina in Gondolete'", a love song inspired by her in youth.

noticed, let me have a minute of them. I have no private nor personal dislike to *Venice*, rather the contrary, but I merely speak of what is the subject of all remarks and all writers upon her present state. Let me hear from you before you start.   Believe me

ever, &c.

P.S.—Did you receive two letters of Douglas Kinnaird's in an endorse from me? Remember me to Mengaldo, Soranzo, and all who care that I should remember them. The letter alluded to in the enclosed, "to the *Cardinal*," was in answer to some *queries* of the government, about a poor devil of a Neapolitan, arrested at Sinigaglia on suspicion, who came to beg of me here; being without breeches, and consequently without pockets for halfpence, I relieved and forwarded him to his country, and they arrested him at Pesaro on suspicion, and have since interrogated me (civilly and politely, however,) about him. I sent them the poor man's petition, and such information as I had about him, which, I trust, will get him out again, that is to say, if they give him a fair hearing.

I *am* content with the article. Pray, did you receive, some posts ago, Moore's lines, which I enclosed to you, written at Paris?

[TO DOUGLAS KINNAIRD]   *R*[*avenn*]*a ⟨May⟩ June 2d. 1821*

My dear Douglas/—Enclosed in confidence is the letter of M[urray] in which you will perceive what he says of *"Negotiation"* or *"Negociation"*—how is this word spelt—with a *t* or a *c*?——By the post I have sent a large tragic packet directed to Murray—and a letter avising you of this expedition.—Having no other copy—I have caused the *Post* to *ensure* it—but they are not quite certain whether their Superiors of Bologna will sanction the insurance to London.—In case of their *not*—the packet will be *sent back* to me from Bologna.—I hope not—but cannot be sure till Thursday next.——I tell you this—that in case it should not arrive before this letter at Murray's this might account for it's temporary delay. However as the insurance is 45—Scudi—(that is to say nearly twelve guineas more or less) I trust that the Pontifical post-masters will forward the packet, especially as it contains nothing political.——

Murray's letter will enable you to judge for yourself;—I *do not* think—that he has lately acted very liberally on those points, but I so dislike disputes or dissentions of the kind—especially at this distance —that I avoid the Subject.—All that I *recollect* to have said of accepting

131

his proposal—amounts to my having replied—"that when the votaries of Apollo are to be treated with whether as physicians or poets—it is usual to deal in *guineas* & not in pounds."—But I am not at all sure that I may *not* have accepted the proposition—*remember that*—and this will be to be found in my letters to him—if it be true.——As it is— I will not declare *off* with him—about "the *Doge*" which is probably at a discount owing to Elliston's obstinacy in playing it against all honourable courtesy—but in future dealings I shall abide by *your* discretion—only requesting you to inform yourself first *well* in that intricate mystery of dealing between Booksellers & authors—before you decide.—I suppose that you know that *they sell* a work *to each other*—at a price far below that which is paid by the public—and of course gain less than the purchaser may be inclined to suppose.—I have no objection to your stating to Mr. Murray—that I have not much applauded his mode of Bargaining.——Indeed I decided more on what you & Hobhouse said—and from my aversion *from* such a disagreeable topic of correspondence—than from his own arguments. —He said—it was *impossible* that *more* could be made of "the Doge" and "the Dante".—What was I to answer?—He would have sent me a shopman's account from his ledger—proving that he had been a loser by selling the whole of the works—for these ten years past.—He did so about *Crabbe*—so Moore told me—who saw his accounts.—— Murray told *Mitchell*[1]—(the Aristophanes) that he had gained *little or nothing*—(except the credit) by *selling my works*—and that *I* was not what the *world supposed me* but—an *avaricious* man enough.—— This Shelley told me about *three years* ago at Venice.——You may tell Murray *this* from *me*—giving *the authority*.—I never reproached him with *this*—though I had some occasion to believe it; for *Shelley* is *truth* itself—and *honour* itself—notwithstanding his out-of-the-way notions about religion.——

You are wrong about Rogers—it was *not* an "attack"—*nor was it* "*wanton*".—Would you have me call him "*young*?"[2]—I alluded to "Human Life" because Bowles had called it a "more beautiful poem than the Pleasures of Memory"—which is false & foolish.—Now you shall be told something about the said Sam.—Moore told me that Sam hesitated for a *year* or *two* whether he should or should *not* insert a line or two in his "Human Life" about me—because of the *public run* being then against me on account of Miss Milbanke.——The shabby rascal!

---

[1] Thomas Mitchell (1783–1815) published the first volume of his translation of *The Comedies of Aristophanes* in 1820; the second volume in 1822.

[2] See April 26, 1821, to Murray.

—first to think that his petty praise imported a doit to me or to others
—and 2dly. *not* to dare to praise—because a man was persecuted.———
It is the moment a brave—or an honest man would say what he *felt*—&
more readily than at another time.———You may also say this publicly.
—I care not a curse for any or all—or each of them.—As Coriolanus
says

> "On fair ground—
> I could beat forty of them."—[3]

As to Rogers you *know* his amiable way of abusing all the world.—
If he wishes for *war*—let him—he shall have it.———

yrs. ever & truly
[Scrawl]

P.S.—Please to recollect that I never begin *without provocation.*—
That once given—they are to be paid off occasionally.—To do as you *have
been done by*—is the only way with those Scoundrels the race of Authors
and in general—they do not come within the Christian dispensation.—
Nothing can equal my contempt of your *real mere unleavened* author. I
never lived with such but with men of the world—and such writers as
were like other people.—Your mere writing is nothing but a *knack*—
out of their trade—they are not even clever.———

[TO THOMAS MOORE]   *Ravenna, June 4th, 1821*

You have not written lately, as is the usual custom with literary
gentlemen, to console their friends with their observations in cases of
magnitude. I do not know whether I sent you my "Elegy on the
recovery of Lady "[Noel]:"—

> Behold the blessings of a lucky lot—
> My play is damn'd, and Lady [Noel] *not.*

The papers (and perhaps your letters) will have put you in possession of Muster Elliston's dramatic behaviour. It is presumed that the
play was *fitted* for the stage by Mr. Dibdin, who is the tailor upon such
occasions, and will have taken measure with his usual accuracy. I hear
that it is still continued to be performed—a piece of obstinacy for which
it is some consolation to think that the discourteous histrio will be out
of pocket.

---

[3] *Coriolanus*, Act III, scene 1.

You will be surprised to hear that I have finished another tragedy in *five* acts, observing all the unities strictly. It is called "Sardanapalus," and was sent by last post to England. It is *not for* the stage, any more than the other was intended for it—and I shall take better care *this* time that they don't get hold on't.

I have also sent, two months ago, a further letter on Bowles, &c.; but he seems to be so taken up with my "respect" (as he calls it) towards him in the former case, that I am not sure that it will be published, being somewhat too full of "pastime and prodigality."[1] I learn from some private letters of Bowles's, that *you* were "the gentleman in asterisks."[2] Who would have dreamed it? you see what mischief that clergyman has done by printing notes without names. How the deuce was I to suppose that the first four asterisks meant "Campbell" and *not* "*Pope*", and that the blank signature meant Thomas Moore. You see what comes of being familiar with parsons. His answers have not yet reached *me*, but I understand from Hobhouse, that *he* (H.) is attacked in them. If that be the case, Bowles has broken the truce, (which he himself proclaimed, by the way,) and I must have at him again.

Did you receive my letters with the two or three concluding sheets of Memoranda?

There are no news here to interest much. A German spy (*boasting* himself such) was stabbed last week, but *not* mortally. The moment I heard that he went about bullying and boasting, it was easy for me, or any one else, to foretel what would occur to him, which I did, and it came to pass in two days after. He has got off, however, for a slight incision.

A row the other night, about a lady of the place, between her various lovers, occasioned a midnight discharge of pistols, but nobody wounded. Great scandal, however—planted by her lover—*to be* thrashed by her husband, for inconstancy to her regular Servente, who is coming home post about it, and she herself retired in confusion into the country, although it is the acme of the opera season. All the women furious against her (she herself having been censorious) for being *found out*. She is a pretty woman—a Countess [Rasponi][3]—a fine old Visigoth name or Ostrogoth.

[1] Farquhar, *The Recruiting Officer*, Act V, scene 1.

[2] Bowles had quoted a gentleman "of the highest literary, etc." as saying that in his pamphlet he (Bowles) had "hit the right nail on the head, and * * * * too." Byron had taken this to refer to Pope, but he was amused to learn from Bowles that he meant Moore. Moore tells the story in a note. (Moore II, 492.)

[3] Moore supplied asterisks for the name; Prothero filled it in.

The Greeks! what think you? They are my old acquaintances—but what to think I know not. Let us hope howsomever.

Yours,
B

R[avenn]a June 8th. 1821

Dear Douglas/—I put it to you once more—if *now* is not the time to sell out of the funds.—Is there no way to persuade the woman's trustees—to get us out of the funds—when no loss would ensue?—Have you cast about for a mortgage?—Surely if they rise to the price at which we bought in—[Bland?] might be persuaded to sell out—even though no immediate mortgage offered for investment.—I enclose you a note for the woman—which I request the favour of you to forward.——By last two posts I sent you *two* letters (*two* I think) apprizing you that I had forwarded to Mr. Murray's address the tragedy of "Sardanapalus" in five acts—and *all* the Unities.—

yrs ever & truly
[Scrawl]

P.S.—The favour of an answer is desired.—I practice yr. egg receipt—does it *nourish* the hair as well as cleanse it? Will you ask Mrs. Leigh—if I did not consign to her care a large topaz—or Cairn Gorme *Seal* with my arms upon it?—If I did—say that I should be glad to have it sent out by some safe conveyance to me.—I also wrote months ago to Murray to send me out *Holmes* the miniature painter (to take my daughter's likeness and another) but he has sent no answer—nor as yet—a single word or document about Elliston's business—so that I know of it only from yr. letters—and a newspaper or two.——

Ravenna 12 Giugno 1821

[Added to a letter in Italian by Lega Zambelli]

Dear Sir,—Tell Count V. Benzone (with my respects to him & to his Mother) that I have received his books—& that I shall *write to thank him* in a few days.—Murray sends me books of travels—I do not know why;—for I have travelled enough myself to know that such books are *full of lies.*—If you come here—you will find me very glad to see you, & very ready to dispute with you—

yrs. [Scrawl]

Dear Murray/—I *have* resumed my "majestic march" (as Gifford is pleased to call it) in "Sardanapalus" which by the favour of Providence and the Post Office should be arrived by this time—if not interrupted. —It was sent on the 2d. June—12 days ago.——Let me know because I had but that one copy.—Can your printers make out the M.S.?—I suppose long acquaintance with my scrawl may help them—if not— ask Mrs. Leigh—or Hobhouse or D[ouglas] K[innaird]—they know my writing.——The whole five acts were sent in one cover—ensured to England—paying forty five scudi *here* for the insurance.——I received some of yr. parcels—the Doge is longer than I expected—pray why did you print the face of M[argarit]a C[ogn]i by way of frontispiece?—It has almost caused a row between the Countess G[uiccioli] and myself.—And pray why did you add a note about the Kelso woman's "Sketches"[1]—Did I not request you to omit it—the instant I was aware that the *writer* was a *female?*—The whole volume looks very respectable—and sufficiently dear in price—but you do not tell me whether it succeeds—your first letter (before the performance) said that it was succeeding far beyond all anticipation—but this was before the piracy of Elliston—which (for anything I know as I have had no news—yr. letters with papers not coming) may have affected the circulation.——I have read Bowles's answer—I could easily reply— but it would lead to a long discussion—in the course of which I should perhaps lose my temper—which I would rather not do with so civil & forbearing an antagonist.—I suppose he will mistake being *silent* for *silenced.*—I wish to know when you publish the remaining things in M.S.?——I do not mean the *prose*—but the verse.—I am truly sorry to hear of yr. domestic loss—but (as I know by experience) all attempts at condolence in such cases are merely varieties of solemn impertinence.—There is nothing in this world but *Time.*

yrs. ever & truly

B

P.S.—You have never answered me about *Holmes* the Miniature painter—can he come or no? I want him to paint the miniatures of my daughter—and two other persons. In the 1st. pamphlet it is printed "*a* Mr. J.S." it should be "Mr. J.S." and not "*a*" which is contemptuous—it is a printer's Error & was not thus written.

[1] See Sept. 8, 1820, note 1, and Sept. 28 (29), 1820, to Murray (*b*) (Vol. 7, pp. 173, 183).

My dear Douglas/—The funds are up to 76——I now repeat & entreat you to urge—contrive—& do something to get us sold out—— surely—Hanson himself—and Bland—and all the crew must be persuaded by this time.—A 1000 thanks for yr. letters—which have been a great consolation.——I have written four or five times.—On the 2d. I sent another tragedy to Murray—"*Sardanapalus*" in five acts. Let me know if it has arrived—as I had no other copy.——I enclose an epistle of Murray—by which you will perceive that he speaks nothing of M[*arino*] F[*aliero*] or of the letter—as having made a hit.—Perhaps he is right.—

yrs. ever & truly
BN

P.S.—I wish to know if Murray does or does not intend to publish the other M.S.S. now in his hands?—they have been so above a year. ——

[In Teresa Guiccioli's hand, signed by Byron]

Carissima Amica—Dalla gentilissima vostra ricevuta collo scorso ordinario ho inteso l'arrivo costi del Sign. Legnani; ed ho provato un' sommo piacere nel leggere le assicurazioni della vostra Amicizia; non già che io ne dubitassi, ma solo per quella specie di sodisfazione che si prova nel sentirsi replicare le cose liete. Per egual modo Voi pure non dovevate aver bisogno d'una mia Lettera per essere certa che io conservassi per Voi quei sentimenti che non potete a meno d'ispirare, e tanto più che le ragioni per confidarvene non avevate a cercarle nelle qualità che vi piace attribuire al mio cuore, ma solo in Voi stessa. Onde io avrei a dolermi del torto che vi fate, se non fosse che la vostra modestia mi è anche più amabile del piacere che avrei a' convincervi del vostro errore.—Solamente desidero che per l'avvenire il mio silenzio non vi mostri più che il mio timore di divenirvi importuno scrivendovi.—

La mia Bambina di cui vi piace sapere stà benissimo, ed è già da quattro mesi in un luogo d'Educazione della Romagna, ove ho preferito metterla piuttosto che lasciarla nelle mani di persone venali, del qual soggiorno Ella si trova contentissima, e mi viene assicurato che sia cresciuta assai. Io spero che non disapproverete ciò che ho fatto; e siate certa che la vostra approvazione non mi sarà il minore compenso che io posso ricavare dalle cure che mi prendo per Lei. Ringraziate il Conte Rangone dei cordiali saluti che per [presso?] Voi mi ha mandati—ed assicuratelo di tutta la mia stima ed Amicizia.—State sana—e credetemi colla maggiore sincerità

D.S.—La Contessina Guiccioli vi ricorda il suo rispetto, e la sua Amicizia.—

Il Vostro Devo. mo Aff. mo S. ed Amico

Byron. Pair d'angleterre

[TRANSLATION]   *Ravenna June 16th 1821*

Very dear Friend—From your very kind letter received with the latest post, I learned of Signor Legnani's[1] arrival there with you; and I experienced an immense pleasure in reading affirmations of your friendship; not of course that I doubted it, but only for that sort of satisfaction one feels in hearing happy things repeated. In like measure you should not have needed a letter of mine to be certain that I cherish for you those sentiments that you cannot help but inspire, nor have you to search into the qualities it pleases you to attribute to my heart for my reasons in confiding them to you, but to yourself alone. Whence I should have to regret the wrong you do yourself, were it not that I hold your modesty more loveable than the satisfaction I would have from convincing you of your error.———I desire only that in the future my silence may not demonstrate more to you than my fear of becoming importunate in writing to you.—

My Child, of whom you inquire, is very well, and has been for four months at a place of Education in Romagna, where I preferred to put her rather than leave her in the hands of venal persons; she is very happy about such a sojourn, and I am assured that she has grown a great deal. I hope you will not disapprove of what I have done; and you may be certain that your approval will not be the least compensation that I can obtain for the care I take on her behalf. Thank Count Rangone for the cordial greetings that he has sent me through you,— and assure him of all my esteem and friendship.—Be healthy—and believe me with the greatest sincerity

Your devoted and affectionate servant and friend

Byron. Peer of England[2]

P.S.—Countess Guiccioli reminds you of her respect, and her friendship.—

[1] Luigi Legnani was a famous tenor.
[2] Translated by Professor Nancy Dersofi.

My dearest A.—What was I to write about? I live in a different
world.—You knew from others that I was in tolerable plight—and all
that.—However write I will since you desire it.——I have put my
daughter in a convent for the present to begin her accomplishments
by reading—to which she had a learned aversion—but the arrangement
is merely temporary till I can settle some plan for her;—if I return to
England—it is likely that she will accompany me—if not—I sometimes
think of Switzerland—& sometimes of the Italian Conventual education;—I shall hear both sides (for I have Swiss Friends—through Mr.
Hoppner the Consul General,—he is connected by marriage with that
country) & choose what seems most rational.——My menagerie—
(which you enquire after) has had some vacancies by the elopement of
one cat—the decease of two monkies and a crow—by indigestion—but
it is still a flourishing and somewhat obstreperous establishment.—
You may suppose that I was sufficiently provoked about Elliston's
behaviour—the more so—as the foreign Journals—the Austrian ones
at least—(who detest me for my politics) had misrepresented the
whole thing.—The moment I knew the real facts from England—
I made these Italical Gentry contradict themselves & tell truth—the
former they are used to—the latter was a sad trial to them—but they
did it—however, by dint of Mr. Hoppner's & my own remonstrances.
Tell Murray that I enclosed him a month ago—(on the 2d.) another
play—which I presume that he has received (as I ensured it at the
post Office) *you* must help him to decypher it—for I sent the only
copy—and you can better make out my griffonnage;—tell him it *must*
be printed—(aye & published too) immediately—& copied out—for
I do not choose to have only that *one* copy.——Will you for the
hundredth time apply to Lady B[yron] about the *funds*—they are now
high—& I could sell out to a great advantage.—Don't forget this—
that cursed connection crosses at every turn my fortunes—my feelings
—& my fame.——I had no wish to nourish my detestation of her &
her family—but they pursue, like an Evil Genius.—I send you an
Elegy upon Lady Noel's *recovery*—made two [here a dozen or more
lines are cut off] the parish register—I will reserve my tears for the
demise of Lady Noel—but the old b——h will live forever because she
is so amiable and useful.——

yrs. ever & [Scrawl]

P.S.—Let me know about Holmes—Oh La!—is he as great a
mountebank as ever?

Dear Sir/—If the man is to be conducted to the *frontier*—and to *lose his bread also,*—with a stain upon his character—I beg leave to submit respectfully to the *Cardinal* that I cannot dismiss him from my service[1] —but will rather let him abide the consequences of a *process.*—I submit it also to his Eminence—that the Sr. Pistocchi[2] has no more right to carry *arms* at *night* & out of *uniform* than the lowest Citizen *off duty.*—If one is to be punished *both* should be punished.—Is it because Mr. Pistocchi is an *officer* that both sides are not to be heard?—it is fit that the man should be allowed to speak in his own defence as the consequences are much more serious to a poor devil of a servant than they can be to another who is independent in his circumstances.—

yrs. ever & truly
BYRON

[TO THOMAS MOORE]   *Ravenna, June 22d, 1821*

Your dwarf of a letter came yesterday. That is right;—keep to your "magnum opus"[1]—magnoperate away. Now, if we were but together a little to combine our "Journal of Trevoux"[2] But it is useless to sigh, and yet very natural,—for I think you and I draw better together, in the social line, than any two other living authors.

I forgot to ask you, if you had seen your own panegyric in the correspondence of Mrs. Waterhouse and Colonel Berkeley?[3] To be sure *their* moral is not quite exact; but *your passion* is fully effective; and all poetry of the *Asiatic* kind—I mean Asiatic, as the Romans called "Asiatic oratory," and not because the scenery is Oriental—must be tried by that test only. I am not quite sure that I shall allow the Miss Byrons (legitimate or illegitimate) to read Lalla Rookh—in the first place, on account of this said *passion*; and, in the second, that they mayn't discover that there was a better poet than papa.

---

1 Byron's servant "Tita" [Battista Falcieri] was arrested for a quarrel in the street with a soldier and Alborghetti warned Byron that the authorities proposed to banish him from the province.

2 The soldier who quarrelled with Tita.

1 Possibly Moore's *Loves of the Angels*, which was not published, however, until 1823.

2 The Jesuits founded a literary journal at Trévoux in 1701 called *Mémoires de Trévoux.*

3 At the Gloucester Assizes in April, 1821, John Waterhouse was awarded £1000 damages for the seduction of his wife by Colonel Berkeley.

You say nothing of politics—but, alas! what can be said?

> The world is a bundle of hay,
> Mankind are the asses who pull,
> Each tugs it a different way,—
> And the greatest of all is John Bull!

How do you call your new project? I have sent to Murray a new tragedy, ycleped "Sardanapalus," written according to Aristotle—all, save the chorus—I could not reconcile me to that. I have begun another, and am in the second act;—so you see I saunter on as usual.

Bowles's answers have reached me; but I can't go on disputing for ever,—particularly in a polite manner. I suppose he will take being *silent* for *silenced*. He has been so civil that I can't find it in my liver to be facetious with him,—else I had a savage joke or two at his service.

* * * * * * * * * * * * * *

I can't send you the little journal, because it is in boards, and I can't trust it per post. Don't suppose it is any thing particular; but it will show the *intentions* of the natives at that time—and one or two other things, chiefly personal, like the former one.

So, Longman don't *bite*.—It was my wish to have made that work of use. Could you not raise a sum upon it (however small), reserving the power of redeeming it, on repayment?

Are you in Paris, or a villaging? If you are *in* the city, you will never resist the Anglo-invasion you speak of. I do not see an Englishman in half a year, and, when I do, I turn my horse's head the other way. The fact, which you will find in the last note to the Doge, has given me a good excuse for quite dropping the least connexion with travellers.[4]

I do not recollect the speech you speak of, but suspect it is not the Doge's, but one of Israel Bertuccio to Calendaro. I hope you think that Elliston behaved shamefully—it is my only consolation. I made the Milanese fellows contradict their lie, which they did with the grace of people used to it.

Yours, &c.

B

[4] In a final note to *Marino Faliero* Byron wrote: "The fact is, that I hold in utter abhorrence any contact with the travelling English. . . . I was persecuted by these tourists even to my riding ground at Lido, and reduced to the most disagreeable circuits to avoid them."

Dear Sir,—A letter from Mr. Murray informs me that a parcel or packet by post (enclosing extracts from the proofs) is directed to my name and Mr. Hoppner's. If such a parcel arrives—or has arrived—I request of yr. goodness to forward it by the post. It contains nothing but what I have said—& the post is the quickest conveyance. Believe me, very truly

yr obliged & obedt. Servt.
BYRON

Dear Sir/—It appears to me that there must be some *clerical* intrigue—of the low priests about the Cardinal to render all this nonsense necessary about a squabble in the street of *words only*—between a Soldier and a Servant.[1] If it is directed against *me*—it shan't succeed—for I desire no better than a *fair* examination of my conduct—as far as connected with the place or the inhabitants. If against the *poor* valet—it is an odious oppression;—I desire no more than a ⟨full⟩ process—for then—they would see the *falsehood* of all the *trash*—about this man—who has *no more to do with political matters than the Man in the Moon*. If you can get this business settled—either *here* (which would be better as shorter) or at Rome[2]——you will not find me less obliged or more ungrateful than you have hitherto found me.—Why can't they decide the matter by an investigation—an arrest—or a reproof?——There was never any objection on my part to his having a punishment proportioned to the offence—but *not* a chastisement the consequences of which might affect the man's prospects through life.—

I wish to know what is to be gained by it?—If they think to get *rid* of *me*—they shan't—for as I am conscious of no fault—I will yield to no oppression; but will go at my own good time when it suits my inclination and affairs.——That they may disgust me—is not difficult—and in that case—it may so happen that more than myself may be disgusted in the end.—I wrote to the Cardinal in the only style that it became me to use.—I am not conscious of being wanting in respect to his age and station,—in other points I used the freedom of

---

[1] See June 22, 1821, to Alborghetti.
[2] Alborghetti did get the business settled and Tita was released, after being held for about three weeks.

Statement due to my own rank—& the circumstances of the business.—
Believe me

yrs. ever & truly
B<small>N</small>

[TO DOUGLAS KINNAIRD]   *Ravenna. June 29th. 1821*

Dear Douglas/—Instead of receiving a letter from you per post—I
have been reading one in the papers—as secondary to Burdett &
Canning.——Pretty fellows! last time they got hit in the thigh—
whereupon these lines *might* be written.—

> Brave Champions! go on with the farce,—
> But reversing the spot where ye bled,
> Last time both got shot in the A—se,
> Now (damn you) get knocked on the head.

Have you got at "Sardanapalus"—or is it arrived?——I am anxious
to know—because I wish to learn if that is the line I ought to continue
in.——From Hobhouse I hear nothing—his last was a long complaint
about Bowles's lines—as if *I* could have helped that.——I am in the
third act of a *third* drama—[1] but Murray is so costive in his communica-
tions—that I doubt whether to go on or no.—*Your* hints about prices—
have sealed him up——& he won't speak in a hurry.—He is a good
fellow—& has a great regard for me—but all men in matters of barter
look upon their bargain*ée* as an Antagonist.—It is human nature, & not
peculiar to Murray nor his profession.—Have you been stirring to get
me out of the funds now they are *as high* as when we bought in?—
"Oh Douglas—Douglas—many a time & oft—["] I might continue
as pathetically as Lady Randolph[2]—& to as much purpose apparently.
——I am not very well—having had a bilious pain in my Stomachic
region for some days.—But I rides & jumbles it off as well as I can—
with exercise & raw eggs.—By the way your *hair* receipt costs me an
egg a day.——Does it nourish as well as embellish the hair?—The
Coronation will be over[3] by the time you have this letter so let me
hear from you.—

yrs. ever & most [Scrawl]

---

[1] *The Two Foscari.*

[2] In John Home's *Douglas* (1757), a popular tragedy, Lady Randolph had been
secretly married to Douglas and bore him a son before Douglas was slain. This
son, raised by a shepherd, came to a tragic end when her second husband Lord
Randolph killed him without knowing his origin.

[3] The coronation of George IV took place on July 19, 1821.

Dear Murray—From the last parcel of books the two first volumes of "Butler's Catholics"[1] are missing.—As the book is *"from* the author" in thanking him for me—mention this circumstance.— Waldegrave and Walpole are not arrived[2]—Scott's novels all safe.— —By the time you receive this letter the Coronation will be over—& you will be able to think of business.—Long before this you ought to have received the M.S.S. of "Sardanapalus".—It was sent on the 2d. Inst. By the way—you must permit me to choose my *own* seasons of publication.—All that you have a right to on such occasions is the mere matter of barter—if you think you are likely to lose by such or such a time of printing—you will have full allowance made for it—on statement.—It is now two years nearly that M.S.S. of mine have been in yr. hands in Statu quo.—Whatever I may have thought (& not being on the Spot nor having any exact means of ascertaining the thermometer of success or failure I have had no *determinate* opinion upon the subject) I have allowed you to go on in your own way—& acquiesced in all your arrangements hitherto. I pray you to forward the proofs of "Sardanapalus" as soon as you can—& let me know if it be deemed press & print-worthy.——I am quite ignorant how far "the Doge" did or did not succeed—yr. first letters seemed to say yes—your last say nothing.—My own immediate friends are naturally partial——one review (Blackwood's) speaks highly of it—another pamphlet calls it "a failure".—It is proper that you should apprize me of this—because I am in the *third* act of a *third* drama—& if I have nothing to expect but coldness from the public & hesitation from your-self——it were better to break off in time.—I had proposed to myself to go on—as far as my Mind would carry me—and I have thought of plenty of subjects.—But *if* I am trying an impracticable experiment— it is better to say so at once.——

So Canning & Burdett have been quarrelling[3]—if I mistake not, the

---

[1] Charles Butler (1750–1832), a Roman Catholic, was admitted to the bar in 1791. He was the first of his faith to be admitted since 1688. He published his *Historical Memoirs respecting the English, Irish and Scottish Catholics from the Reformation to the Present Time* (4 Vols.) in 1819–1821.

[2] See Feb. 1, 1821, to Kinnaird, notes 1 and 2.

[3] Sir Francis Burdett was wounded in the thigh in a duel with James Paull over the candidature for Westminster in 1807. When Canning fought Lord Castlereagh in 1809, he was also wounded in the thigh. The quarrel Byron referred to did not lead to a duel, for Burdett wrote a letter to Canning which satisfied him. Burdett had said that it was no wonder that Canning should defend a system (in opposing reform of Parliament) by which he and his family got so much public money.

last time of their single combats—each was shot in the thigh by his Antagonist, & Their Correspondence might be headed thus—by any wicked wag.—

> Brave Champions! go on with the farce!
> Reversing the spot where you bled,
> Last time both were shot in the *a—se*—
> *Now* (damn you) get knocked on the *head*!

I have not heard from you for some weeks—but I can easily excuse the silence from the occasion.—Believe me

yrs. ever & truly
B

P.S.—Do you or do you not mean to print the M.S.S. Cantos—Pulci &c.?—

P.S. 2d.—To save you the bore of writing yourself—when you are "not i' the vein"[4] make one of your Clerks send a few lines to apprize me of arrivals &c.—of M.S.S.—& matters of business.—I shan't take it ill—& I know that a bookseller in large business—must have his time too over-occupied to answer every body himself.—

P.S. 3d.—I have just read "John Bull's letter"[5]—it is diabolically *well* written—& full of fun and ferocity.—I must forgive the dog whoever he is.—I suspect three people—one is *Hobhouse*—the other—Mr. Peacock (a very clever fellow) and lastly Israeli—there are parts very like Israeli—& he has a present grudge with Bowles & Southey &c. There is something too of the author of the Sketch-book in the Style. Find him out. The packet or letter addressed to Mr. H[oppner] has never arrived & never will.—You should address directly to *me here* & by the *post*.——

[TO JOHN MURRAY]   *July 4th. 1821*

This is the note of acknowledgment for the promise *not* to continue D[on] J[uan].[1] She says in the P.S. that she is only sorry D. J. does not *remain* in Hell (or go there). The *dolore* in the first sentence refers

---

4 *Richard III*, Act IV, scene 2.

5 The author of this anonymous pamphlet was J. G. Lockhart, later the son-in-law and biographer of Sir Walter Scott. See Alan Lang Strout, *John Bull's Letter to Lord Byron*, 1947.

1 Written on the back of a note from Teresa reminding Byron of his promise not to continue *Don Juan*.

merely to a bilious attack which I had some days ago, and of which I got better.

Ravenna, July 5th, 1821

How could you suppose that I ever would allow any thing that *could* be said on your account to weigh with *me*? I only regret that Bowles had not *said* that you were the writer of that note, until afterwards, when out he comes with it, in a private letter to Murray, which Murray sends to me.[1] D—n the controversy!

> "D—n Twizzle,
>   D—n the bell.
> And d—n the fool who rung it—Well!
> From all such plagues I'll quickly be delivered."[2]

I have had a friend of your Mr. Irving's—a very pretty lad—a Mr. Coolidge, of Boston—[3] only somewhat too full of poesy and "entusy-musy." I was very civil to him during his few hours' stay, and talked with him much of Irving, whose writings are my delight. But I suspect that he did not take quite so much to me, from his having expected to meet a misanthropical gentleman, in wolf-skin breeches, and answering in fierce monosyllables, instead of a man of this world. I can never get people to understand that poetry is the expression of *excited passion*, and that there is no such thing as a life of passion any more than a continuous earthquake, or an eternal fever. Besides, who would ever *shave* themselves in such a state?

I have had a curious letter to-day from a girl in England (I never saw her), who says she is given over of a decline, but could not go out of the world without thanking me for the delight which my poesy for several years, &c. &c. &c. It is signed simply N. N. A. and has not a word of "cant" or preachment in it upon *any* opinions. She merely says that she is dying, and that as I had contributed so highly to her existing pleasure, she thought that she might say so, begging me to *burn* her *letter*—which, by the way, I can *not* do, as I look upon such a letter, in such circumstances, as better than a diploma from Gottingen. I once had a letter from Drontheim in *Norway*[4] (but not from a dying

---

[1] See June 4, 1821, to Moore, note 1.
[2] George Colman the Younger, *Broad Grins* (1811). Byron has quoted, slightly inaccurately, from "The Elder Brother".
[3] See "Detached Thoughts", No. 25, (Vol. 9).
[4] See "Detached Thoughts", No. 34, (Vol. 9).

woman), in verse, on the same score of gratulation. These are the things which make one at times believe one's self a poet. But if I must believe that * * * * *, and such fellows, are poets also, it is better to be out of the corps.

I am now in the fifth act of "Foscari" being the third tragedy in twelve months, besides *proses*; so you perceive that I am not at all idle. And are you, too, busy? I doubt that your life at Paris draws too much upon your time, which is a pity. Can't you divide your day, so as to combine both? I have had plenty of all sorts of worldly business on my hands last year, and yet it is not so difficult to give a few hours to the *Muses*. This sentence is so like * * * * that—

Ever, &c.

If we were together, I should publish both my plays (periodically) in our *joint* journal. It should be our plan to publish all our best things in that way.

[TO JOHN MURRAY]   *R[avenn]a July 6th. 1821*

Dear Sir/—In agreement with a wish expressed by Mr. Hobhouse— it is my determination to omit the Stanza upon the *horse* of *Semiramis*[1] —in the fifth Canto of D[on] J[uan].—I mention this in case you are or intend to be the publisher of the remaining Cantos.—By yesterday's post I ought in point of [time] to have had an acknowledgement of the [arrival] of the M.S.S. of "Sardanapalus".—If it *has* arrived & you have delayed the few lines necessary for this—I can only say that you are keeping two people in hot water—the postmaster here—because the packet was insured—& myself because I had but that one copy.— I am in the *fifth* act of a play on the subject of the Foscaris—father and Son.—Foscolo can tell you their story.

I am yrs. [Scrawl]

P.S.—At the particular request of the Countess G[uiccioli] I have promised *not* to continue Don Juan.—You will therefore look upon these 3 cantos as the last of that poem.—She had read the two first in the French translation—& never ceased beseeching me to write no more of it.—The reason of this is not at first obvious to a superficial

---

[1] *Don Juan*, Canto V, stanza 61. Queen Caroline, whose trial for adultery with her courier Bartolommeo Bergami, came up in August and lasted until November, was too clearly referred to in the stanza.

observer of FOREIGN manners[,] but it arises from the wish of all women to exalt the *sentiment* of the passions—& to keep up the illusion which is their empire.—Now D. J. strips off this illusion—& laughs at that & most other things.—I never knew a woman who did not protect *Rousseau*—nor one who did not dislike de Grammont— Gil Blas & all the *comedy* of the passions—when brought out naturally. —But "King's blood must keep word" as Serjeant Bothwell says.[2]— Write you Scamp! Your parcel of *extracts* never came & never will— you should have sent it by the post—but you are growing a sad fellow and some fine day we shall have to dissolve partnership. Some more *Soda* powders.—

[TO JOHN CAM HOBHOUSE]   R[avenn]a July 6th. 1821

My dear H/—I have written by this post to Murray to omit the stanza to which you object.[1]—In case he should forget—you can jog his memory. I have also agreed to a request of Madame Guiccioli's *not* to continue that poem further.—She had read the French translation and thinks it a detestable production.—This will not seem strange even in Italian morality—because women all over the world always retain their Free masonry—and as that consists in the illusion of the Senti- ment—which constitutes their sole empire—(all owing to Chivalry— & the Goths—the Greeks knew better) all works which refer to the *comedy* of the passions—& laugh at Sentimentalism—of course are pro- scribed by the whole *Sect.*—I never knew a woman who did not admire Rousseau—and hate Gil Blas & de Grammont and the like—for the same reason.—And I never met with a woman English or foreign who did not do as much by D. J.—As I am docile—I have yielded and promised to confine myself to the "high flying of Buttons" (you remember Pope's phrase)[2] for the time to come.—You will be very glad of this—as an earlier opponent of that poem's publication.——I

---

[2] Scott's *Old Mortality*, Chapter 6.

[1] Hobhouse had written to Byron on June 21, 1821: "By the way, do not cut at poor Queeney in your Don Juan about Semiramis and her Courser courier. She would feel it very much, I assure you."

[2] Pope's phrase was in a letter of July 15, 1716, concerning the *Iliad* translation: "I appeal to the People, as my rightful judges and masters; and if they are not inclin'd to condemn me, I fear no arbitrary high-flying proceedings from the small Court-faction at Button's." (Sherburn, *Correspondence of Alexander Pope*, I, 306.) Button's Coffee House was the meeting place of a Whig group, too worshipful of Addison to suit Pope. Pope and Gay engaged in a lively war of wit with the members of Addison's "little Senate at Button's".

only read your Canningippic[3] in the papers—but even there it was worthy of anything since those against Anthony.——You must not give letters to me.—I have taken an oath against being civil, ever since—— you will see my reason in the last note to Marino Faliero.— I have sent to England a tragedy a month ago—& am in the *fifth* act of another.—Murray has not acknowledged its arrival—I must one day break with that Gentleman—if he is not the civiler.— Of Burdett's affair I cannot judge—so I made an epigram on it—which I sent to Douglas K[innair]d. By the way now the *funds are up, stir him* up—and the bloody trustees.—It would give me pleasure to see some of you that I might gossip over the late revolt—(or rather revol*ting*) transactions of these parts.—Things are far from quiet even now.—Have you seen my "Elegy on the *recovery* of Lady Noel"—

> "Behold the blessings of a lucky lot!
> My play is damned—and Lady Noel *not.*"

Do you know that your bust was sent to England (via *Livorno*) months ago? Let me hear from or of you

yrs. [Scrawl]

P.S.—Fletcher is turned Money lender—& puts out money (*here*) at 20 per cent—Query—will he get it again? *Who* knows?

[TO JOHN MURRAY]   *R[avenn]a July 7th. 1821*

Dear Sir/—Enclosed are two letters from two of yr. professional brethren.—By one of them you will perceive that if you are disposed to *"buy justice"* it is to be sold (no doubt as *"Stationary"*) at his Shop.——Thank him in my name for his good will—however—and good offices—and say that I *can't* afford to "purchase justice"—as it is by far the dearest article in these very dear times.—

yrs. ever [Scrawl]

[TO JOHN MURRAY]   *R[avenn]a July 9th. 1821*

Dear Sir/—The enclosed packet came *quite open* so I suppose it is no breach of confidence to send it back to *you* who must have seen it before.—Return it to the Address—explaining in what state I

---

[3] See May 20, 1821, to Hobhouse, note 2.

149

received it.———What is all this about *Mitylene*[1] (where I never was in my life) "Manuscript Criticism on the Manchester business" (which I never wrote) "Day & Martin's patent blacking" and a "young lady who offered &c."—of whom I never heard.—Are the people mad or merely drunken?———I have at length received your packet—& have nearly completed the tragedy on the Foscaris.—Believe me

yours very truly
B

        Luglio 12 1821

Mio Caro Ruggiero [sic]—Tu sei padrone della Teresa per diritto—e di me per dovere ed amicizia.—Ma viste le circonstanze io crederei bene per *prudenza* anche—che Ella non partisse per alcuni giorni.—Se tu insisti—ella cederà—come io—che non ho—nè debbo avere che una voce in questo affare.———Ma i passa-porti sono equivoci—la presenza di lei non può giovare nulla—per impedirli, se loro vogliono molestarti—nè per consolarti—poiche non vorresti vedere una donna isolata in tale situazione.—Se accade del bene noi ti raggiungeremo, se⟨de⟩ del male—anche ti raggiungeremo in qualunque circonstanza—ed io mi farei un dovere trovarti anche se fosse in fortezza.—Ma ti prego non precipitare la cosa per ora,—e particolarmente pensare di tutto ciò che potrebbe accadere alla Teresa priva di te e di Pierino—in un paese inimico.———Per me io non ho altro a dire senochè desiderare vederti e Pierino ben' presto—ciò che farò o in un paese o l'altro.—Sta Sano e credemi sempre il

tuo aff.mo amico
BYRON

P.S.—Ti rimando il pacco di *quest' oggi*—che la Teresa ti ebbe fatto rimandarmi.—Serviti liberamente non solamente di quello—ma di tutto il mio.—Tu farai come tu vuoi—ma in ogni modo ricordati—che si arriva del ⟨distacco tra⟩ male al la Teresa ⟨e me⟩—che non era colpa mia.

[TRANSLATION]   *July 12th. 1821*

My dear Ruggiero—You are Teresa's master by right—and mine by duty and friendship.—But in view of the circumstances I should

---

[1] Probably the spurious "account of Lord Byron's residence in the Island of Mitylene" printed with *The Vampyre* in 1819, revived and printed along with other supposed compositions of Byron.

think it better, also for prudence's sake, for her not to leave for a few days.[1] If you insist, she will give way and so will I—who have not and should not have a voice in the matter. But the passports are equivocal—her presence will not be of any use to prevent them if they want to molest you, or to console you—for you would not want to see a woman left alone in such a situation.

If things go well we shall join you; if ill—even then we shall join you, in any circumstances whatever—and I shall consider it my duty to find you, even if you are in prison.—

But I beg you not to precipitate matters for the present, and particularly to think of all that might happen to Teresa, deprived of you and of Pierino—and in enemy country.——

For my part I have no more to say except that I hope to see you and Pierino very soon—which I will do in one place or another.—
Keep well and believe me always

Your most affectionate friend
BYRON

P.S.—I am returning today's packet—which Teresa made you return to me. Make use freely not only of that, but of everything of mine.—

You will do as you wish—but in any case remember—that if any separation occurs[2] between Teresa and me—it will not be my fault.

[TO JOHN MURRAY]   *July 14th. 1821*

Dear Sir/—According to yr. wish I have expedited by this post two packets addressed to J. Barrow Esqre. Admiralty &c.[1]——The one contains the returned proofs with such corrections as time permits of "Sardanapalus".—The other contains the tragedy of "the two Foscari" in five acts. the argument of which Foscolo or Hobhouse can explain to you—or you will find it at length in P. Daru's history of Venice,—

---

[1] When the Gambas, father and son, were exiled following the abortive revolution in the Romagna, Teresa refused to leave without Byron, and he wrote on her behalf to her father. But when she was threatened to be shut up in a convent, Byron persuaded her to join her father and brother in Florence.

[2] Teresa tried to erase this phrase and make the letter read: "if any harm comes to Teresa".

[1] Sir John Barrow (1764–1848), Secretary of the Admiralty, was a friend of Murray and a founder of the Royal Geographical Society. He sometimes contributed to Murray's *Quarterly Review*. Packets sent in his care would apparently be facilitated in transportation and would save postage.

also more briefly—in Sismondi's *I[talian] R[epublics]*. An outline of it is in the Pleasures of Memory[2] also.—The name is a dactyl "Fŏscărĭ".——Have the goodness to write by return of Post which is essential.——I trust that "Sardanapalus" will not be mistaken for a *political* play—which was so far from my intention that I thought of nothing but Asiatic history.—The Venetian play too is rigidly historical.— My object has been to dramatize like the Greeks (a *modest* phrase!) striking passages of history, as they did of history & mythology.— You will find all this very *un*like Shakespeare—and so much the better in one sense—for I look upon him to be the *worst* of models—though the most extraordinary of writers.—It has been my object to be as simple and severe as Alfieri—& I have broken down the *poetry* as nearly as I could to common language.—The hardship is that in these times one can neither speak of kings or Queens without suspicion of politics or personalities.——I intended neither.——I am not very well—and I write in the midst of unpleasant scenes here—They have without trial—or process—banished several of the first inhabitants of the cities—here and all around the Roman States—amongst them many of my personal friends—so that every thing is in confusion & grief;—it is a kind of thing which cannot be described without equal pain as in beholding it.——You are very niggardly in your letters.—

yrs. truly [Scrawl]

P.S.—In the first soliloquy of Salamenes—read—

"⟨Which are⟩ at once his *Chorus* and his Council['"]

"Chorus" being in the higher dramatic sense—meaning his accompaniment—& not a mere *musical* train.—

[TO DOUGLAS KINNAIRD] *July 14th. 1821*

My dear Douglas/—You perhaps did right in not forwarding the letter—which was none of the tenderest.[1]—Open—& read it—and forward it not.—You must excuse my impatience about the funds.— you *forget* that you must have a further power of Attorney to sell out—

[2] Rogers referred to the story of the Foscaris in *The Pleasures of Memory* and in his poem *Italy*.
[1] Byron had enclosed a harsh letter to Hanson, who had opposed an Irish mortgage. See Feb. 1, 1821, to Kinnaird.

and in the interval of a Courier's expedition—the funds may fall—
or the Courier may fall—or—what can I say?—I should approve of the
Exchequer bills. So my lady has been civil—that's news—& new—
however it is her child's interest—& as such no great stretch of
politeness.——With regard to M[urray] you will please to recollect
that I never meant any *comparison*. I sent his letter to show you his
way of thinking.—Mine is this.—I believe M. to be a good man with a
personal regard for me.—But a bargain is in its very essence a *hostile*
transaction.—If I were to come to you—Douglas—& say—"lend me
five hundred pounds"—you would either do it—or give a good reason
why you would not.—But I come and say—"Douglas—I have a
carriage & horses—or a library—or what you will—give me five
hundred pounds for them"—you first enquire if they are worth it—&
even if they are—do not all men try to abate the price of all they buy?—
I contend that a bargain even between brethren—is a declaration of
war.—Now this must be much more so in a Man like M. whose
business is nothing but a perpetual speculation on what will or will not
succeed—& can have no steady returns being a matter of opinion. I
have no doubt that he would lend or give—freely—what he would
refuse for value received in M.S.S.——So do not think too hardly
of him.—I do not know myself to what he alludes—nor do I wish to
know.—Your manner is quick—as is the case with all men of any
vivacity—and *he* might feel perhaps a turn of the lip—or a short reply
—which Hobhouse would only make a long letter about—and I should
only keep in mind for six months—and then pay you off in your own
coin on a fit opportunity.——Now these are resources which the great
M. has not—neither is he on that equality of feeling with you—(as
doubtless neither in rank) which can admit of that agreeable give and
take—which you and I and all of our Chorus—have long reciprocated.
It is different with me—a publisher becomes identified almost with his
authors—and can say any thing—or hear any thing.——And now
there approacheth new barter.—By this post is forwarded (with the
returned proofs of "Sardanapalus") the tragedy M.S.S. of "the two
Foscari" in five acts.—When you have read both and formed your
opinion—I leave to you the discretionary power of poundage & pence.
—Perhaps it were as well to publish them first and settle afterwards
according to success—if there be any.—You will perceive that I have
kept aloof from the Stage as before. By the time you receive this the
Coronation will have subsided and you may have leisure to think of
such things.——I write out of spirits—for they have been banishing
(without trial) half the inhabitants & many of my friends amongst

153

them of this country—as politicians.—I hope that this will find you in good humour.

yrs ever & aftly. [Scrawl]

Ravenna July 15th. 1821[1]

Madame—I am about to request a favour of your Grace, without the smallest personal pretensions to obtain it.—It is not however for myself—and yet I err—for surely what we solicit for our friends—is— or ought to be—nearest to ourselves.——If I fail in this application— my intrusion will be it's own reward—if I succeed—your Grace's reward will consist in having done a good action—& mine in your pardon for my presumption.—My reason for applying to you is this— your Grace has been long at Rome—and could not be long any where without the influence and the inclination to do good.——Amongst the list of exiles on account of the late suspicions—and the intrigues of the Austrian Government (the most infamous in history) there are many of my acquaintances in Romagna & some of my friends.—Of these more particularly are the two Counts *Gamba*—(father & Son) of a noble and respected family in this city.—In common with thirty or more of all ranks—they have been hurried from their homes without process— without hearing—without accusation.——The father is universally respected & liked—his family is numerous & mostly young—& these are now left without protection.—His Son is a very fine young man— with very little of the vices of his age or climate—he has I believe the honour of an acquaintance with yr. Grace—having been presented by Madame Martinetti.—He is but one and twenty—& lately returned from his studies at Rome.—Could your Grace—or would you—ask the repeal of both—or at least of *one* of these from those in power in the holy City? They are not aware of my solicitation in their behalfs—but I will take it upon me to say—that they shall neither dishonour your goodness—nor my request. If only one can be obtained—let it be the father—on account of his family.—I can assure your Grace—and the very pious Government in question—that there can be no danger in this act of—*clemency*——shall I call it?—It would be but *Justice* with us— but *here*!—let them call it—what they will.——I cannot express the obligation which I should *feel*——I say *feel* only—because I do not see

[1] This is misdated February 15 in *LJ*, V, 237.

how I could repay it to your Grace.—I have not the slightest claim upon you—unless perhaps through the memory of our late friend Lady Melbourne—I say *friend* only—for my *relationship* with her family has not been fortunate for them nor for me.—If therefore you should be disposed to grant my request I shall set it down to your tenderness for her who is gone—& who was to me the best & kindest of friends.——The persons for whom I solicit—will (in case of success) neither be in ignorance of their protectress—nor indisposed to acknowledge their sense of her kindness by a strict observance of such conduct as may justify her interference.—If my acquaintance with your Grace's character were even slighter than it is—through the medium of some of our English friends—I had only to turn to the letters of Gibbon (now on my table) for a full testimony to it's high & amiable qualities.—I have the honour to be with great respect

yr. G[race]'s most obedt. very Humble Servt.

BYRON

P.S.—Pray excuse my scrawl which perhaps you may be enabled to decypher from a long acquaintance with the handwriting of Lady Bessborough.—I omitted to mention that the measures taken here have been as *blind* as impolitic—this I happen to *know*.—Out of the *list* in Ravenna—there are at least *ten* not only innocent—but even opposite in principles to the liberals. It has been the work of some blundering Austrian spy—or angry priest to gratify his private hatreds.—Once more—yr. pardon.—

[TO JOHN MURRAY]   *R[avenn]a July 22d. 1821*

Dear Murray/—By this post is expedited a parcel of notes—addressed to J. Barrow Esqre. &c.—Also by ye. former post—the returned proof of S[ardanapalus]—and the M.S.S. of the "two Foscaris."—Acknowledge these.—The printer has done wonders—he has read what I cannot—my own handwriting.——I *oppose* the "delay till Winter"—I am particularly anxious to print while the *Winter theatres* are *closed*—to gain time in case they try their former piece of politeness.——Any *loss*—shall be considered in our contract—whether occasioned by the season or other causes—but print away—and publish.—I think they must own that I have more *styles* than one. ——"Sardanapalus" is however almost a comic character—but for that matter—so is Richard the third.—Mind the *Unities*—which are

155

my great object of research. I am glad that Gifford likes it—as for "the Million"[1]—you see I have carefully consulted anything but the *taste* of the day—for extravagant "coups de theatre".—Any probable loss—as I said before—will be allowed for in our accompts.—The reviews (except one or two, Blackwood's for instance) are cold enough—but never mind those fellows——I shall send them to the right about—if I take it into my head.—Perhaps that in the Monthly is written by Hodgson—as a reward for having paid his debts and travelled all night to beg his mother in law (by his *own* desire) to let him marry her daughter,—though I had never seen her in my life, it succeeded.—But such are mankind—and I have always found the English *baser* in some things than any other nation.—You stare—but it's true—as to *gratitude*;—perhaps—because they are prouder—& proud people hate obligations.——

The tyranny of the government here is breaking out—they have exiled about a thousand people of the best families all over the Roman States.—As many of my friends are amongst them—I think of moving too—but not till I have had your answers—continue *your address* to me *here* as usual—& quickly.——What you will *not* be sorry to hear is— that the *poor* of the place—hearing that I mean to go—got together a petition to the Cardinal—to request that *he* would request me to *remain*. I only heard of it a day or two ago—& it is no dishonour to them nor to me—but it will have displeased the higher powers who look upon me as a Chief of the Coalheavers. They arrested a servant of mine for a Street quarrel with an Officer (they drew upon one another knives & pistols) but as *the Officer* was out of uniform—& in the *wrong* besides—on my protesting stoutly—he was released.—⟨As⟩ I was not present at the affray—which happened by night near my stables.——My man (an Italian) a very stout—& not over patient personage would have taken a fatal revenge afterwards if I had not prevented him. As it was he drew his stiletto—and—but for passengers —would have carbonadoed the Captain—who (I understand) made but a poor figure in the quarrel—except by beginning it.——He applied to me—and I offered him any satisfaction—either by turning away the man or otherwise, because he had drawn a knife. He answered that a reproof would be sufficient.—I reproved him—and yet— after this—the shabby dog complained to the *Government*—after being quite satisfied as he said.—*This* roused me—and I gave them a remonstrance which had some effect.—If he had not enough—he

---

[1] cf. *Hamlet*, Act II, scene 2; "the play, I remember, pleased not the million."

should have called me *out*—but that is not the Italian line of conduct,—the Captain has been reprimanded—the servant released—& the business at present rests there.—Write & let me know of the arrival of [Scrawl]

P.S.—You will of course publish the two tragedies of Sardanapalus & the Foscaris together.—You can afterwards collect them with "Manfred", and "the Doge"—into the works.—Inclosed is an additional note.—

Ravenna. July 23d. 1821

My dear Hoppner/—This country being in a state of proscription—and all my friends exiled—or arrested—the whole family of Gamba—obliged to go to Florence for the present—the father & Son for politicians—(& the Guiccioli because menaced with a *Convent*—as her father is *not* here—) I have determined to remove to Switzerland—and they also.—Indeed my life here is not supposed to be particularly safe—but that has been the case for this twelve-month past—and is therefore not the primary consideration.———I have written by the post to Mr. Hentsch Jr.[1] the Banker of Geneva—to provide (if possible) a house for me—and another for Gamba's family (the father son and daughter) on the *Jura* side of the Lake of Geneva—furnished—& with stabling (for *me* at least) for eight horses.—I shall bring Allegra with me.—Could you assist me or Hentsch in his researches? The Gambas are at Florence but have authorized me to treat for them.———You know—or do not know that they are great patriots—and both—but the Son in particular very fine fellows.—*This* I know—for I have seen them lately in very awkward situations—*not* pecuniary —but personal—and they behaved like heroes, neither yielding nor retracting.———You have no idea what a state of oppression this country is in—they arrested above a thousand of high & low—throughout Romagna—banished some—& confined others—without *trial—process*—or even *accusation*!! Every body says they would [have] done the same by me if they dared proceed openly. My motive however for removing, is because *every one* of my acquaintance to the amount of hundreds almost have been exiled.———Will you do what you can in looking out for a couple of houses—*furnished* and conferring with

---

[1] Byron's letter to Hentsch (July 22, 1821) was sold at auction at Sotheby's Dec. 14, 1917 (no quotations); its present location is unknown.

157

Hentsch for us? We care nothing about Society—and are only anxious for a temporary and tranquil asylum, and individual freedom.—Believe me

ever & truly yrs.
BYRON

P.S.—My best respects to Mrs. Hoppner. I have sent two dramas to England—one upon "Sardanapalus"—the other—upon "the two *Foscaris*" (a Venetian story) both in five acts.—Address to me at Ravenna as usual.

P.S.—Can you give me an idea of the comparative expences of Switzerland and Italy? which I have forgotten.—I speak merely of those of decent *living—horses*, &c.—& not of luxuries or high living. Do *not* however decide any thing positive till I have your answer—as I can then know how to think upon these topics of transmigration &c. &c. &c.

[TO DOUGLAS KINNAIRD] *R[avenn]a July 23d. 1821*

Dear Douglas/—By the inclosed you will see what Gifford thinks of "Sardanapalus". He approves of it.—M[urray] wants to delay publishing—till *Winter*.—This I *oppose*—he must publish *directly* while the *Winter theatres are shut*.—By this time you will have seen the play of "the Two Foscari's" also.—[We] will make any allowance for a loss in the sale by a difference of season in the publication.—I was very glad by yr. short letter to see that you liked Sardanapalus.—But don't abuse the "*Unities*"—there can be no drama without an approach to them.—The rest is barbarism.——Pray let me hear from you

yrs. ever
BN

P.S.—You see Murray has been candid about the Sale of "the Doge".—I leave you to deal with him about the M.S.S. now in his hands.——I have told him that we will abate for any deduction made by the season—though I can't see why people should read less in the country than when they are in town.——The funds—the funds—the funds—

[TO COUNTESS TERESA GUICCIOLI] *R[avenn]a Luglio 26 o 1821*

Mia Teresa/—Ti prego calmarti, ed andare avante colla certezza—che dovressimo rivederci tra poco.—Se non in Ravenna—combin-

eremmo per la Svizzera quando mi viene la risposta da Ginevra.—Jeri
ò veduto il *Zio* C[avalli] che da delle speranze—Tonino *è a Roma ciò è
certo.*–Intanto non cedere a un' dolore cosi irragionevole—ma pensa di
consolare il tuo padre e fratello.—Mi rincresce della lontananza della
Duchessa—della bontà di quale sperava molto—ma forse se può fare
egualmente senza di lei.——Il tuo progetto di tornare qui solo per
rivederci un istante—sarebbe una vera pazzia—mi pare che con un
tale proposizione tu hai desiderio di farti mettere in *convento*—come
venne minacciato.—Ti amo e ti amerò—come ti ho sempre amato—
ma non posso incoraggire un' delirio cosi fatale come sarebbe il tuo
ritorno il giorno dopo la tua partenza.—Lega ti scriverà accludendo
due lettere della posta di oggidi—che io ho ricevuto per te—come tu
dicesti.——Mille cose a Ruggiero e Pierino—scrivi spesso—e presto.
—Saluta il Sr. Costa e la sua consorte—ai quali sono gratissimo della
loro amicizia per la tua famiglia.—"Figlia consolati—sterge le
lacrime"——e credemi ("crede B[yron]" tu sai è la parola di mia
famiglia) sempre e tutto il tuo

amico am.te
B

P.S.—Pet. . . . mettiti in buon' umore—le cose anderanno meglio
che tu pensi.—Ti ringrazio per il fiore accluso—che ebbe conservato
molto il suo *odorino.*—Tutto qui è come era al'tuo partire.——

[TRANSLATION] *Ravenna, July 26th, 1821*

My Teresa: Pray calm yourself and continue your journey,[1] in the
certainty that we shall see each other again soon. If not in Ravenna,
then we shall arrange about Switzerland, as soon as I get an answer
from Geneva.—Yesterday I saw Uncle C[avalli] who gives some hope
——Tonino[2] is in *Rome, that is certain.* Meanwhile don't give way to
such unreasonable grief—but think of consoling your father and your
brother.

I am sorry about the Duchess's absence[3]—I had hoped much from
her kindness—but perhaps we may do as well without her.—Your

---

[1] Byron had finally persuaded Teresa to leave Ravenna, where she was threatened
with incarceration in a convent, to join her father and brother in Florence, but after
arriving in Bologna she proposed returning for one night to see Byron again; but
she was still in danger in the Papal States and he urged her to continue her journey.

[2] Marchese Antonio Cavalli, a cousin of Teresa, was a leading Carbonaro.

[3] See July 15, 1821, to the Duchess of Devonshire.

plan of coming back here to see each other for a moment would be real folly—such a proposal really makes me think that you wish to be put in a *convent*—as was threatened.

I love you and shall love you as I have always loved you—but I cannot encourage such fatal madness as your return here would be, the day after your departure.—

Lega will write to you enclosing two letters of today's post which I have received for you—as you asked.—

A thousand messages to Ruggero and Pierino.—Write often and quickly. Greet signor Costa[4] and his wife, to whom I am very grateful for their friendship to your family.

"My daughter, be comforted, dry your tears"—and believe me (crede B. you know is my family motto) ever and entirely your friend and lover

B

P.S.—Little gossip—get into a good humour—things will go better than you think——Thank you for the flower, which has kept much of its scent——Everything here is as it was at your departure.

[TO COUNTESS TERESA GUICCIOLI]   *L[ugli]o 29 1821*

Mia Teresa/—Voi siete partita coll' intenzione di ritrovare la vostra famiglia in Firenze.—Questo fu il solo partito rispettabile o ragionevole per voi nelle circonstanze attuali. Cosa vi fa trattenervi in Bologna? io non so—e se lo sapessi—non lo potrei approvare.——Vi *raccomando* dunque di bel nuovo di *proseguire* il viaggio per tutte le ragioni. Col vostro padre siete salva—e dappiù—fate il vostro dovere come figlia.—Dove siete, io non vedo che una donna senza appoggio— e *non* ⟨d'un molto buon cuore che⟩ dovete lasciare stare il suo padre nel' esilio senza fare un viaggio di 18 ore per consolarlo.—Se credete di essere sicura dalle tentative gia fatte (e per fare ancora) per mettervi in un' ritiro—finche rimanete nei *stati del Papa*—*Sbagliate*.—Sono sempre il vostro

a.a.

B

P.S.—Spero sentire che siete partito per Firenze—allora vi scriverò in dettaglio.—

---

4 Professor Costa was Teresa's old teacher and a Gamba family friend, with whom she stayed in Bologna.

My Teresa: You left with the intention of joining your family in Florence—that was the only respectable and reasonable excuse for you in the present circumstances. What is detaining you in Bologna? I do not know, and if I knew—I could not approve.———Once again I *urge* you to continue your journey, for every reason. With your father you are safe—and besides—you are doing your duty as a daughter. Where you are, I can only see a woman without support, and not very kind, who leaves her father in exile without taking an 18 hours' journey to console him.—If you believe that you are safe from the attempts already made (and that would be made again) to put you away in a convent so long as you remain in the *Papal States—you are mistaken.*[1]

I am always your friend and lover

B

P.S.—I hope to hear that you have left for Florence—then I will write to you in detail.

[TO ELIZABETH, DUCHESS OF DEVONSHIRE] *Ravenna. July 30th. 1821*

Madam/—The enclosed letter which I had the honour of addressing to your Grace unfortunately for the subject of it—and for the writer—arrived after your Grace's departure.—I venture to forward it to Spa—in the hope that you may be perhaps tempted to interest yourself in favour of the persons to whom it refers by writing a few lines to any of yr. Roman acquaintances in power.—Two words from your Grace—I cannot help thinking would be sufficient—even if the request were still more presumptuous. I have ye. honour to be with greatest respect

yr. most obedt. very humble Servt.
BYRON

[TO JOHN MURRAY] *R[avenn]a July 30th. 1821*

Dear Sir/—Enclosed is the best account of the Doge Faliero—which was only sent to me from an old M.S.S. the other day.—Get it translated and append it as a note to the next edition.[1]—You *will*

---

[1] After receiving this letter Teresa finally left for Florence.

[1] Marino Sanudo's *Vite dei Doge*, translated by Francis Cohen, was published as an appendix to *Marino Faliero*. There is no record of this account from an old manuscript.

perhaps be pleased to see that my conceptions of his character were correct—though I regret not having met with this extract before.— You will perceive that he himself said exactly what He is made to say— about the Bishop of Treviso.[2]—You will see also that "he spoke very little and then only words of rage and disdain" after his arrest—which is the case in the play—except when he breaks out at the close of Act fifth.—But his speech to the Conspirators—is better in the M.S.S. than in the play—I wish that I had met with it in time.——Do not forget this note, with a translation.—

In a former note to the Juans—speaking of Voltaire I have quoted his famous "Zaire—tu pleures"—which is an error—it should be "Zaire *vous pleurez*"[3]—recollect this—& recollect also that your *want* of *recollection* has permitted you to publish the note on the Kelso traveller[4]—which *I had positively desired you not*—for proof of which I refer you to my letters.—I presume that you are able to lay your hand upon these letters—as you are accused publicly in a pamphlet of showing them about. I wait your acknowledgment of the packets containing "the Foscaris"—notes—&c. &c.—now your Coronation is over—perhaps you will find time. I have also written to Mr. Kinnaird to say that I expect the two tragedies to be published speedily—and to inform him—that I am willing to make any abatement on your statement of loss liable to be incurred by publishing at an improper season. ——I am so busy here about these poor proscribed exiles—who are scattered about—and with trying to get some of them recalled—that I have hardly time or patience to write a short preface—which will be proper for the two plays.——However I will make it out—on receiving the next proofs.—

yrs. ever
[Scrawl]

P.S.—Please to append the letter about *the Hellespont*[5] as a note to your next opportunity of the verses on Leander &c. &c. &c. in Childe Harold.—Don't forget it amidst your multitudinous avocations— which I think of celebrating in a dithyrambic ode to Albemarle Street. Are you aware that Shelley has written an elegy on Keats—and accuses the Quarterly of killing him?—

---

[2] *Marino Faliero*, Act I, scene 2.
[3] In an intended note on Bacon's inaccuracies intended for *Don Juan*, Canto V, stanza 147, See Jan. 8, 1821, to Murray, and *LJ*, V, 600.
[4] See *Poetry*, IV, 471.
[5] See Feb. 21, 1821, to Murray.

Who killed John Keats?
　　I, says the the Quarterly
So savage & Tartarly
　　　　⟨Martyrly⟩
　　'Twas one of my feats—
Who ⟨drew the [pen?]⟩ shot the arrow?
　　The poet-priest Milman
(So ready to kill man)
Or Southey or Barrow.—

You know very well that I did not approve of Keats's poetry or principles of poetry—or of his abuse of Pope—but as he is dead—omit *all* that is said *about him* in any *M.S.S.* of mine—or publication.—His Hyperion is a fine monument & will keep his name—I do not envy the man—who wrote the article—your review people have no more right to kill than any other foot pads.—However—he who would die of an article in a review[6]—would probably have died of something else equally trivial—the same thing nearly happened to Kirke White[7]— who afterwards died of consumption.

[TO PERCY BYSSHE SHELLEY]   [*July 30–31? 1821*]

[First page missing] . . . omitted. The impression of Hyperion upon my mind was—that it was the best of his works.—Who is to be his editor? It is strange that Southey who attacks the reviewers so sharply in his Kirk White—calling theirs "the ungentle craft"—should be perhaps the killer of Keats.[1]—Kirke White was nearly extinguished in the same way—by a paragraph or two in "the Monthly"—Such inordinate sense of censure is surely incompatible with great exertion— have not all known writers been the subject thereof?—

　　　　　　　　　　　　　　　　　yrs. ever & truly
　　　　　　　　　　　　　　　　　　　B

P.S.—If moving at present should be inconvenient to you[2]—let me settle that—draw upon me for what you think necessary—I should do so myself on you without ceremony—if I found it expedient.—Write directly.—

---

[6] See *Don Juan*, Canto XI, stanza 60.
[7] The young Nottingham poet who died in 1806 at the age of 21.
[1] It was not Southey but John Wilson Croker who wrote the devastating review of Keats's *Endymion* in the *Quarterly Review* in 1818.
[2] Byron had invited Shelley to pay him a visit at Ravenna.

I had certainly answered your last letter, though but briefly, to the part to which you refer, merely saying, "damn the controversy;" and quoting some verses of George Colman's, not as allusive to you, but to the disputants. Did you receive this letter? It imports me to know that our letters are not intercepted or mislaid.

Your Berlin drama is an honour,[1] unknown since the days of Elkanah Settle, whose "Empress of Morocco" was represented by the Court ladies, which was, as Johnson says, "the last blast of inflammation" to poor Dryden, who could not bear it, and fell foul of Settle without mercy or moderation, on account of that and a frontispiece, which he dared to put before his play.[2]

Was not your showing the Memoranda to * * [Lady Holland?] somewhat perilous?[3] Is there not a facetious allusion or two which might as well be reserved for posterity?

I know S[chlegel] well—that is to say, I have met him occasionally at Copet. Is he not also touched lightly in the Memoranda? In a review of Childe Harold, Canto 4th, three years ago, in Blackwood's Magazine, they quote some stanzas of an elegy of S[chlegel]'s on Rome, from which they say that I *might* have taken some ideas.[4] I give you my honour that I never saw it except in that criticism, which gives, I think, three or four stanzas, sent *them* (they say) for the nonce by a correspondent—perhaps himself. The fact is easily proved; for I don't understand German, and there was I believe no translation—at least, it was the first time that I ever heard of, or saw, either translation or original.

I remember having some talk with S[chlegel] about Alfieri, whose merit he denies. He was also wroth about the Edinburgh Review of Goethe, which was sharp enough, to be sure. He went about saying,

---

[1] There had been a spectacle based on Moore's *Lalla Rookh* at the court of Berlin in which the Emperor and Empress took part.

[2] Dryden took his revenge in the second part of *Absalom and Achitophel*, and Settle replied in *Absalom Senior*.

[3] Moore wrote in his diary for July 6, 1821: "I yesterday gave Lady Holland Lord Byron's 'Memoirs' to read." (*Moore Memoirs*, Vol. III, p. 251.)

[4] A note in *Blackwood's Edinburgh Magazine* (Vol. III, p. 222) says: "We had lately sent to us a translation of an Elegy by William Augustus Schlegel, from which our correspondent supposes that Lord Byron has borrowed not a little of the spirit, and even of the expressions, of the Fourth Canto." But the writer of the note discounted the similarities. Byron was particularly sensitive to any suggestion of plagiary.

too, of the French—"I meditate a terrible vengeance against the French—I will prove that Moliere is no poet."[5]

I don't see why you should talk of "declining." When I saw you, you looked thinner, and yet younger, than you did when we parted several years before. You may rely upon this as fact. If it were not, I should say *nothing*, for I would rather not say unpleasant *personal* things to any one—but, as it was the pleasant *truth*, I tell it you. If you had led my life, indeed, changing climates and connexions—*thinning* yourself with fasting and purgatives—besides the wear and tear of the vulture passions, and a very bad temper besides, you might talk in this way—but *you*! I know no man who looks so well for his years, or who deserves to look better and to be better, in all respects. You are a * * *, and what is perhaps better for your friends, a good fellow. So don't talk of decay, but put in for eighty, as you well may.

I am, at present, occupied principally about these unhappy proscriptions and exiles, which have taken place here on account of politics. It has been a miserable sight to see the general desolation in families. I am doing what I can for them, high and low, by such interest and means as I possess or can bring to bear. There have been thousands of these proscriptions within the last month in the Exarchate, or (to speak modernly) the Legations. Yesterday, too, a man got his back broken, in extricating a dog of mine from under a mill-wheel. The dog was killed, and the man is in the greatest danger.[6] I was not present—it happened before I was up, owing to a stupid boy taking the dog to bathe in a dangerous spot. I must, of course, provide for the poor fellow while he lives, and his family, if he dies. I would gladly have given a much greater sum than that will come to that he had never been hurt. Pray, let me hear from you, and excuse haste and hot weather.

Yours, &c.

* * * * *

You may have probably seen all sorts of attacks upon me in some gazettes in England some months ago. I only saw them, by Murray's

---

[5] Schlegel had disparaged Molière's character and abilities as a dramatist in his *Lectures on Dramatic Art and Literature* (translation by John Black, London, 1815, Vol. II, pp. 40–41).

[6] The man's name was Balani. He died eleven days after the accident and Byron pensioned his widow. (*LJ*, V, 335n.)

bounty, the other day. They call me "Plagiary," and what not.[7] I think I now, in my time, have been accused of *every* thing.

I have not given you details of little events here; but they have been trying to make me out to be the chief of a conspiracy, and nothing but their want of proofs for an *English* investigation has stopped them. Had it been a poor native, the suspicion were enough, as it has been for hundreds.

Why don't you write on Napoleon?[8] I have no spirits, nor "estro" to do so. His overthrow, from the beginning, was a blow on the head to me. Since that period, we have been the slaves of fools. Excuse this long letter. *Ecco* a translation literal of a French epigram.

> Egle, beauty and poet, has two little crimes,
> She makes her own face, and does *not* make her rhymes.

I am going to ride, having been warned *not* to ride in a particular part of the forest on account of the ultra-politicians.

Is there no chance of your return to England, and of *our* Journal? I would have published the two plays in it—two or three scenes per number—and indeed *all* of mine in it. If you went to England, I would do so still.

[TO JOHN MURRAY]   R[avenn]a *August 4th. 1821*

Dear Sir/—I return the proofs of the 2d. pamphlet. I leave it to your choice and Mr. Gifford's to publish it or not with such omission as he likes.[1]—You must however omit the whole of the observations against the *Suburban School*—they are meant against Keats and I cannot war with the dead—particularly those already killed by Criticism. Recollect to omit all that portion in *any case*.—Lately I have sent you several packets which require answer—you take a gentlemanly interval to answer them.—

yrs &c,
BYRON

P.S.—They write from Paris that Schlegel is making a fierce book against *me*—what can I have done to the literary Col-captain of late

---

[7] A series of articles on Byron's alleged plagiarisms appeared in the *Literary Gazette* (Feb. 24, March 3, 10, 17, 31, 1821). The author was A. A. Watts.

[8] Napoleon died May 5, 1821.

[1] The second letter on Bowles was not published until 1835.

Madame?—*I* who am neither of his country nor his horde?—Does this Hundsfot's intention appal you? if it does—say so.—It don't *me*—for if he is insolent—I will go to Paris and thank him;—there is a distinction between *native* Criticism—because it belongs to the Nation to judge and pronounce on natives,—but what have *I* to do with Germany or Germans neither my subjects nor my language having anything in common with that Country?—He took a dislike to me—because I refused to flatter him in Switzerland—though Madame de Broglie[2] begged me to do so—"because he is so fond of it.["]——"Voila les hommes!"—

[TO COUNT PIETRO GAMBA]   *A*[*gost*]*o* 4. *1821*

Mio Caro Pietro—Mille grazie per la vostra lettera gratissima.—Non posso rispondere tutto ciò che debbo e vorrei dire.—La sua Eccellenza sarà arrivata. [Several words blotted out] che. [word erased] —Mi ha scritto 1000 ingiurie da Bologna—perche io d'accordo con tutti i savj—e tutti i suoi amici e parenti—la consigliava di giungere a Firenze, per ritrovare voi e il suo Padre.—La cosa era assolutamente neccessaria—se ella non voleva essere messa in Convento.—Domandate di tutti.—Non vedo nessuno—le mie passeggiate vedove sono *ben' seccanti*;—ho colpito colla pistola—due *scarpe nuove* del' poveretto l'altro jeri—ciò che mi costò dodici *pauole*! Ho visto per la strada un' giorno la Tuda—che pareva una peccorella 'smarrita—un' poco losca —e molto sentimentale per causa di vostro abandono—mi confessò di essere varie volte da voi &c. &c. ma chi sa se questo è vero.—La sua bellezza non fu pero ⟨tante⟩ tale da dare del' invidia nè anche a quella più—gelosa delle donne—la sua Eccellenza.——La Martini è 'sparita dalla finestra solita—in conseguenza del' esilio del' amato bene—in vece di lei—ho veduto *Santino* Fabbri—*la*—ciò che mi veniva indicato di più sensi che quella della *vista*.—Intanto tutte le vostre numerose vedove sono inconsolabili——non si sente che dei sospiri—ciò che fa un' poco d'aria—cosa piac[evole] in questa stagione. ——Lega avrà scritta a Pappa—tutte le nuove—e le speranze—ed i passi—che pensiamo fare—io intanto sono e sarò sempre il vost[r]o affe. ed obl. amico

[Scrawl]]

² Madame de Staël's daughter

P.S.—1000 cose a Pappa—Vivete felici.—[Seven lines heavily crossed out. Only the beginning is legible: "Mi scrivono da Parigi che . . ."] Questo fu scritto prima del' arrivo del' vostro preg.mo—Io aspetto una risposta da Svizzera dove scrissi prima della partenza della Teresa—intanto stiamo a vedere un' poco—la precipitazione non può se' non pregiudicare alla vostra famiglia e a tutti quanti.—Lega ha ordine di scrivere più in dettaglio.——

[TRANSLATION] *August 4th. 1821*

My dear Pietro—A thousand thanks for your very welcome letter. —I cannot answer all that I should say, or would wish to,—Her Excellency ought to have arrived . . . . [line erased by Teresa]

She has written me a thousand insults from Bologna—because in agreement with every sensible person and with all her friends and relations, I advised her to go to Florence, to join you and her father.— The thing was absolutely necessary—if she did not want to be put in a convent.—Ask anyone.—

I am seeing no one—my widower's rides are very tedious; I put holes in *two new shoes* of that poor devil with my pistol the day before yesterday—which cost me *twelve pauls.* One day I saw Tuda on the road—who looked like a lost lamb—squinting a little—and very sentimental about your desertion—She confessed that she had been with you several times, etc. etc.—but who knows if it is true.—Her beauty was however not such as to awaken envy in even the most jealous of women, Her Excellency.

The Martini has disappeared from her usual window—in consequence of the exile of her beloved. Instead of her—I saw Mrs. Santino Fabbri there—of whom I was made aware by more senses than that of sight.—For the rest, all your numerous widows are inconsolable—one hears nothing but sighs—which makes a little breeze—a pleasant thing in this weather.

Lega will have written to Papa all my news and hopes and the steps we propose to take. Meanwhile I am and always shall be your affectionate and obliged friend.

P.S.—1000 messages to Papa. Be happy. [Here seven lines have been completely erased by Teresa, which began "They write me from Paris that' . . . . . .] This was written before the arrival of yours. I am awaiting an answer from Switzerland where I wrote before

Teresa's departure. Meanwhile let us wait a bit and see—Haste can but do harm to your family and to all of us. Lega has been told to write more in detail.—

Agosto 4, 1821

Teresa Mia/—Spero che tu ti trovi bene a Firenze—e salva coi tuoi parenti.—Lega nella lettera che scrive a Pappa per questo ordinario—spiegherà in dettaglio le ragioni le quali rendevano urgente la tua partenza da Bologna.——Basta dire—che Costa—Cavalli—e tutti quanti i tuoi amici erano persuasissimi che fosse il solo partito nelle tue delicatissime circonstanze.—Per me, io non ho niente di rimproverarmi in questi consigli—nè da rispondere alle ingiurie con quali ti ha piaciuta onorarmi nelle ultime tue lettere.——Ho ricevuto una lettera nobile e consolante da Pierino;—pare che egli mi conserva la sua amicizia—che sarà sempre reciproca dalla parte mia.——Qui facciamo tutto che possiamo per il ritorno del' Conte Ruggiero;—io ho spedito la lettera alla D[uchessa] di D[evonshire] che ora si trova a Spa presso Liege—ma che potrebbe scrivere di la a Roma.——Non ho risposta finora alle mie lettere di Ginevra;—aspetto le tue nuove con impazienza.——Per me—io non istò nè bene nè male;—la mia speranza naturalmente è voltata a voi altri.——non vedo nessuno—vivo coi miei libri e coi cavalli.—Senza tradurre tante pagine di "Corinna"—nè sforzare tanta apparanza del' romanesco—ti assicuro che ti amo come t'ho sempre amato, si vedrà col' tempo—chi sarà il più instancabile nel' amarci;—ma in eloquenza ti cedo per due ragioni—1 o—non conosco la lingua—2 o—troppe parole danno sempre da sospettare—ed i grandi *predicatori* del' sentimento esaggerato limitano la practica di loro massime alla Cattedra.—l'amor vero dice poco. Ti prego di salutare cordialmente Pappa e Pierino—e pregarli commandarmi in tutto—come loro (e il tuo) amico più sincero ed aff. mo

B

Ravenna, August 4th, 1821

My Teresa—I hope that you are happy in Florence—and safe with your relations. Lega, in the letter he is writing to Papa by this post, will explain in detail the reasons which rendered urgent your departure from Bologna.—It is enough to say that Costa, Cavalli, and all your friends were persuaded that it was the only decision possible in your very delicate situation. For my part, I have nothing to reproach myself with, as to this advice—nor to reply to the insults with which it has pleased you to honour me in your recent letters.

I have received a noble and comforting letter from Pierino; it appears that he is preserving his friendship for me, which will always be reciprocated by me.

Here we are doing all we can for the return of Count Ruggero. I have sent off the letter to the D[uchess] of D[evonshire] who is now at Spa near Liege—but who could write from there to Rome. I have had no answer as yet to my letters from Geneva. I am awaiting your news with impatience.

As for me—I am neither well nor ill; my hopes are naturally turned towards you all.—I don't see anyone—I live with my books and my horses.

Without translating so many pages of *Corinne*, or forcing so great a semblance of romance, I assure you that I love you as I always have loved you; time will show, which of us will be the most untiring in our love. But in eloquence I give way to you for two reasons—firstly, I don't know the language—secondly, too many words are always suspect—the great *preachers* of exaggerated sentiment limit the practice of their maxims to their pulpit;—true love says little.

Please salute Papa and Pierino cordially and beg them to command me in everything—as their (and your) most sincere and affectionate friend.

B

[TO COUNT PIETRO GAMBA]   *Ravenna 5 Agosto 1821*

[Postscript to letter of Lega Zambelli to Pietro Gamba]

Mio Caro Pietro—Sarebbe impossibile per me partire in questo momento—prima del' arrivo delle miei lettere—e d'un parente del Allegra—che aspetto momentaneamente da Pisa—per decidere sopra il destino della bambina. La vostra impazienza e [è] forse naturale—ma non me pare necessaria nelle circonstanze questa gran' fretta andare non si sa dove.—In 10 giorni debbo avere una risposta da Ginevra per le due case.—sempre e tutto

[Scrawl]

170

August 5th. 1821

It will be impossible for me to leave just now—before the arrival of my letters and of a relation of Allegra's—whom I am expecting at any moment from Pisa, to decide about the child's future. Your impatience is perhaps natural—but it doesn't seem to me necessary, under the circumstances, to be in so great a hurry to go one does not know where. In ten days I ought to have an answer from Geneva about the two houses. Always and entirely.

[TO PERCY BYSSHE SHELLEY] *[August 5? 1821]*[1]

D[ea]r S.—I wrote to you last week.

yrs. ever
B

[TO DOUGLAS KINNAIRD] *R[avenn]a August 7th. 1821*

My dear Douglas/—It is fit that you should be informed that up to the present writing—I have *not* received the half year's fee of mine stocks.—And it is also fitting that you should extract me from the said Stocks—which sit very heavily upon my slumbers of secure property.—And I have also written to say that Mr. Murray must publish the two plays immediately—and that we will *abate a part* if the sale is hurt by the season.—And I could wish that you would come to a decisive arrangement with that Gentleman—who has much the air of shuffling a good deal with me—Cannot he say at *once*—I *will*—or I *can not?*—I should not take offence but merely another publisher.—We must actually come to some sort of explanation with him—for I cannot go on in this way.——And pray say so—for I desire no mysteries—if I *do not write to him*—in these terms—it is because I choose to deal with him through *you* as my trustee and Attorneo—and for no other reason—and not from any underhand wish.—Nay—it is a *delicacy* to him to treat through a third person—because he can state *objections* to *you*—which regard for my feelings might prevent him from doing to myself. Believe me ever & truly yrs.

B

1 This note must have been written just before Shelley arrived at Ravenna for a visit to Byron. It is attached to a cover addressed to Shelley and post marked "8 Agosto" (the date of its arrival in Pisa). Shelley arrived at ten in the evening on August 6.

Dear Sir/—I send you a thing—which I scratched off lately—a mere buffoonery—to quiz "the Blues"[1] in two literary eclogues.—If published it must be *anonymously*—but it is too short for a separate publication—and *you* have no miscellany that I know of—for the reception of such things.—You may send me a proof if you think it worth the trouble—but don't let *my* name out—for the present—or I shall have all the old women in London about my ears—since it sneers at the solace of their antient Spinsterstry.—Acknowledge this—& the various packets lately sent—

              yrs. [Scrawl]

Dear Sir/—By last post I forwarded a packet of [to?] you[;] as usual you are avised by this post.—I should be loth to hurt Mr. Bowles's feelings by publicising the second pamphlet—and as he has shown considerable regard for mine—we had better suppress it altogether— at any rate I would not publish it without letting him see it first—and omitting all such matter as might be *personally* offensive to him.— Also all the part about the Suburb School must be omitted—as it referred to *poor Keats* now slain by the Quarterly Review.——If I do not err—I mentioned to you that I had heard from Paris—that Schlegel announces a meditated abuse of me in a criticism.—The disloyalty of such a proceeding towards a foreigner who has uniformly spoken so well of Me. de Stael in his writings—and who moreover has nothing to do with continental literature or Schlegel's country and countrymen—is such—that I feel a strong inclination to bring the matter to a *personal* arbitrament—provided it can be done—without being ridiculous or unfair.——His intention however must be first fully ascertained before I can proceed—and I have written for some information on the subject to Mr. Moore.—The Man was also my personal acquaintance—and though I refused to flatter him grossly (as Me. de B[roglie] requested me to do) yet I uniformly treated him with respect—with much more indeed than any one else—for his peculiarities are such that they one and all laughed at him—and especially the Abbe Chevalier di Breme—who did nothing but make

---

[1] *The Blues, A Literary Eclogue* was published in *The Liberal* No. III, pp. 1–24, in 1823.

me laugh at him so much behind his back—that nothing but the politeness on which I pride myself in society—could have prevented me from doing so to his face.——He is just such a character as William the testy in Irving's New York.[1]——But I must have him out for all that—since his proceeding (supposing it to be true) is ungentlemanly in all it's bearings—at least in my opinion—but perhaps my partiality misleads me.—It appears to me that there is a distinction between *native* and *foreign* criticism in the case of living writers—or at least should be,—I don't speak of *Journalists* (who are the same all over the world) but where a man with his name at length sits down to an elaborate attempt to defame a foreigner of his acquaintance—without provocation—& without legitimate object—for what can I import to the Germans?—What effect can I have upon their literature?—Do you think me in the wrong?—if so—say so.

yours
[Scrawl]

P.S.—I mentioned in my former letters—that it was my intention to have the two plays published *immediately*.—Acknowledge the various packets.—I am extremely angry with *you*—I beg leave to add for several reasons too long for present explanation. I have just been turning over the homicide review of *J. Keats*.—It is harsh certainly and contemptuous but not more so than what I recollect of the Edinburgh R[eview] of "the Hours of Idleness" in 1808. The Reviewer allows him "a degree of talent which deserves to be put in the right way" "rays of fancy" "gleams of Genius" and "powers of language". —It is harder on L. Hunt than upon *Keats* & professes fairly to review only *one* book of his poem.—Altogether—though very provoking it was hardly so bitter as to kill—unless there was a morbid feeling previously in his system.——

[TO COUNT PIETRO GAMBA]   *R[avenn]a. A[gost]o 9 o 1821*

Mio Caro Pietro/—I vostri sentimenti vi fanno onore, ma nonostante io ritengo la mia opinione sul' riguardo del Conte R[uggero] il vostro padre—e la Teresa.—Mi basta però di avere esposto le mie ragioni—se siate decisi partire—partite—io verrò.—M'avrebbe più

[1] The chronicles of William the Testy (Wilhelmus Pieft) appeared in Irving's *A History of New York, by Diedrich Knickerbocker.*

173

piaciuto—sarebbe stato anche assai meglio per tutti quanti se avreste avuto la pazienza aspettare la risposta da Ginevra.—Allora avreste saputo dove andare precisamente—in una casa—in vece di trovarvi in una miserabile locanda piena di viaggi[a]tori.—Per mi stesso—l'idea di ritornare in Svizzera è disgustossima—per tante ragioni—delle quali sarete ben accorto quando siamo la—e sarà troppo tardi.— Teresa dovrebbe senza altro—accompagnare il suo padre e fratello— ma nonostante quella protezione—io credo che ella si troverà in una situazione assai penosa—per le dicerie dei buoni Ginevrini—ed i viaggiatori Inglesi—per tutti i due dei quali basta per delle persone essere della *mia conoscenza* per essere esposte alla più infame calonnia. —Io sperai—e anche sono persuaso—che con un poco di tempo e coraggio—il vostro padre potrebbe tornare a R[avenn]a e la Teresa anche senza disturbi per uno o l'altra.—La Teresa scrive a me delle vere pazzie—come se io volessi abandonare &c. &c.—se ebbi quell' intenzione—perche la pregava di partire da R[avenn]a—da B[ologn]a? in pochi giorni—ella sarebbe rinchiusa in un' ritiro e l'affare finito— senza che io ebbi la minima colpa—nei occhi del' mondo.—Sicura-mente non mi sarei dato tante premure per una donna con cui meditava una separazione.

Finora non è venuta risposta—non sono venuti i miei cambiali— i quali per certo non sarebbe bene lasciare girando il paese dopo la mia partenza—sono tre ordinarie che dovrebbe essere arrivati—e la tardanza mi sorprende e disgusta.—Non sono necessarie per me adesso—perche n'ho abbastanza—ma intanto non piace troppo di non sapere niente di una somma di qualche migliaia di Scudi—la quale nel' corso ordinario dei affari—dovrebbe essere già arrivata—20 giorni fa.—Mi preme di più perche la Svizzera è forse il paese più caro in Europe pei stranieri----il popolo essendo il più furbo e birbante sulla terra—in tutto ciò che risguarda il denaro—e l'inganno—e l'avarizia.——Io non suggeriva un' soggiorno in quel paese se non colla idea di un' assoluta necessità di lasciare l'Italia—e solamente perche v è il paese più vicino.—Questa *necessità* di partenza non esiste più—il governo della Toscana—è assai mite—assai—assai più del' governo attuale di Ginevra—che adesso è sotto il giogo dei anti-liberali.——Un' mio amico qui scrive alla mia richiesta a Teresa— delle ragioni forti pei quali sarebbe meglio di rimanere in Italia.— Credetemi con' pienissimo stima ed' amicizia sempre il vostro

a e S.
[Scrawl]

My Dear Pietro—Your sentiments do you honour, but nevertheless I keep my own opinion regarding Count R.—your father—and Teresa. It is enough for me, however, to have expressed my reasons. If you are determined to go—go—and I will come,—I should have been much better pleased, and it would have been much better for everyone, if you had had the patience to wait for an answer from Geneva. Then you would have known precisely where to go—to a house—instead of finding yourself in a miserable inn full of travellers. As for myself—the idea of returning to Switzerland is most unpleasant—for many reasons—which you will become well aware of when we are there and it will be too late.—Teresa should certainly go with her father and her brother—but in spite of that protection—I am afraid that she will find herself in a very painful situation—on account of the gossip of all the good citizens of Geneva—and of the English travellers—for both of whom it is enough that people should enjoy *my acquaintance* for them to be exposed to the most infamous calumny. I hoped—and am still convinced—that with a little time and courage—your father will be able to return to R[avenna] and Teresa too, without trouble for either of them.

Teresa writes to me like a lunatic—as if I wished to give her up, etc. etc. If I had had that intention—why did I beg her to leave R[avenna] and B[ologna]? In a few days—she would have been shut up in a convent—and the affair finished—without its being in the least my fault—in the eyes of the world. Assuredly I would not have taken so much trouble for a woman from whom I was planning a separation.

So far no answer has come—and my banker's drafts have not arrived, which certainly it would not be desirable to leave trailing around the country after my departure. They ought to have come three posts ago, and the delay surprises and annoys me. For me they are not necessary at present—for I have enough. But meanwhile I don't much like not knowing what has happened to a sum of several thousand scudi— which in the ordinary course of events should have arrived twenty days ago. It matters the more to me because Switzerland is perhaps the dearest county in Europe for foreigners, its people being the most canny and rascally in the world about all that has to do with money— and deceitfulness—and avarice. I only suggested a stay in that country because there seemed to be an absolute necessity for leaving Italy— and only because it is the nearest country. This *necessity* to leave no longer exists. The government of Tuscany is very mild—far, far

milder than the present government of Geneva—which is now under
the yoke of the anti-liberals.

A friend of mine here is writing, at my request, to Teresa—some
forcible reasons why it would be better to stay in Italy.[1]

Believe me with the most complete esteem and friendship always
your friend and servant

[TO DOUGLAS KINNAIRD]   R[avenn]a. A[gost]o 10th. 1821

My dear Douglas/—To my great surprize and not to my pleasure—
the half-year's fee is not arrived.—Oons! what do you mean?—and
why do you not get out of the Stocks? which are falling again?——
Murray has behaved very handsomely to Moore about the memoirs—[1]
or memoranda—as you may know by this time.——I wrote to you
lately—pray let me have my *fee*—and let me know what you think
to ax Murray for the M.S.S. His good conduct to Moore has almost
reconciled [me] to him again.——My respects to Hobhouse and all
friends

yrs. in haste and very truly
[Scrawl]

[TO JOHN MURRAY]   Ravenna. August 10th. 1821

Your conduct to Mr. Moore is certainly very handsome; and I
would not say so if I could help it, for you are not at present by any
means in my good graces.

With regard to additions, &c., there is a Journal which I kept in
1814 which you may ask him for; also a Journal, which you must get
from Mrs. Leigh, of my journey in the Alps, which contains all the
germs of Manfred. I have also kept a small Diary here for a few
months last winter, which I would send you, and any continuation.
You would easy find access to all my papers and letters, and do *not*
neglect this (in case of accidents) on account of the mass of confusion

---

[1] Shelley had arrived at Ravenna on August 6. Byron asked him to write to
Teresa to convince her that Switzerland was not a desirable residence for exiles.
Shelley's letter and his subsequent visit to her in Florence were successful in getting
the Gambas to settle in Pisa instead.

[1] Moore wrote in his diary for July 27, 1821: "Received also a letter from
Murray, consenting to give me two thousand guineas for Lord Byron's *Memoirs*,
on condition that, in case of survivorship, I should consent to be the editor."
(Moore, *Memoirs*, Vol. III, p. 260).

in which they are; for out of that chaos of papers you will find some curious ones of mine and others, if not lost or destroyed. If circumstances, however (which is almost impossible), made me ever consent to a publication in my lifetime, you would in that case, I suppose, make Moore some advance, in proportion to the likelihood or non-likelihood of success. You are both sure to survive me, however.

You must also have from Mr. Moore the correspondence between me and Lady B., to whom I offered the sight of all which regards herself in these papers. This is important. He has *her* letter, and a copy of my answer. I would rather Moore edited me than another.

I sent you Valpy's letter to decide for yourself, and Stockdale's[1] to amuse you. *I* am always loyal with you, as I was in Galignani's affair, and *you* with me—now and then.

I return you Moore's letter, which is very creditable to him, and you, and me.

Yours ever,
B

[TO COUNTESS TERESA GUICCIOLI] *R[avenn]a A[gost]o 10 o 1821*

Amor Mio/—Ti prego di non rendere la nostra infelicità più grande colle rimprovere non meritate.—Io sono sempre stato fidele e leale a te e a tutta la tua famiglia.—La Lettera del' mio amico scritta alla mia richiesta—sarà un esposizione veracissima—delle tantissime ragioni per non esporci ad una residenza nei stati della Svizzera.—Non ho mai pensato di dividermi da te—ma lasciami un' poco di tempo e di libertà di pensare per noi—e sopra tutto per te.—La mia lettera a Pierino contiene ciò che ho da dire sopra quei argomenti.—Non dico altro.—Amami come ti amo.

tutto tuo——

[TRANSLATION] *Ravenna. August 10th. 1821*

My Love—Pray do not render our unhappiness greater by unmerited reproaches. I have always been faithful and loyal to you and to all your family. My friend's letter, written at my request, will be a very veracious statement of the numerous reasons for not exposing

[1] Abraham John Valpy and John Joseph Stockdale had apparently made some publishing proposals to Byron.

177

ourselves to residing in the states of Switzerland. I have never thought of separating myself from you—but leave me a little time and freedom to think [what is best] for us—and above all for you. My letter to Pierino contains what I have to say on this subject. I will not say any more.——

Love me as I love you. Entirely yours.——

[TO JOHN MURRAY]   *R[avenn]a August 13th. 1821*

Dear Sir/—I think it as well to remind you that in "the *Hints*"—all the part which regards Jeffrey & the E[dinburgh] R[eview] must be *omitted*.—Your late mistake about the Kelso-woman induces me to remind you of this—which I appended to your power of Attorney six years ago—viz.—to *omit* all that could touch upon Jeffrey in that publication—which was written a year before our reconciliation in 1812.——Have you got the Bust?—I expect with anxiety the proofs of the two Foscaris

yrs. [Scrawl]

P.S.—Acknowledge the various packets.

[TO COUNTESS TERESA GUICCIOLI]   *R[avenn]a A[gost]o 13 o 1821*

Carissima—Le lettere da Ginevra non sono favorevoli a nostra partenza.—Lo Stato è pieno di Inglesi—e ogni casa occupata—e così sarà per più di cinquanta giorni ancora, fin al' 8bre.—Dappiù—Ginevra e tutti i contorni suoi sono pieni di Inglesi anche per tutto l'inverno.—Tu conosci se io poteva vivere nella stessa atmosfera con quella razza.——Ti prego dunque abandonare quell' idea—e persuadere R[uggero] e P[ierino] di fare altro tanto.—Si può stabilirsi in Toscana ed assai meglio per ogni rapporto.——La lettera di mio amico—per l'ultimo espresso—ti avrà spiegata la mia situazione in quel paese di Svizzera—nel anno 1816.—— Se vuoi rinovare quelle persecuzioni che sarebbero dirette con' eguale furia contro di te—non hai che andare in Svizzera.——Io conservo ancora la speranza che con' un poco di tempo e pazienza il tuo padre potrebbe essere richiamato in sua patria—ed allora tu puoi accompagnarlo.—Se Pierino è deciso di viaggiare—non mi oppongo—per certo egli sarebbe assai più contento viagg[i]ando senza tanti impegni e senza fare la cattiva figura che farebbe—se *noi* due eravamo della sua compagnia.——In ogni modo—Se papa non può tornare—possiamo stabilirsi in Toscana. ——In questo punto ricevo la tua lettera per mezzo di uno dei *richiemati*—Già avrete la mia risposta—il tuo padre cerca un paese *libero*—dove lo troverà—per certo non in Svizzera—dove esigliano di nuovo i già *esigliati*! Il mio primo desiderio sarebbe che egli tornara a Ravenna—il secondo (ma anche quello assai mal volontieri) che si stabiliva in Toscana—la Svizzera non mi pare niente adattata—ed io pensai solamente di quel paese come preferibile a *San Leo*—adesso che non v'è più pericolo di quello per lui—l'andare in Svizzera sarebbe —ma—ho già esposto tutto nelle lettere passate.—Sempre e tutto tuo

[Scrawl]

P.S.—M'è venuta una lettera della Benzona chi ti saluta—anche il suo Beppe;—saluta Pierino e Papa della parte mia.——

[TRANSLATION]   *Ravenna. August 13th. 1821*

Dearest—The letters from Geneva are not favourable to our departure. The State is full of English people—and every house is occupied—and so it will be for over fifty days more—until October.

Besides, Geneva and all its surroundings are full of English people, even in the winter. You know whether I could live in the same air as that race——Pray therefore abandon that plan—and persuade Ruggero and Pietro to do the same. We can establish ourselves in Tuscany; it will be much better from every point of view.——

My friend's letter by the last messenger will have explained to you my situation in that country, Switzerland, in 1816. If you wish to renew my persecution, which would now be directed with equal fury against you, you have only to go to Switzerland. I still hope that with a little time and patience your father may be allowed to return to his own country—and that you will be able to go with him. If Pierino is determined to travel—I do not oppose it. Certainly he would be much better off in his travels without so many ties—and without cutting the sorry figure that he would cut, if we were in his company.——At any rate—if Papa is not allowed to return, we can establish ourselves in Tuscany.

At this point your letter has come, by the hand of one of the returned exiles. By now you will have had my answer. Your father is looking for a *free* country—where will he find it? Certainly not in Switzerland—where they exile once more those who have already been exiled.

My first choice would be for him to return to Ravenna. The second (but even that unwillingly), that he should establish himself in Tuscany—Switzerland does not seem to be at all suitable and I only thought of that country as preferable to San Leo.[1] Now that there is no more danger for him—to go to Switzerland would be—but—I have already expressed all this in my preceding letters. Always and ever yours

P.S.—I had a letter from the Benzoni, who greets you—so does her Beppe.[2] Greet Pierino and Papa for me.

[TO COUNT GIUSEPPE ALBORGHETTI]   *August 15th. 1821*

Dear Sir/—An English Gentleman & friend of mine[1] has this day been refused admittance into the Duomo by the *Campanaro* in the most insolent manner.—As I have not the honour of personal acquaintance with the Archbishop I should thank you to represent this to him—whatever his feelings may be towards me—I presume that he does not encourage his people's insults to strangers.—especially as I never encourage or protect mine in such things. The readiness of your authorities to inculpate my servants on all occasions will not permit me to pass over this.—If the Archbishop chastises his insolent dependent, it is well—if *not*—I will find means—to punish him at any cost.——Excuse my troubling *you*—but as I do not know the Prelate personally—& *you* do—I thought my application would come better thus—than by a direct address.—If he or others suppose that political circumstances have at all diminished my power to make myself properly respected—they will discover the difference.—Believe me very truly yours—dear Sir—

[Scrawl]

[TO DOUGLAS KINNAIRD]   *R[avenn]a August 16th. 1821*

My dear Douglas/—The fee is arrived.—There *"will* be a Turkish war"—and yet you tell me not to be disturbed "about the funds"?—

---

[1] A fortress near Rimini used for political prisoners.
[2] Count Giuseppe Rangone, Cavalier Servente of the Countess Benzoni.
[1] Shelley.

It may be a very good jest to you "a prosperous Gentleman"[1] but for one who thinks as I do—and is situated as I am—it is not so agreeable a landscape.——I shall certainly (as I have always told you) never be easy (but who is?) in my mind till we are out of the Stocks.——You do not say that you have seen the "two Foscaris"—I am afraid that you will not like them.—With regard to Murray I leave you to deal with him—I am glad that you approve of what I said.—You tell me no news—when & where the Rochdale is to be tried or if it has been—& how that old Serpent the She Noel does in her health & years.—But never mind.——You talk of Kean? is he arrived? Whether he is or not —can matter little—the Doge never was nor could be a Stage play.— It is contrary to my *plan*—which is quite different.—I trust that they won't meddle with the new tragedies—that would be carrying things too far.—

Yours ever & truly

B

[TO JOHN MURRAY]   *R[avenn]a August 16th. 1821*

Dear Sir/—I regret that Holmes can't or won't come—it is rather shabby—as I was always very civil & punctual with him—but he is but one rascal more—one meets with none else, amongst the English. —You may do what you will with my answer to Stockdale[1]—of whom I know nothing—but answered his letter civilly—you may open it—& burn it or not—as you please.—It contains nothing of consequence to any-body.—How should I—or at least *was* I then to know that he was a rogue?—I am not aware of the histories of London and it's inhabitants.—Your more recent parcels are not yet arrived—but are probably on their way—I sprained my knee the other day in swimming —and it hurts me still considerably.——I wait the proofs of the M.S.S. with proper impatience.——So you have published—or mean to publish the new Juans? an't you afraid of the Constitutional Association of Bridge street?[2]—when first I saw the name of *Murray,*—I

---

[1] *Macbeth*, Act I, scene 3.

[1] John Joseph Stockdale (1770–1847) had published some of Shelley's early poems.

[2] The Constitutional Association was a kind of vigilante group formed to prosecute offences against the church and state. It particularly looked out for "seditious" and "blasphemous" publications and harassed booksellers and publishers. John Hunt was later prosecuted and convicted for publishing Byron's *Vision of Judgment*. Charles Murray was one of the active attorneys for the Association.

—— thought it had been yours—but was solaced by seeing that Synonime is an Attorneo—and that you are not one of that atrocious crew.——

I am in great discomfort about the probable war—and with my damned trustees not getting me out of the funds.—If the funds break—it is my intention to go upon the highway—all the other English professions are at present so ungentlemanly by the conduct of those who follow them—that open robbery is the only fair resource left to any man of principles;—it is even honest in comparison—by being undisguised.——I wrote to you by last post to say that you had done the handsome thing by Moore and the Memoranda. You are very good as times go—and would probably be still better but for "the March of events" (as Napoleon called it) which won't permit anybody to be better than they should be.—Love to Gifford—Believe me

yrs ever & [Scrawl]

P.S.—I restore Smith's[3] letter—*whom* thank for his good opinion.

A[mor] M[io]—Le mie lettere sono arrivate. Dunque v'è poco trattenermi qui.—La mia intenzione è di prendere una casa in Pisa dove sarà dei quartieri per la famiglia tua—e la mia—separati—ma vicini.—Se ciò non ti piace—dimmi—e si prenderà una casa separata per tutti i dui.——Questa lettera sarà portata dal' Inglese che adesso sta qui—il quale partirà domane.—Egli spiegerà a tutti quanti—molte cose difficili e lunghe nel' scrivere—che non è il mio talente nelle lingue *non* barbare.——Quando tutto è deciso—spediro una parte della servitù coi effetti più pesanti, *mobili* &c. necessarj per la casa.—Poi verrò coi altri.—Saluta Papa e Pietro—

sono sempre
[Scrawl]

P.S. Se avete preso un' quartiere in Prato—e si trova la casa per me, è l'istesso;—ma Pisa sarebbe il miglior' soggiorno—secondo a ciò che mi dicono.—Io lascio Ravenna così mal-volontieri—e così persuaso che la mia partenza non può che condurre da un' male a un' altro più grande,—che non ho cuore di scriver' altro in questo punto.—

[3] James Smith, brother of Horace, and joint author of the *Rejected Addresses*.

Ravenna August [16th] 1821

My Love—My letters have arrived, so there is little to keep me here. My intention is to take a house in Pisa where there will be apartments for your family—and for me—separate, but near. If that does not please you—tell me—and we will take a separate house for each of us. This letter will be taken to you by the Englishman who is here now, and is leaving tomorrow.[1] He will explain to everyone many things difficult and lengthy to set down in writing, which is not my talent in a language *not* barbarous. When all is decided, I will send a part of the household with the heavier effects, furniture, etc., needed for the house—then I will come with the others.—

Greet Papa and Pietro—I am always

P.S.—If you have found an apartment in Prato—and can find a house for me, it will do as well—but Pisa would be a more agreeable place to stay in—according to what I am told. I am leaving Ravenna so unwillingly—and so persuaded that my departure can only lead from one evil to a greater one—that I have no heart to write any more just now.—

[TO COUNT PIETRO GAMBA] *Ravenna 17 Agosto 1821*

[Added to a letter of Lega Zambelli to Pietro Gamba]

Caro Pietro—Ecco il risultato dei pensieri più ragionevoli che io posso formare nelle circonstanze attuali.—Io partirò pero molto mal'volontieri da Ravenna—persuaso—che la mia partenza non può fare altro che male alla Teresa in ogni maniera.—L'imbarazzo—(come sempre accade dove entra il bel' sesso)—è sommo—per lei e per noi—per quella ragione.—Sarebbe stato 1000 volte più rispettabili e prudente—se Ella e il Conte Ruggiero potrebbero tornare qui.—Ma la volontà di dio—o del' diavolo—e della santissima Lucrezia di Imola —e dei santissimi Nonni sia fatta!—Maledetti siano tutti i Nonni—e Lucrezia di Imola e d'altra che mai furono nel' Mondo!—Mille cose a Papa.——

[TRANSLATION] *August 17th. 1821*

Dear Pietro—Here is the result of the most reasonable ideas that I can form under the present circumstances. I shall, however, leave

[1] Shelley.

Ravenna most unwillingly—being convinced that my departure can do nothing but injure Teresa in every way.

The embarrassment (as always happens where the fair sex is concerned) is very great for her and for us—for that reason it would have been a thousand times more respectable and prudent—if she and Count Ruggero could have returned here. But the will of God—or of the devil—or of the most sainted Lucrezia of Imola[1]—and the most sainted grandparents—be done! A curse on all grandparents—on Lucrezia of Imola and of any where else in the world!

A thousand greetings to Papa.——

[TO COUNTESS TERESA GUICCIOLI]   A[gost]o 20 o 1821

Mia Cara T.—Io ho scritto per ogni ordinario.—Non abbiamo spedito dei altri espressi—per non esporre quei poveri diavoli—alla infame oppressione che l'ultimo incontrava per la sua strada.——Il Signor S[helley] dovrebbe essere già a Firenze—e avrà spiegato le mei intenzioni.——Se le lettere non sono capitate—biasimate la posta e non noi altri.—Lega scriverà a Papa e Pierino per affari.——Salutate tutti i dui e credetemi sempre

[Scrawl]

P.S.—Qui non sono nuove—senoche quel' buffo di Cocardino ha rimandato i due richiamati.—La colpa di Ranuzzi fu di essere *rivale* di un frate—questo si sa—il *"bel* paese"!!——

[TRANSLATION]   *August 20. 1821*

My dear T.—I have written by every post. We have not sent any other couriers, so as not to expose those poor devils to the infamous oppression which the last one met with on the road. Mr. S[helley] must have arrived in Florence already, and will have explained my intentions. If the letters have not arrived—blame the post and not us. Lega will write to Papa and Pierino on business. Greet both of them and believe me always.

[Scrawl]

---

[1] Count Ruggero Gamba's sister, married to Count Ginnasi of Imola. Byron felt that the Gamba relations disapproved of his liaison with Teresa.

P.S.—Here there is no news—except that that buffoon Cocardino[1] has sent back the two men recalled. The fault of Ranuzzi was that he was a *rival* of a monk. That is known—the *"beautiful* country"!!

My dear Douglas/—I have received the enclosed proposal from Mr. Murray which I can *not* accept.——He offers me for *all*—the sum he once offered for ⟨separate⟩ two cantos of D[on] Juan.—I will accept nothing of the kind—unless he advances very considerably, [or] —unless the things have completely failed.—This *you* can inform yourself of—and act accordingly.—With regard to what his friend says of *"Simplicity"*—I study to be so.—It is an experiment whether the English *Closet*—or *mental* theatre will or will not bear a *regular* drama instead of the melo-drama.——Murray's offer falls short by *one half* of the fair proposal—all things considered.——However I leave you a free discretion & will satisfy any agreement of *yours*— confident that it will be honest & loyal to both parties.

yrs. ever & truly
[Scrawl]

P.S.—Inclosed is a letter from Miss Boyce[1]—she was a transient piece of mine—but I owe her little on that score—having been myself at the short period I knew her in such a state of mind and body—that all carnal connection was quite mechanical & almost as senseless to my senses as to my feelings of imagination.——Advance the poor creature some money on my account & deduct it from your books quoad banker for me.——Allow me to remind you that up to 1819—*all* the *offers* came from our part—& *not* from Murray's—*he* offered for the third Canto of C[hilde] H[arold]—*twelve hundred* & then came up to two thousand.— For the 4th. he gave at once two thousand five hundred—& both yourself & H[obhous]e & yr. brother thought that I might have obtained more. ——If *we* are *down* in the scribbling world—say so *at once*—and I will withdraw from the Arena without a word further.—Excuse my ignorance—which comes from my foreign residence. As I am about it—take one more quotation from yr. *own* letters. "I think that Murray ought to offer you *more* than any *other* bookseller—now it is my belief

---

[1] A nickname for the Cardinal.
[1] Byron had a brief affair with Susan Boyce, a minor actress at Drury Lane, while he was connected with the sub-committee of management in 1815. See Marchand, Vol. II, pp. 548–550.

that he bids you *less.*—You may be *sure* that I have *good authority* for *what I say*"—&c. &c. &c.——Now my dear Dougal there are your own words—& after them *what can "I say?"* when not *three months* after you wrote to me something very like the reverse of yr. former expressions so recently transmitted?—

[TO JOHN MURRAY]   R[avenn]a *August 23d. 1821*

Dear Sir/—Enclosed are the two notes corrected.—With regard to the charges about the "Shipwreck"[1]—I think that I told both you and Mr. Hobhouse years ago—that [there] was not a *single circumstance* of it—*not* taken from *fact*—not indeed from any *single* shipwreck —but all from *actual* facts of different wrecks.—Almost all Don Juan is *real* life—either my own—or from people I knew.——By the way much of the description of the *furniture* in Canto 3d. is taken from *Tully's Tripoli*[2]—(pray *note this*)—and the rest from my own observation.——Remember I never meant to conceal this at all—& have only not stated it because D[on] Juan had no preface nor name to it.— If you think it worth while to make this statement—do so—in your own way.—*I* laugh at such charges—convinced that no writer ever borrowed less—or made his materials more his own.——Much is Coincidence[;] for instance—Lady Morgan (in a really *excellent* book I assure you on Italy) calls Venice an *Ocean Rome*[3]—I have the very same expression in *Foscari*[4]—& yet *you* know that the play was written months ago & was sent to England.—The "Italy" I received only on the 16th. Inst.——Your friend—like the public is not aware that my dramatic Simplicity is *studiously* Greek—& must continue so—*no* reform ever succeeded at first.——I admire the old English dramatists —but this is quite another field—& has nothing to do with theirs.—I

[1] Byron's indebtedness for his shipwreck scenes in the second canto of *Don Juan* to Sir J. G. Dalyell's *Shipwrecks and Disasters at Sea* (1812) was pointed out by the *Monthly Review.* (Vol. III, Aug. 1821, pp. 19–22).

[2] Richard Tully's *Narrative of a Ten Years' Residence at the Court of Tripoli* was the source of some of Byron's description of the furnishings of the Pirate Lambro's palace in *Don Juan*, Canto III, stanzas 67–69.

[3] Lady Morgan called Venice "the Rome of the ocean" in her *Italy* (Galignani edition, 1821, Vol. III, pp. 263–264.)

[4]   "Their antique energy of mind, all that
                       Remained of Rome for their inheritance
                       Created by degrees an ocean-Rome."
                                   The Two Foscari, Act. III, scene 1.

want to make a *regular* English drama—no matter whether for the Stage or not—which is not my object—but a *mental theatre*————

yrs. [Scrawl]

P.S.—*Can't* accept your courteous offer.[5]————

For Orford and for Waldegrave
You give much more than me you *gave*
Which is not fairly to behave
My Murray!

Because if a live dog, 'tis said,
Be worth a Lion fairly sped,
A *live lord* must be worth *two* dead,
My Murray!

And if, as the opinion goes,
Verse hath a better sale than prose—
Certes, I should have more than those
My Murray!

But now—this sheet is nearly crammed,
So—if *you will*—*I* shan't be shammed,
And if you *wont*—*you* may be damned,
My Murray!

These matters must be arranged with Mr. Douglas K[innaird].—He is my trustee—and a man of honour.—To him you can state all your mercantile reasons which you might not like to state to me personally —such as "heavy season" ["]flat public" "don't go off"—["]Lordship writes too much—Won't take advice—declining popularity—deductions for the trade—make very little—generally lose by him—pirated edition—foreign edition—severe criticisms. &c.["] with other hints and howls for an oration—which I leave Douglas who is an orator to answer.———You can also state them more freely—to a third person—as between you and me they could only produce some smart postscripts which would not adorn our mutual archives.———I am sorry for the Queen[6]—and that's more than you are.———Is the bust arrived?

[TO COUNTESS TERESA GUICCIOLI]   *A*[gost]*o 24 o 1821*

Mia Teresa/—Lega avrà informato Pierino e Papa dei nostri preparativi per partire per Pisa.—Io non posso aggiungere altro.

---

[5] Murray had offered 2000 guineas for three cantos of *Don Juan, Sardanapalus,* and *The Two Foscari.*

[6] Queen Caroline, wife of George IV, died August 7, 1821.

Quando tutto è accommodati a Pisa—ed i mobili sono arrivati &c. &c. allora partiremo.——Tu sai che le miei lettere non sono lunghe quasi mai—e non aspetterai molto da questa—sapendo che io ho tante cose da pensare.—Io non niego che parto—molto mal volontieri—prevedendo dei mali assai grandi per voi altri—e *massima per te.*— Altro non dico—lo vedrai.——

Sono [Scrawl]

P.S.—Saluta P. e Papa.

[TRANSLATION]   *August 24th. 1821*

My Teresa—Lega will have told Pierino and Papa about the preparations for our journey to Pisa. I have nothing more to add. When everything is arranged in Pisa and the furniture has arrived, etc., then we shall start.

You know that my letters are hardly ever long—and will not expect very much from this one—knowing that I have a great deal to think about. I do not deny that I am leaving very unwillingly—foreseeing very serious evils for you all—and especially *for you.* I will not say more—you will see.

I am

P.S.—Greet Pietro and Papa.

[TO THOMAS MOORE]   *Ravenna, August 24th, 1821*

Yours of the 5th only yesterday, while I had letters of the 8th from London. Doth the post dabble into our letters? Whatever agreement you make with Murray, if satisfactory to *you,* must be so to me. There need be no scruple, because, though I used sometimes to buffoon to myself, loving a quibble as well as the barbarian himself (Shakespeare, to wit)—"that, like a Spartan, I would sell my *life* as *dearly* as possible"[1]—it never was my intention to turn it to personal, pecuniary account, but to bequeath it to a friend—yourself—in the event of survivorship. I anticipated that period, because we happened to meet, and I urged you to make what was possible *now* by it, for reasons which are obvious. It has been no possible *privation* to me, and therefore does not require the acknowledgments you mention. So, for God's sake, don't consider it like * * * * * * * * *

---

[1] Unidentified.

By the way, when you write to Lady Morgan, will you thank her for her handsome speeches in her book about *my* books? I do not know her address. Her work is fearless and excellent on the subject of Italy—pray tell her so—and I know the country. I wish she had fallen in with *me*, I could have told her a thing or two that would have confirmed her positions.

I am glad that you are satisfied with Murray, who seems to value dead lords more than live ones. I have just sent him the following answer to a proposition of his:—

> For Orford and for Waldegrave, &c.

The argument of the above is, that he wanted to "stint me of my sizings,"[2] as Lear says—that is to say, *not* to propose an extravagant price for an extravagant poem, as is becoming. Pray take his guineas, by all means—*I* taught him that. He made me a filthy offer of *pounds* once, but I told him that, like physicians, poets must be dealt with in guineas, as being the only advantage poets could have in the association with *them*, as votaries of Apollo. I write to you in hurry and bustle, which I will expound in my next.

Yours ever, &c.

P.S.—You mention something of an attorney on the way to me on legal business. I have had no warning of such an apparition. What can the fellow want? I have some lawsuits and business, but have not heard of any thing to put me to the expense of a *travelling* lawyer. They do enough, in that way, at home.

Ah, poor Queen! but perhaps it is for the best, if Herodotus's anecdote is to be believed [3] * * * * * * * * * * * *

Remember me to any friendly Angles of our mutual acquaintance. What are you doing? Here I have had my hands full with tyrants and their victims. There never *was* such oppression, even in Ireland, scarcely!

[TO PERCY BYSSHE SHELLEY] *R[avenn]a A[gust]o 26th. 1821*

My dear Shelley/—Conclude for the house then forthwith.[1]—I wish that there were two more *stalls*—for I have *eight* horses.—We are in

[2] *King Lear*, Act II, scene 4: "to scant my sizes".
[3] Herodotus, I, 31. The goddess Hera taught her priestess Cydippe that death was a higher boon than life.
[1] The Casa Lanfranchi in Pisa.

all the agonies of packing.——If my furniture be not sufficient pray engage for some more—and if any money is necessary—draw on me at sight;—you had better *clinch* the Padrone of the palazzo—lest he rise in his price or play some trick with some others of the hectic English.——Do the essential and I will approve & sanction yr. proceedings.

yrs. ever
BYRON

P.S.—I mean to send off all furniture before setting out.——My respects to Mrs. S[helley] &c. &c. &c. Let me know the road without passing through Florence.——

[TO COUNTESS TERESA GUICCIOLI]   *R[avenn]a A[gost]o 26 o 1821*

Teresa Mio—Stiamo preparando—Si v è della lentezza sarà di quel' benedetto Lega—il quale abandono alle tue rimprovere. Ti prego di stare in buon' umore—verrò il momento che posso.—Sperando rivederti egualmente [word erased]. e meno pic . . . Sono sempre il tuo a—a in e

[Scrawl]

P.S.—1000 Saluti alle altre due Eccelenze maschie—ciò è a papa e Pierino.——Scrivo a Sh[elley] per firmare la casa.—

[TRANSLATION]   *Ravenna August 26th. 1821*

My Teresa—We are getting ready—If there is any delay it will be that blessed Lega's—whom I abandon to your reproaches. Pray be in good humour. I will come to you the moment I can. Hoping to see you equally [word erased] and less p. . . .[1] I am always your friend and lover for ever.

P.S.—A thousand greetings to the two male Excellencies—that is Papa and Pierino. I am writing to Shelley, to settle on the house.

---

[1] Byron had written "Pettegola"—gossip, but Teresa erased the word and wrote "pic. . ." the first letters of piccinina—"little one'" which has the connotations of small and pretty.

Dear Douglas/—By last post I apprized you of Murray's offer (two thousand g[uinea]s) for the two plays—& the Juans—the which I have declined referring him to you for further—or any treaty.——I declined it in the following lyrics.—

> For Orford and for Waldegrave
> You give more than to me you gave
> Which is not fairly to behave—
> > My Murray!
>
> Because—if a live dog—'tis said,
> Be fairly worth a Lion sped,
> A *live lord* must be worth *two dead*,—
> > My Murray!
>
> And if, as the Opinion goes,
> Verse hath a better sale than prose,
> Certes, I should have more than those—
> > My Murray!
>
> But now—this page is nearly crammed,—
> So, if *you will*, *I* shan't be shammed,
> And if you *wont*, *you* may be damned,
> > My Murray!

I trust more to your prose than my verse however—so pray confer with him in your most oratorical style;—I begin to think that they are only peremptory personages like yourself—who can deal with these Worldlings.——This offer does seem to me very scrubby—considering all things—he never once refers nor seems to think of the Bowles pamphlet—(though I do *not* mean to charge for *it*) but behaves as he did about Galignani's business—when I did him a handsome service quite gratuitously—& needlessly—and he never even acknowledged my civility by a word of thanks.——However you will be guided by circumstances—& let me know—I desire nothing but fair play on all sides.—I have told him to state to *you* his mercantile reasons—& that he will be answered—or his reasons admitted. ——I remember he once wanted to persuade me that I had *given him* the *Giaour* & Bride of Abydos—because for a *year* I had not come to any agreement—nor accepted his offer.——It is some time that I have not heard from Hobhouse.—Moore writes to me that a lawyer or lawyer's Clerk passed through Paris some weeks ago on his way to me *on business*.——Is there such an Envoy to your knowledge and on

what mission?—It is odd that you should not have given me notice.—
Let me hear from you.

yrs. ever & faithly
[Scrawl]

P.S.—The Queen! is she any loss to your house in the way of
business?—Poor woman!—She is at rest from them now.—

[TO JOHN MURRAY (a)]   R[avenn]a August 31st. 1821

Dear Sir/—I have received the Juans—which are printed so *carelessly*
especially the 5th. Canto—as to be disgraceful to me—& not creditable
to you.—It really must be *gone over again* with the *Manuscript*—the
errors are so gross—words added—changed—so as to make cacophony
& nonsense.——You have been careless of this poem because some of
your Synod don't approve of it—but I tell you—it will be long before
you see any thing half so good as poetry or writing.——Upon what
principle have you omitted the *note* on Bacon & Voltaire? and one of
the concluding stanzas sent as an addition? because it ended I suppose
—with—

"And do not link two virtuous souls for life
Into that *moral Centaur* man & wife?["]

Now I must say once for all—that I will not permit any human being
to take such liberties with my writings—because I am absent.—I
desire the omissions to be replaced (except the stanza on Semiramis)
particularly the stanza upon the Turkish marriages—and I request
that the whole be carefully *gone over* with the M.S.S.—I never saw such
stuff as is printed—Gu*ll*eyaz—instead of Gu*lb*eyaz &c. Are you aware
that Gu*lb*eyaz is a real name—and the other nonsense?—I copied the
Cantos out carefully—so that there is *no* excuse—as the Printer reads
or at least *prints* the M.S.S. of the plays without error.——If you have
no feeling for your own reputation pray have some little for mine.——
I have read over the poem carefully—and I tell you *it is poetry.*—Your
little envious knot of parson-poets may say what they please—time
will show that I am not in this instance mistaken.——
    Desire my friend Hobhouse to correct the press especially of the
last Canto from the Manuscript—as it is—it is enough to drive one
out of one's senses—to see the infernal torture of words from the original.—For instance the line

192

"And pair their rhymes as Venus yokes her doves["]
is printed—

"and *praise* their rhymes &c.—["]

also "precarious" for "precocious"—and this line stanza 133.—

"And this strong extreme effect—to tire no longer."

Now do turn to the Manuscript—& see—if I ever made such a *line*—it
is *not verse.*——No wonder the poem should fail—(which however *it
wont* you will see)[1] with such things allowed to creep about it.——
Replace what is omitted—& correct what is so shamefully misprinted,
—and let the poem have fair play—and I fear nothing.——I see in the
last two Numbers of the Quarterly—a strong itching to assail me—
(see the review of the *"Etonian"*)[2] let it—and see if they shan't have
enough of it.——I don't allude to Gifford—who has always been my
friend—& whom I do not consider as responsible for the articles
written by others.—But if I do not give Mr. Milman—⟨Mr. Southey⟩
—& others of the crew something that shall occupy their dreams!—
[line crossed out] I have *not* begun with *the* Quarterers—but let them
look to it.—As for *Milman*[3] (*you* well know I have not been unfair to
his poetry ever) but I have lately had some information of his critical
proceedings in the Quarterly which may bring that on him which he
will be sorry for.—I happen to know *that* of him—which would
annihilate him—when he pretends to preach *morality*—*not* that *he* is
immoral—because he *isn't*—having in early life been once too much
so.—And dares he set up for a preacher? let him go and be priest to
Cybele.——

You will publish the plays—when ready—I am in such a humour
about this printing of D[on] J[uan] so inaccurately—that I must close
this.

yrs. [Scrawl]

[1] Cantos III, IV, and V of *Don Juan* were published together by Murray on
August 8, 1821, and their success was immediate. "The booksellers' messengers
filled the street in front of the house in Albemarle Street, and the parcels of books
were given out the window to their obstreperous demands." (Smiles, Vol. I, p.
413.)

[2] *Quarterly Review*, Vol. XXV, p. 106. There is an oblique reference to works in
the Whistlecraft style, "and if our literature is to be disgraced (as is threatened)
by the publication of an English Pucelle, we do not wish to see, in a work like *The
Etonian*, any thing which may, in the most distant degree, remind us of such
compositions."

[3] Henry Hart Milman, afterwards Dean of St. Pauls and a voluminous writer
of religious histories, had published several volumes of verse and was a frequent
contributor to the *Quarterly Review*.

P.S.—I presume that you have *not* lost the *stanza* to which I allude? it was sent afterwards look over my letters—& find it.—The *Notes* you can't have lost—you acknowledged them—they included eight or nine corrections of Bacon's mistakes in the apothegms.—And now I ask once more if such liberties taken in a man's absence—are fair or praise-worthy?—As for *you* you have no opinions of your own—& never had—but are blown about by the last thing said to you no matter by whom.—

[TO JOHN MURRAY] (*b*)   [*August 31? 1821*]

Dear Sir/—The enclosed letter is written in bad humour—but not without provocation.—However—let it (that is the bad humour) go for little—but I must request your serious attention to the abuses of the printer which ought never to have been permitted.—You forget that all the fools in London (the chief purchasers of your publications) will condemn in me the stupidity of your printer.—For instance in the Notes to Canto fifth—"the *Adriatic* shore of the Bosphorus" instead of the *Asiatic*!! All this may seem little to you—so fine a gentleman with your ministerial connections—but it is serious to me—who am thousands of miles off—& have no opportunity of not proving myself the fool yr. printer makes me—except your pleasure & leisure forsooth. The Gods prosper you—& forgive you for I wont.

[Scrawl]

[TO DOUGLAS KINNAIRD]   *R[avenn]a A[gost]o 31st. 1821*

My dear Douglas/—I write only two words to say that the new Don Juans are so full of gross *misprints*—especially the 5th Canto—that I must beg you & Hobhouse to go over it with the M.S. & correct the whole.—Words—added—misplaced—mispelt—& in short—a frequent disfigurement.—To Mr. Murray I have written very freely by this post on the topic.———He has also taken the liberty to omit some notes—& a stanza (not that upon the Queen—*that* I *ordered* to be omitted at Hobhouse's desire)—now—I have told him—& I beg to repeat it through you—that I will not allow any earthly being to take such liberties with me—because I am absent—it is a personal insult—

& not to be suffered.——Will you tell Hobhouse that I will think upon the *literary* part of the letter, & believe me yours ever & in haste

[Scrawl]

P.S.—Let the plays be published when the preface arrives.——

[TO J. MAWMAN][1]   *R[avenna] A[gost]o 31st. 1821*

Ld. Byron presents his Compliments to Mr. Mawman & would be particularly glad to see that Gentleman if he can make it convenient to call at half past *two* tomorrow afternoon.——Ld. B. takes the liberty of sending his Carriage & horses in case Mr. M. would like to make the round of the remarkable buildings of Ravenna.——

[TO COUNTESS TERESA GUICCIOLI]   [*September? 1821*]

[Postscript of letter from Lega Zambelli to Countess Guiccioli]
  Teresa Mia/—Mi maraviglio che siete degnata scrivere per una cameriera che già rifiutava di venire da te—e che è poco meno di una p[uttana]—publica.——Non ho tempo dirti altro per ora—Scrivimi—amami—&c. &c.

[Scrawl]

[TRANSLATION]   [*September? 1821*]

My Teresa—I am surprised that you should have condescended to write about a maid who had already refused to go to you—and who is little else than a public wh[ore]. I have no time to say more now. Write to me—love me, &c. &c.

[TO DOUGLAS KINNAIRD]   *Ravenna. Septr. 1st. 1821*
[Intended dedication of *Marino Faliero* to Douglas Kinnaird][1]

My dear Douglas/—I dedicate to you the following tragedy—rather on account of your good opinion of it—than from any notion

---

[1] J. Mawman was a London bookseller and publisher who had sold copies of Byron's first published poems, *Hours of Idleness*. He was perhaps the Joseph Mawman who published *An Excursion to the Highlands of Scotland* in 1805.
[1] This dedication was apparently intended for a second edition of *Marino Faliero*, but it was not published until 1832 in Murray's edition of Byron's collected works.

of my own that it may be worthy your acceptance.—But if it's
merits were ten times greater than they possibly can be—this offering
would still be very inadequate acknowledgement of the notice and
steady friendship with which for a series of years you have honoured

your obliged & affectionate friend
BYRON

[TO J. MAWMAN]   *Septr. 1st. 1821*

Mr. Mawman is requested to show this copy to the publisher and
to point out the gross printer's blunders, *some* of which only the author
has had time to correct. They did not exist in the M.S.S. but are owing
to the carelessness of the printer, etc.[1]

[TO THOMAS MOORE]   *Ravenna, September 3d, 1821*

By Mr. Mawman (a paymaster in the corps, in which you and I are
privates) I yesterday expedited to your address, under cover one, two
paper books[1] containing the *Giaour*-nal, and a thing or two. It won't
all do—even for the posthumous public—but extracts from it may. It is
a brief and faithful chronicle of a month or so—parts of it not very
discreet, but sufficiently sincere. Mr. Mawman saith that he will, in
person or per friend, have it delivered to you in your Elysian fields.

If you have got the new Juans, recollect that there are some very
gross printer's blunders, particularly in the fifth Canto,—such as
"praise" for "pair"—"precarious" for "precocious"—"Adriatic" for
"Asiatic"—"case" for "chase"—besides gifts of additional words and
syllables, which make but a cacophonous rhythmus. Put the pen
through the said, as I would mine through * * [Murray]'s ears, if I
were alongside him. As it is, I have sent him a rattling letter, as
abusive as possible. Though he is publisher to the "Board of *Longitude*," he is in no danger of discovering it.

---

[1] Written in a copy of Cantos III, IV, and V of *Don Juan* given to Mawman.
[1] According to Mawman one of the paper books contained some additions to
Byron's Memoirs. (*LJ*, V, 355n.) The other, Moore says (II, 522) "contained a
portion, to the amount of nearly a hundred pages, of a prose story, relating the
adventures of a young Andalusian nobleman, which had been begun by him, at
Venice, in 1817." Moore quoted an extract from it. The story was a transparent
account of the separation from Lady Byron, in great detail, with only the names
fictional.

I am packing for Pisa—but direct your letters *here*, till further notice.

Yours ever, &c.

[TO JOHN MURRAY (*a*)] *Septr. 4th. 1821*

Dear Sir/—Enclosed are some notes &c.—You will also have the goodness to hold yourself in readiness to publish the long delayed letter to *Blackwood's*[1] &c. but previously let me have a proof of it—as I mean it for a separate publication.—The enclosed note you will annex to the Foscaris.—also the dedications.——

yrs.

[TO JOHN MURRAY (*b*)] *R[avenn]a Septr. 4th. 1821*

Dear Sir/—By Saturday's post I sent you a fierce and furibund letter upon the subject of the printer's blunders in Don Juan.—I must solicit your attention to the topic—though my wrath hath subsided into sullenness.——Yesterday I received Mr. Mawman—a friend of yours —& because he is a friend of *yours*—and that's more than I would do in an *English* case—except for those whom I honour.—I was as civil as I could be among packages—even to the very chairs & tables—for I am going to *Pisa* in a few weeks—& have sent & am sending off my chattels.——It regretted me—that my books & every thing being packed—I could not send you a few things I meant for you but they were all sealed & baggaged—so as to have made it a Month's work to get at them again.—I gave him an envelope with the Italian Scrap in it alluded to in my Gilchrist defence[1]—Hobhouse will make it out for you—& it will make you laugh—& him too—the *spelling* particularly.—The "*Mericani*" of whom they call me—the "Capo" (or Chief) mean "Americans"—which is the name given in *Romagna* to a part of the Carbonari—that is to say of the *popular* part, the *troops* of the Carbonari.——They are originally a society of hunters in the forest—who took that name of Americans—but at present comprize some thousands &c. but I shan't let you further into the secret, which

---

1 The reply to *Blackwood's Edinburgh Magazine* was not published until 1832 in Murray's collected edition.

1 See May 10, 1821, to Murray, note 1. The "Italian Scrap" was an anonymous letter threatening him with assassination.

may be participated with the postmasters. Why they thought me their Chief—I know not—their Chiefs are like "Legion—being Many"[2].——However it is a post of more honour than profit—for now that they are persecuted—it is fit that I should aid them—and so I have done as far as my means will permit.——They will rise again some day—for these fools of the Government are blundering—they actually seem to know *nothing*; for they have arrested & banished many of their *own* party—& let others escape—who are not their friends.—What thinkst thou of Greece?——Address to me *here* as usual—till you hear further from me.——By Mawman I have sent a journal to Moore—but it won't do for the public—at least a great deal of it won't—*parts* may.——I read over the Juans—which are excellent.—Your Synod was quite wrong—& so you will find by and bye.—I regret that I do not go on with it—for I had all the plan for several cantos—and different countries & climes. You say nothing of the *note* I enclosed to you—which will explain why I agreed to discontinue it—(at Madame G[uiccioli]'s request) but you are so grand and sublime & ⟨furiously⟩ occupied that one would think instead of publishing for "the Board of *Longitude*" that you were trying to discover it.——Let me hear that Gifford is *better*—he can't be spared either by you or me.—Enclosed is a note which I will thank you *not* to forget to acknowledge and to publish.

yrs. [Scrawl]

[TO DOUGLAS KINNAIRD]   *Ravenna. Septr. 4th. 1821*

My dear Douglas/—I intend to dedicate the "two Foscaris" to Walter Scott—"Sardanapalus" to Goethe—& "Faliero" to you.[1]— The two first I have sent to Murray—your own I enclose to *you* that you may see it first—& accept it or not. If content—send it to *Murray*. —You are a Good German—I am not even a bad one—but would feel greatly obliged if you would write two lines to the "Grosser Mann" at my request—to tell him my intent & ask his leave.—See the inscription at Murray's—it goes by this post.—

yrs ever [Scrawl]

[2] *St. Mark*, V: 9.
[1] When *Sardanapalus, The Two Foscari*, and *Cain* were published together on Dec. 19, 1821, the first two appeared without dedications. *Cain* was dedicated to Sir Walter Scott. The dedication to "The Illustrious Goethe" first appeared in Murray's edition of 1829.

Cara P[ettegola]—Quel' Lega non ha fatto nessun' progresso nei preparativi—dunque gridatelo bene.—Per me io non aspetto che per vedere terminata questo affare dei mobili &c.——Cosa è divenuto di Papa e Pierino? sono a Pisa?—La tua lettera non parla di loro.—— Amami—e credimi   +

[Scrawl]

P.S.—Oggi ho portato Lega alla Marina per insegnarlo a nuotare— puoi imaginare quel' prete nel' mare.—

[TRANSLATION]   *September 4th. 1821*

Dear P[ettegola—(gossip)]—That man Lega has not gone on with the preparations—so scold him well. For my part I am only waiting to see the business of the furniture, etc., finished. What happened to Papa and Pierino? Are they in Pisa? Your letter does not speak of them.——

Love me and believe me

P.S.—Today I took Lega to the beach to teach him to swim—you can imagine that priest in the sea.

[TO OCTAVIUS GILCHRIST]   *Ravenna. Septr. 5th. 1821*

Sir/—I have to acknowledge the arrival of yr. three pamphlets[1] "from the author" whom I thank very sincerely for the attention.—— The tone which Mr. Bowles has taken in this controversy has been so different with the different parties—that we are perhaps none of us fair personal judges of the subject.—Long before I had seen Mr. B's answers to myself—or the last pamphlet of the three which you have sent to me—I had written an answer to his attack upon yourself— which perhaps you may have seen—(or at any rate may see if you think it worth the trouble) at Mr. Murray's.——As it was somewhat savage—on reading Mr. Bowles's mild reply—to me, I suppressed it's publication, recollecting also that you were perfectly competent to your own defence—and might probably look upon my interference as

---

[1] The first of Gilchrist's pamphlets was a reply to an attack by Bowles on him for a review of *Spence's Anecdotes* in the *Quarterly Review* for October, 1820. From that point on the controversy between Bowles and Gilchrist became bitter.

impertinent.——I have not read Mr. Bowles's "Sequel" to which your third pamphlet refers.——Mr. Bowles has certainly not set *you* an example of forbearance in *controversy*—but in *society* he really is what I have described him—but as we are all mad upon some subject or other—and the only reason why it does not appear in *all* is that their insane chord has not been struck upon;—our Editor seems to have been touched upon the score of Pope—and for that reason it is a thousand pities that he ever meddled with him.——By the way—to refer to myself—I think you might as well have omitted the mention of Don Juan and Beppo and Little &c. as more indecent than the "Imitation from Horace" of Pope—for two reasons—firstly they are *not so* indecent by any means—as for example—

> "And if a tight young girl will serve the turn
> In arrant pride continues still to *churn*"[2]

—
or
—

> "What pushed poor E—— on the imperial whore
> 'Twas but to be where Charles had been before['']"[3]

and in the next place—as I had been fighting Pope's battles as well as I could it was rather hard in an *ally* to bring in an "odious comparison" at the expence of his auxiliary.——However this is a trifle—and if Pope's moral reputation can be still further elevated at the expence of mine—I will yield it as freely—as I have always admired him sincerely——much more indeed than you yourself in all probability—for *I* do not think him inferior to Milton——although to state such an opinion publicly in the present day—would be equivalent to saying that I do not think Shakespeare without the grossest of faults—which is another heterodox notion of my entertainment.—Indeed I look upon a proper appreciation of Pope as a touchstone of taste—and the present question as not only whether Pope is or is not in the first rank of our literature—but whether *that* literature shall or shall not relapse into the Barbarism from which it has scarcely emerged for above a century and a half.—I do not deny the natural powers of Mind of the earlier dramatists—but I think that their service as a *standard* is doing irreparable mischief.——It is also a great error to suppose the *present* a *high* age of English poetry—it is equivalent to the age of *Statius* or *Silius Italicus* except that instead of imitating the Virgils of our

[2] Misquoted from Pope's "Sober Advice from Horace", lines 151–152.
[3] Pope's "Sober Advice from Horace", lines 81–82.

language—they are "trying back" (to use a hunting phrase) upon the Ennius's and Lucilius's who had better have remained in their obscurity.—Those poor idiots of the Lakes too—are diluting our literature as much as they can——in short——all of us more or less (except Campbell & Rogers) have much to answer for—and I don't see any remedy.——But I am wandering from the subject— which is to thank you for your present & to beg you to believe me your

> obliged & very faith[fu]l Servt.
> BYRON

Is it not odd that hitherto Pope has been edited only by *priests?* Warburton—Warton—Bowles?—at least I know no others.—

P.S.—I saw Mr. Mawman the other day;—he tells me that the Booksellers have engaged Roscoe[4] to edite Pope—and I think the choice is a very judicious one.—Roscoe has all the elegance and classical turn of mind requisite to do Pope justice.—Hitherto he has only been edited by his enemies or by Warburton who was a polemical parson and as fit to edite Poetry as Pope to preach in Gloucester Cathedral.— The Attorney-bishop did him no good—& Warton & Bowles have done him harm. Mr. Mawman tells me that Roscoe is requested (by the publishers) to keep the Controversy with Mr. Bowles &c. quite out of sight—& not to allude to it at all.—This is the *quietest* way— but whether it is the best I know not.—I suppose it is.——Mr. Mawman seemed indignant at Bowles's edition which he said "was a treachery to his employers who had paid him to edite Pope—and not to defame him.—['] He wondered that I had not put this more strongly in a letter—but how was I to know it?—It seemed to me inconceivable that they could *publish* such an edition without being aware of it's *tendency*—and thus tacitly approving it with their "Imprimatur".——

[TO JOHN MURRAY] [*Sept. 5? 1821*]

Dear Sir/—Will you have the goodness to forward the enclosed to Mr. Gilchrist—whose address I do not exactly know—*If* that Gentleman would like to see my *second* letter to *you*—on the attack upon himself—you can forward him a copy of the proof.—

> yrs. [Scrawl]

4 William Roscoe (1753–1832) had written a *Life of Lorenzo de' Medici* (1795) and *Life and Pontificate of Leo the Tenth* (1805). He started his edition of Pope in 1822.

[Postscript to letter of Lega Zambelli to Count Gamba]

Amico Preg.mo—*Io* non ho detto che *"possa"*—ho detto che lo *fa*—secondo a ciò che mi riferiscono.—Quel' buffo di Lega conta le cose in sua maniera.—Dappiù il Signor Lega fa tutto ciò che egli *"possa"* (o *può*)—per *ritardare* la mia partenza.—Ciò scrivo—perche sapete la sola ragione che mi trattenga qui per ora, è la lentezza di Lega. Sono sempre il vostro amico affmo.

[Scrawl]

1000 Saluti alla Teresina.

[TRANSLATION]   *September 5th, 1821*

Most Honoured Friend—*I* did not say *"he might"*—I said he *was doing it*—according to what I am told.

That buffoon Lega tells things in his own way. Besides Mr. Lega does all this—so that he *may* (or *can*) delay my departure. I am writing this, so that you may know that the only reason that is keeping me here now is Lega's slowness. I am always your affectionate friend. 1000 greetings to Teresa.

[TO PERCY BYSSHE SHELLEY]   *R[avenn]a Septr. 8th. 1821*

Dear Shelley/—They pretend here to *two hundred Scudi* for the carriage of about *two thirds* of my furniture *only*, & *not for the whole*.—As this seems to me very exorbitant—(and indeed whether it be so or no) I should prefer that *you* sent me from Pisa—*waggons horses & drivers* according to the fairest contract you can make with them for me. I will sanction it—be it more or less.—It is the same thing as the drivers &c. must *return* here—and the Tuscans will only have to come here first.——The number of waggons wanted on the whole will be *eight*—the number of *beasts*, what they please—the baggage is heavy—but whether drawn by horses—mules—or oxen, is indifferent to me.——It was for *six* cars only that the Indigenous masters of horse asked two hundred crowns—i.e. half a year's rent of the house for a transport of chattels.——Send me Etrurians at their own price—for of the two—I prefer being cheated by the new comers to continuing to

202

minister to the antient Scoundrels of this venerable city.——When I talked to you about purchase of *other moveables*—I meant such as may be requisite—to complete mine in a new mansion.——Of course I meant things requisite—according to the *premises*—and did not mean to limit the [price?] to an exact sum or to a few Scudi more or less according to what was wanted.——Of course you have seen *this* house & *that* house & can judge.—You may do it now—or wait till I come as you please.—Believe me

yours ever & truly
BYRON

P.S.—Expedite the Baggage Waggons—we wait only now for those to march.——Make my remembrances to every body I don't know—& my respects to all I do.——

[TO OCTAVIUS GILCHRIST] *R[avenn]a Septr. 8th. 1821*

Sir/—Some days ago I enclosed to Mr. Murray a letter to your address. Since this occurred I perceive by some advertisements at the close of yr. pamphlets that you have published some works upon the older dramatists.—As my remarks upon *them* in my letter might appear *indirectly* to reflect upon this, I hasten to assure you that I was not aware of the circumstance till my letter was written—& that it merely contains a private & *unpopular* opinion of mine expressed simply with reference to Pope.—Renewing my thanks for ye. present I am

yr. obliged & very humble Servt.
BYRON

P.S.—Excuse this scrawl—for I cut the finger of my *pen*-hand against a Sea-shell in diving yesterday.—

[TO JOHN MURRAY] *Septr. 9th. 1821*

Dear Sir/—Please to forward the enclosed also to Mr. Gilchrist.— I cut my finger in diving yesterday against a sharp shell & can hardly write.—Last week I sent a long note (in English) to the play—let me have a *proof of it*—but as I am in haste—you can publish the plays with the *whole of it, except the part referring* to *Southey* to which I wish to add something—& we will then append the whole to a re-print.—All the part down to where it begins on that rascal—will do for publication without my reviewing it—that is to say if yr. printer will take pains, & not be careless as about the new Juans.—Let me hear that Gifford is better & your family well.—

yrs. [Scrawl]

[TO COUNTESS TERESA GUICCIOLI]   R[avenn]a S[ettembr]e 9bre[sic] 1821

Eccellenza Pic . . . . ./ La Duchessa di Devonshire ha scritto l'acchiusa—che sarà tradotta da Sr. S[helley]—se quella ti preme.—La prego di mandarmila in dietro—dopo averla letta. Pei maestri della *lingua Inglese*—sarebbe meglio per ora evitare l'ocasione di dar' luogo alle dicerie.—Tu non conosci lo stato dei partiti in Inghilterra—e le orrori che dicono di Shelley e di me—e se non hai un' poco di riguardo I Inglesi di Pisa e di Firenze diranno che *essendo stanco io*—ti ho consegnato a lui.—Ti dico questo schietto e netto—in tante parole—per farti conoscere—a cosa può condurre la minima imprudenza.—Dunque essendo avisato—dipende da te di condurti come vuoi.——Noi andiamo facendo dei preparativi per lasciare Ravenna—ciò che forse sarà ben' inutile—ed in ogni modo è stato sempre *contrarissimo* a miei pensieri.—Un' poco di pazienza avrebbe ristabilito tutto, come vedrai della lettera (della dama) acchiusa.—Bisogna anche pensare di due cose—la prima è—che se papa è richiemato—io *torno in' quel' istante* a R[avenna]—e la seconda è—che se egli viene richiemato *prima di* mia partenza—io non parto.——Per le spese della casa nuova—&c. Io li pagarei 1000 volte volontieri per non avere il disturbo di traslocarmi per delle inezie.—Per quello non sarà difficoltà.—

Sono sempre [Scrawl]

Saluti Papa e Pierino &c.

[TRANSLATION]   *September 9th, 1821*

Excellency P[ettegola-gossip]. . . .—The Duchess of Devonshire has written the enclosed, which Mr. S[helley] will translate, if it interests you. Pray return it to me after reading. As for teachers of the English language, it would be better for the present to avoid giving any occasion for gossip. You do not know the state of the factions in England—and the horrible things that are said about Shelley and me—

and if you are not careful the English in Pisa and Florence will say that, *being tired of you,* I handed you on to him. I say this frankly and openly, in so many words. So, having been warned—it depends on you to behave as you think best.

We are making preparations to leave Ravenna—which may well be quite useless—and has in any case been entirely *contrary* to my ideas. A little patience would have put everything right, as you will see from the enclosed letter (of the lady).

We must also think of two things—the first is—that if Papa is recalled from exile *I shall return that instant* to Ravenna—and the second is—that if he is recalled *before my departure*—I shall not leave. As to the cost of the new house, etc. I would pay them willingly 1000 times so as not to have the trouble of moving for nothing. About that there will be no difficulty.

I am always

Greet Papa and Pierino &c.

[TO JOHN MURRAY]   *Ravenna. Septr. 10th. 1821*

Dear Sir/—By this post I send you three packets containing "Cain" a Mystery—(i.e. a tragedy on a sacred subject) in three acts.—I think that it contains some poetry—being in the style of "Manfred". Send me a proof of the whole by return of *post.*—If *there is time*—publish it with the other *two*—if not print it separately & as soon as you can.— Of the dedications (sent lately) I wish to transfer that to Sir Walter Scott to *this* drama of *"Cain"*—reserving that of the "Foscaris" for another, for a particular reason—of which more by & bye. Write—

yrs. [Scrawl]

[TO DOUGLAS KINNAIRD]   *R[avenna] Septr. 11th. 1821*

Dear Douglas/—By this post—there goes to Mr. Murray—a drama in three (long) acts—called "Cain" full of poesy—& pastime.—— I avise you that you may apprize & deal with him accordingly. It is in my very fiercest Metaphysical manner—like "Manfred" and all that. Let me know of it's arrival—for I am anxious—& Murray is as lazy and indolent as suits a parvenu;—if I were alongside of him—I could deal with him—but as it is—I must trust to your stimuli properly applied to that illustrious coxcomb of yesterday's crop.——Touch him up like a man of family.—

Yours ever (in haste) but faithfully & truly
[Scrawl]

P.S.—If you don't see to him directly, he will play some trick—and pretend that it is not arrived to avoid an addition to his disbursements &c.—He has been shuffling lately like a Conjuror.—

[TO JOHN MURRAY]   *Ravenna Septr. 12th. 1821*

Dear Sir/—By Tuesday's post—I forwarded in three packets—the drama of "Cain" in three acts—of which I request the acknowledgment when arrived.—To the last speech of Eve in the last act (i.e. where she curses Cain) add these three lines to the concluding one—

> "May the Grass wither from thy foot! the Woods
> Deny thee shelter! Earth a home! the Dust
> A Grave! the Sun his light! and Heaven her God!['']

There's as pretty a piece of Imprecation for you, when joined to the lines already sent—as you may wish to meet with in the course of your business.—But don't forget the addition of the above three lines which are clinchers to Eve's speech.——Let me know what Gifford thinks (if the play arrives in safety) for I have a good opinion of the piece as poetry—it is in my gay metaphysical style & in the Manfred line.— You must at least commend my facility & variety—when you consider what I have done within the last fifteen months—with my head too full of other and mundane matters.—But no doubt you will avoid saying any good of it—for fear I should raise the price upon you— that's right—stick to business! Let me know what your other ragamuffins are writing—for I suppose you don't like starting too many of your Vagabonds at once.—You may give them the start for any thing I care.——If this arrives in time to be added to the other two dramas publish them *together*—if not—publish it separately—in the *same* form —to tally for the purchasers.—Let me have a proof of the whole speedily.—It is longer than "Manfred".——

Why don't you publish my *Pulci*?—the very best thing I ever wrote —with the Italian to it.——I wish I was alongside of you—nothing— is ever done in a man's absence—every body runs counter—because they *can*.——If ever I *do* return to England (which I shan't though) I shall write a poem to which "English Bards['']" &c. shall be New Milk

206

in comparison.—Your present literary world of mountebanks stands in need of such an Avatar.—but I am not yet quite bilious enough——a season or two more—and a provocation or two—will wind me up to the point—and then have at the whole set!—I have no patience with the sort of trash you send me out by way of books—except Scott's novels—& three or four other things I never saw such work—or works.—Campbell is lecturing—Moore idling—Southey twaddling—Wordsworth driveling—Coleridge muddling—Joanna Baillie piddling—Bowles quibbling—squabbling—and sniveling.—Milman will *do*—if he don't cant too much—nor imitate Southey—the fellow has poesy in him—but he is envious—& unhappy, as all the envious are.—Still he is among the best of the day.—Barry Cornwall will do better by & bye—I dare say—if he don't get spoilt by green tea—and the praises of Pentonville—& Paradise Row.[1]——The pity of these men is—that they have never lived either in *high life* nor in *solitude*—there is no medium for the knowledge of the *busy* or the *still* world.—If admitted into high life for a season—it is merely as *spectators*—they form no part of the Mechanism thereof.—Now Moore and I—the one by circumstances & the other by birth—happened to be free of the corporation—& to have entered into its pulses and passions "quarum partes fuimus".—Both of us have learnt by this much which nothing else could have taught us.——

yrs. [Scrawl]

P.S.—I saw one of your brethren—another of the Allied Sovereigns of Grub-Street—the other day—viz—Mawman the Great—by whom I sent due homage to your imperial self.—Tomorrow's post may perhaps bring a letter from you—but you are the most ungrateful and ungracious of correspondents.—But there is some excuse for you—with your perpetual levee of politicians—parson-scribblers—& loungers——some day I will give you a *poetical* Catalogue of them.—The post is come—no letter—but never mind.—How is Mrs. Murray & Gifford?—Better?—Say *well*.——My Compliments to Mr. Heber[2] upon his Election.——

[1] Pentonville was then a good-class district in the parish of St. James, Clerkenwell, which arose about the year 1775 after the formation of New Road (now Pentonville Road). Its name came from the fact that it passed through fields belonging to Henry Penton. Paradise Row once stood in the Chelsea area, fashionable in the 18th century. In general Byron was referring to middle class suburbs.

[2] Richard Heber (1773–1833) was elected M.P. for the University of Oxford on Aug. 24, 1821. He was a book collector and a founder of the Athenaeum Club.

My dear Douglas/—It is odd that Murray has not shown you the
Foscari's—Probably he is afraid that you should like it—& be a cause
of raising the price.—I have corrected the proofs—returned them to
England—and *refused* an offer he made me.——By tuesday's post I
sent him another tragedy on the subject of *"Cain"* but in the Manfred
& metaphysical style.—Desire him to let you see it as soon as he can.
—Also the Foscari's.—You must really pursue him

> "As when a Gryphon in the Wilderness
> Follows an Arimaspian.—[''][1]

Follow the Arimaspian Murray—who seems as reluctant to part with
"Gold" as the rest of his Nation.——He has been shuffling—& trying
to make a bargain with me apart from yr. knowledge—which shan't
be.—If Claughton has paid Hanson—-let Hanson pay the money into
yr. bank.—I presume you know by receipts—(they should be amongst
my papers with Hobhouse) that in 1813 he had of my money on account
two thousand seven hundred pounds—besides the *five thousand* that he has
received from *you* as trustee.—Now surely we should have *a bill* before
further payménts.—Claughton's money should go to the Creditors.—
You must dun Sir Jacob—an old fellow with thousands a year—& the
Noel estate too (which ought to have been mine) demurring to pay
a hundred pound or two!!—It can't be—& it shan't be—it is shabby—
scabby—scrubby—& must not be permitted.——If you choose to let
Hanson have a fair proportion ought [out] of Claughton's payment—I
object not—but in proportion to the other Creditors. I have seen nothing
in the papers of his mis-management of the Portsmouth estates—but it
is a great disadvantage to me to have such a solicitor.—However he was
made so when I was ten years old—& I have no help for it.—In case
of taxing his bill—all these little things—would weigh with the
taxers thereof (i.e. the Portsmouth Mismanagements &c.) and with a
jury in case of an appeal to one.——Kean is right to act de Montfort[2]
—I prayed him to do so a hundred times in 1815. But *I* will have
nothing to do with the Doge—why should he act it? I did not—and do
not write for the stage & would not alter a line—to draw down the
upper Gallery into the pit—in thunder—if it could be so.——You

---

[1] *Paradise Lost*, Book II, line 843. According to ancient legend the Arimaspians
were one-eyed people of Scythia who fought with Gryphons for the possession of
the gold in the neighbourhood.

[2] *De Montfort* was the most popular of Joanna Baillie's *Plays of the Passions*, this
one displaying the passion of hate.

are a fine fellow & my zealous friend & ally—also a very good Judge of dramatic effect—but surely the past experience shows that in the present state of the English Stage—no production of mine can be adapted to an audience.—How is Hobhouse? better I hope—tell me so.—

yrs. ever & affectly.
BYRON

P.S.—I am very anxious about the funds—there is no reasoning about such things.

P.S.—Murray by system for some time avoids letting me have any favourable news, in *his* line.—For instance I learned from an Englishman—that notwithstanding the *row*—the popularity & sale of the *two first Juans*—had been excessive.—Of all this he told me nothing. Of the new cantos—I only know that he published them in a disparaging way—& they are printed in so slovenly a manner with regard to *printers' errors*—that no wonder if they don't succeed—but as yet I hear nothing whether they succeed or not.—There is poetry in them though—though I say it.——Let me hear how Hobhouse is—as soon as you can conveniently—I hope we shall have no vacancies for Westminster. Let him get well!

[TO AUGUSTA LEIGH] *R[avenn]a. Septr. 13th. 1821*

My dearest A./—From out the enclosed as well as the former parcel—(a few posts ago) select some of the *best-behaved* curls—and set them in a golden locket for Ada my daughter.—Round the locket let there be this Italian inscription—"*Il Sangue non è mai Acqua.*" — And do not let the engravers blunder.——It means "Blood is never water"—and alludes merely to relationship—being a common proverb.—I should wish her to wear this—that she may know she has (or had) a father in the world.—Let the bill for the locket be sent to Mr. Kinnaird—& let him deduct it from my accounts.——Do this and prosper!—

yrs. ever
[Scrawl]

[TO LADY BYRON] *R[avenn]a Septr. 14th. 1821*

By this post I have sent to Augusta—to make up into a locket for Ada—some of my hair—I suppose that you have no objection—if you have you can state it to Mrs. Leigh—I wish you to send to Mrs. Leigh's some of the child's in return to be forwarded to me in a letter of Augusta's—it will come very safely by the post—I am anxious to see it's *colour*, for the *print*—gives no information of that, and the picture has not yet been sent by Murray.——You will not forget to let her learn Italian—& be *musical*—that is if she has an ear & a heart for the latter.—The former will not be difficult, and perhaps by the time that she and I may meet (if ever we meet) it will be nearly necessary to converse with me—for I write English now with more facility than I speak it—from hearing it but seldom. It is the reverse with my Italian which I can speak fluently—but write incorrectly— having never studied it & only acquired it by ear.——I keep up my English as well as I can by scribbling however.—Murray has at present three tragedies of mine in hand (*not* for the stage you may easily suppose) one of them—on the subject of "Cain" is I think poetical enough.—The other two are in a simpler and severer style.— I am trying an experiment—which is to introduce into our language— the *regular* tragedy—without regard to the Stage—which will not admit of it—but merely to the *mental* theatre of the reader.—As yet— I have had no great success—people looking upon it as a treason to the wild old English drama—which however is a separate and distinct thing—and has as little to do with the question—as Tasso with Ariosto ——they are not of the same genus.——If you see Joanna Baillie— tell her that *Kean* is going at last to act De Montfort—which I urged him to a hundred times in 1815—this I hear by the way—& am very happy—regretting that I cannot see him.—They want me to alter "the Doge" for Kean—which I have refused (to Douglas Kinnaird) [indeed?] the Stage is not my object—and even interferes with it—as long as it is in it's present state.——Alfieri's "Philip" and "Mirrha" when well acted (as I have seen them) appeared to me much more classical exhibitions than our own wild pantomimes—but this may be prejudice.—

I won't trouble you more about the funds—but give up the matter in despair——I have done what I could for the extrication of the property from what I conceive a precarious state—& must now be content to pay the penalties of absence and my own folly in tying up the greater part of my future against the advice of all about me.—— Your Mr. Bland seems a tolerably impracticable gentlemen——but I have no claim upon him—even for common civility.—Believe me

yrs. very [truly?]
BYRON

P.S.—We have had sad work here since the spring—exiles—proscriptions—and all the routine of ill Success.—Most of my friends have been proscribed more or less—and I escaped as they said themselves merely by being too notorious a person as a stranger to be assailed without a regular trial,—and any thing like an *open* proceeding is contrary to the genius of this government and to the disposition of the neighbouring Tiberius of Austria.—I did all I could to forward the views of the patriots—& was prepared to cast in my lot with them—they were within three days of rising—when the cowardice and treachery of the Neapolitans ruined all.——The Italians never can unite—that is their bane.—as I think I told you last summer.—The reason that I wrote to you so anxiously about Augusta &c. was that we expected business daily;—and it would not then have been a time to be "bothering you about family matters"—as Sir Lucius says.[1]——At present I am going into Tuscany—and if the Greek business is not settled soon—shall perhaps go up that way.—The Chief of the Athenian Insurgents is Demetrius Zograffo—who was my Servant for a long time—and with me in London—when I first knew you in 1812.—He was a clever but not an enterprising man—but circumstances make men.—But my going will depend upon more certain information than is yet to be obtained—things are so disguised there.—

[TO DOUGLAS KINNAIRD]   *Septr. 15th. 1821*

Dear Douglas/—The quantum of poesy of mine yet unaccounted for in Murray's hands—amounts to (*including* the three new Cantos of D.J.) at an *under* computation to *ten thousand lines of verse.*—There are the three Juans—(three thousand lines) the three plays—at an average at least *two* thousand lines each—the translation from Pulci *seven hundred*—the Hints from Horace as many—with the Po and one or two smaller pieces.—It will be nearer twelve than ten thousand fairly reckoned.—(Marino Faliero contained three thousand five hundred lines or four hundred & fifty I forget which). Now you know how much Scott & Moore received for poems not exceeding in length six thousand or seven thousand lines.—Campbell for his *prose* upon the *poets*—the same with them.—Orford & Waldegrave little less.—You can judge better than me—if my name has sunk below *theirs*—or if I should or should not be upon the same level.—Murray's proposal to

---

[1] Sir Lucius O'Trigger in Sheridan's *The Rivals*, Act V, scene 3.

me was *two thousand*—which to say the least of it—proves either *his* or *my* degradation.—To be sure the sum is worth more than all the poetry that ever was written *in fact*—but is it so in proportion to the present prices paid to other writers?—Whatever *you* settle I will sanction, as I presume you will do it mainly with a view to the balance of both the parties.—You say that you have information or can have it to decide by. You see I have not included the *pamphlet.* which he *took* without a word of thanks or acknowledgement. He is welcome however.

yrs. ever

[TO COUNTESS TERESA GUICCIOLI]   *Ravenna 15. 7bre. 1821*

[Added to a letter of Lega Zambelli to Teresa]

Eccellenza Pettegola/—Tu hai fatta bene gridare questo buffone—e farei meglio ancora rimproverarlo dappiù.—Egli non è di buona fede— Intanto non aspettiamo che l'arrivo dei vetturali per spedire la robba. Per il primo ordinario ti scriverò piu.—Sono sempre il tuo.

a.—a. in e.
[Scrawl]

P.S.—Saluti le due Eccellenze virili; e di a Pierino che ho delle cose di dirlo che lo farebbero ridere se non fosse un' Venerdi—come lo è quest' oggi—dunque mi trattengo per rivederlo—o per scriverlo per un' altra occasione.——Ti bacio [some words erased] 1100 volte.—

[TRANSLATION]   *Ravenna. 15 Sept. 1821*

Gossip Excellency—You have done well to scold the buffoon—and will do better still to scold him some more. He is not in good faith— meanwhile we are only waiting for the carriers to get the things off. I will write more by the first post. I am always your friend and lover for ever.

P.S.—Greet the two manly Excellencies; and tell Pierino that I have some things to tell him which would make him laugh if it were not Friday, as it is today, so I shall wait to see him—or to write on some other occasion. I kiss you [words erased by Teresa] 1100 times.

[Addition to Lega Zambelli's note to the Countess Guiccioli]

Eccellenza Pettegola/—Siamo tutti preparando—imballando–sudando—bestiammiando &c. *ando*——Mi ha costato due ore di mettere in ordine i archivi delle lettere di vostra Eccellenza—essendo almeno cinque cento;—una piena traduzione di Corinna—ossia—la Pettegola, romanzo di S. E. La N. D. Ca. G. D. T. G. nata G. G. e R. P.——Amami sempre tuo e tutto

[Scrawl]

P.S.—1000 cose a Papa, e l'Eccellenza fraterna—Continua a gridare Lega—che lo merita più ogni giorno.

[TRANSLATION]   *September 17. 1821*

Gossip Excellency—We are all preparing—packing—sweating—swearing—and other-*ings*.

It has cost me two hours to put in order the archives of your Excellency's letters—being at least five hundred; a full translation of *Corinne*—i.e. *The Gossip*, the romance of Her Excellency Our Lady Countess Gaspara Domenica Teresa Guiccioli, born Gamba Ghiselli and Respected Gossip. Love me. Always and entirely yours.

P.S.—1000 messages to Papa and the fraternal Excellency. Go on scolding Lega—who deserves it more every day.

[TO THOMAS MOORE]   *Ravenna, September 17th, 1821*

The enclosed lines[1] as you will directly perceive, are written by the Rev. W. L. B. ＊＊ [Bowles]. Of course it is for *him* to deny them if they are not.

Believe me, yours ever and most affectionately,

B

P.S.—Can you forgive this? It is only a reply to your lines against my Italians. Of course I will *stand* by my lines against all men; but it is heart-breaking to see such things in a people as the reception of that unredeemed ＊＊＊＊＊＊＊ in an oppressed country.[2] *Your* apotheosis is

---

[1] *The Irish Avatar.*

[2] The poem expressed Byron's indignation both that such an enthusiastic reception was given to George IV by the Irish, and that the King made his triumphal entry of Dublin while the Queen lay dead in London.

now reduced to a level with his welcome, and their gratitude to Grattan is cancelled by their atrocious adulation of this, &c., &c., &c.

I am in all the sweat, dust, and blasphemy of an universal packing of all my things, furniture, &c. for Pisa, whither I go for the winter. The cause has been the exile of all my fellow Carbonics, and, amongst them, of the whole family of Madame G., who, you know, was divorced from her husband last week [year?], "on account of P. P. clerk of this parish,"[1] and who is obliged to join her father and relatives, now in exile there, to avoid being shut up in a monastery, because the Pope's decree of separation required her to reside in *casa paterna*, or else, for decorum's sake, in a convent. As I could not say, with Hamlet, "Get thee to a nunnery," I am preparing to follow them.

It is awful work, this love, and prevents all a man's projects of good or glory. I wanted to go to Greece lately (as every thing seems up here) with her brother, who is a very fine, brave fellow (I have seen him put to the proof), and wild about liberty. But the tears of a woman who has left her husband for a man, and the weakness of one's own heart, are paramount to these projects, and I can hardly indulge them.

We were divided in choice between Switzerland and Tuscany, and I gave my vote for Pisa, as nearer the Mediterranean, which I love for the sake of the shores which it washes, and for my young recollections of 1809. Switzerland is a curst selfish, swinish country of brutes, placed in the most romantic region of the world. I never could bear the inhabitants, and still less their English visitors; for which reason, after writing for some information about houses, upon hearing that there was a colony of English all over the cantons of Geneva, &c., I immediately gave up the thought, and persuaded the Gambas to do the same.

By the last post I sent you "The Irish Avatar,"—what think you? The last line—"a name never spoke but with curses and jeers"—must run either "a name only uttered with curses or jeers," or "a wretch never named but with curses or jeers." *Becase* as *how*, "spoke" is not grammar, except in the House of Commons; and I doubt whether we can say "a name *spoken*," for *mentioned*. I have some doubts, too, about "repay,"—"and for murder repay with a shout and a smile." Should

[1] Pope's *Memoirs of P. P., Clerk of this Parish.*

it not be, "and for murder repay him with shouts and a smile," or "*reward* him with shouts and a smile?"

So, pray put your poetical pen through the MS. and take the least bad of the emendations. Also, if there be any further breaking of Priscian's[2] head, will you apply a plaister? I wrote in the greatest hurry and fury, and sent it you the day after; so, doubtless, there will be some awful constructions, and a rather lawless conscription of rhythmus.

With respect to what Anna Seward calls "the liberty of transcript," —when complaining of Miss Matilda Muggleton, the accomplished daughter of a choral vicar of Worcester Cathedral, who had abused the said "liberty of transcript," by inserting in the Malvern Mercury, Miss Seward's "Elegy on the South Pole," as her *own* production, with her *own* signature, two years after having taken a copy, by permission of the authoress—with regard, I say, to the "liberty of transcript," I by no means oppose an occasional copy to the benevolent few, provided it does not degenerate into such licentiousness of Verb and Noun as may tend to "disparage my parts of speech"[3] by the carelessness of the transcribblers.

I do not think that there is much danger of the "King's Press being abused" upon the occasion, if the publishers of journals have any regard for their remaining liberty of person. It is as pretty a piece of invective as ever put publisher in the way to "Botany."[4] Therefore, if *they* meddle with it, it is at *their* peril. As for myself, I will answer any jontleman—though I by no means recognise a "right of search" into an unpublished production and unavowed poem. The same applies to things published *sans* consent. I hope you like, at least, the concluding lines of the *Pome?*

What are you doing, and where are you? in England? Nail Murray —nail him to his own counter, till he shells out the thirteens. Since I wrote to you, I have sent him another tragedy—"Cain" by name— making three in MS. now in his hands, or in the printer's. It is in the Manfred, metaphysical style, and full of some Titanic declamation;— Lucifer being one of the dram. pers., who takes Cain a voyage among the stars, and, afterwards, to "Hades," where he shows him the phantoms of a former world, and its inhabitants. I have gone upon the

---

[2] Priscianus, Roman grammarian (c. 450 A.D.) taught grammar at Constantinople.

[3] Sheridan, *The Rivals*, Act III, scene 3. Mrs. Malaprop says: "What do you think of that?—an aspersion upon my parts of speech!"

[4] Botany Bay, Australia, the destination of transported felons.

notion of Cuvier,[5] that the world has been destroyed three or four times, and was inhabited by mammoths, behemoths, and what not; but *not* by man till the Mosaic period, as, indeed, it proved by the strata of bones found;—those of all unknown animals, and known, being dug out, but none of mankind. I have, therefore, supposed Cain to be shown, in the *rational* Preadamites, beings endowed with a higher intelligence than man, but totally unlike him in form, and with much greater strength of mind and person. You may suppose the small talk which takes place between him and Lucifer upon these matters is not quite canonical.

The consequence is, that Cain comes back and kills Abel in a fit of dissatisfaction, partly with the politics of Paradise, which had driven them all out of it, and partly because (as it is written in Genesis) Abel's sacrifice was the more acceptable to the Deity. I trust that the Rhapsody has arrived—it is in three acts, and entitled "A Mystery," according to the former Christian custom, and in honour of what it probably will remain to the reader.

Yours, &c.

[TO JOHN MURRAY]   R[avenn]a Septr. 20th. 1821

Dear Murray/—You need not send "the Blues" which is a mere buffoonery never meant for publication.—The papers to which I allude in case of Survivorship,—are collections of letters &c. since I was 16 years old—contained in the trunks in the care of Mr. Hobhouse.——This collection is at least doubled by those I have now here; all received since my last Ostracism. To these I should wish the Editor to have access—*not* for the purpose—of *abusing confidences*—nor of *hurting* the feelings of correspondents living—or the memories of the dead—but there are things which would do neither—that I have left unnoticed or unexplained—& which (like all such things) Time only can permit to be noticed or explained—though some are to my credit. The task will of course require delicacy—but that will not be wanting if Moore and Hobhouse survive me—and I may add— yourself—and that you may all three do so—is I assure you—my very sincere wish.—I am not sure that long life is desirable for one of my temper & constitutional depression of Spirits—which of course I

---

[5] The reference is to Cuvier's "Essay on the Theory of the Earth", translated in 1813 by Robert Kerr.

216

suppress in society—but which breaks out when alone—& in my writings in spite of myself. It has been deepened perhaps by some long past events (I do not allude to my marriage &c. on the contrary *that* raised them by the persecution giving a fillip to my Spirits) but I call it constitutional—as I have reason to think it.—You know—or you do *not* know—that my maternal Grandfather (a very clever man & amiable I am told) was strongly suspected of Suicide———(he was found drowned in the Avon at Bath) and that another very near relative of the same branch—took poison—& was merely saved by antidotes.———For the first of these events—there was no apparent cause—as he was rich, respected—& of considerable intellectual resources—hardly forty years of age—& not at all addicted to any un-hinging vice.— It was however but a strong suspicion—owing to the manner of his death—& to his melancholy temper.———The *second had* a cause—but it does not become me to touch upon it;—it happened when I was far too young to be aware of it—& I never heard of it till after the death of that relative—many years afterwards.—I think then that I may call this dejection—*constitutional.*———I had always been told that in *temper* I more resembled my maternal Grandfather than any of my *father's* family———that is in the gloomier part of his temper —for he was what you call a good natured man, and I am not.—

The Journal here I sent by Mawman to Moore the other day—but as it is a mere diary only *parts* of it would ever do for publication.—— The other Journal of the tour in 1816—I should think Augusta might let you have a copy of—but her nerves have been in such a state since 1815—that there is no knowing.———Lady Byron's people and Ly. Caroline Lamb's people—and a parcel of that set—got about her, & frightened her with all sorts of hints & menaces—so that she has never since been able to write to *me* a *Clear common letter*—and is so full of mysteries and miseries—that I can only sympathize—without always understanding her.—All my loves too make a point of calling upon her—which puts her into a flutter (no difficult matter) and the year before last I think Lady F[rances] W[edderburn] W[ebster] mar-ched in upon her—& Lady O[xford] a few years ago spoke to her at a party—and these and such like calamities have made her afraid of her shadow.———It is a very odd fancy that they all take to her———it was only six months ago—that I had some difficulty in preventing the Countess G[uiccioli] from invading her with an Italian letter.—I should like to have seen Augusta's face with an Etruscan Epistle—& all it's Meridional style of "issimas" and other superlatives—before her.—

I am much mortified that Gifford don't take to my new dramas—to be sure they are as opposite to the English drama as one thing can be to another—but I have a notion that if understood they will in time find favour (though *not* on the stage) with the reader.——The Simplicity of plot is intentional—and the avoidance of *rant* also—as also the compression of the Speeches in the more severe situations.—What I seek to show in "the Foscari's" is the *suppressed* passions—rather than the rant of the present day.——For that matter

> "Nay if thou'lt mouthe
> I'll rant as well as thou"—[1]

would not be difficult—as I think I have shown in my younger productions—*not dramatic* ones to be sure.—But as I said before I am mortified that Gifford don't like them—but I see no remedy——our notions on the subject being so different.—How is he? well I hope—let me know.—I regret his demur the more that he has been always my grand patron and I know no praise which would compensate me in my own mind for his censure.—I do not mind *reviews* as I can work them at their own weapons.

yrs. ever & truly
B

P.S.—By the way—on our next settlement (which will take place with Mr. Kinnaird) you will please to deduct the various sums for *books*—packages *received* and *sent*—the *bust*—tooth-powder &c. &c. expended by you on my account.——Hobhouse in his preface to "Rimini" will probably be better able to explain my dramatic system—than I could do—as he is well acquainted with the whole thing.——It is more upon the Alfieri School than the English.——I hope that we shall not have Mr. Rogers here—there is a mean minuteness in his mind & tittle-tattle that I dislike—ever since I *found him out* (which was but slowly) besides he is not a good man——why don't he go to bed?—what does he do travelling? The Journal of 1814 I dare say Moore will give or a copy.—Has "Cain" (the dramatic third attempt) arrived yet? Let me know.—Address to me at *Pisa*—whither I am going.——The reason is that all my Italian friends here have been exiled and are met there for the present—and I go to join them, as agreed upon for the Winter.——

[1] *Hamlet*, Act V, scene 1.

After the stanza on Grattan,[1] concluding with "His soul o'er the freedom implored and denied," will it please you to cause insert the following "Addenda," which I dreamed of during to-day's Siesta:

Ever glorious Grattan! &c. &c. &c.

I will tell you what to do. Get me twenty copies of the whole carefully and privately printed off, as *your* lines were on the Naples affair. Send me *six*, and distribute the rest according to your own pleasure.

I am in a fine vein, "so full of pastime and prodigality!"—So here's to your health in a glass of grog. Pray write, that I may know by return of post—address to me at Pisa. The gods give you joy!

Where are you? in Paris? Let us hear. You will take care that there be no printer's name, nor author's, as in the Naples stanza, at least for the present.

[TO JOHN MURRAY]   *Ravenna Septr. 24th. 1821*

Dear Murray/—I have been thinking over our late correspondence and wish to propose the following articles for our future.—1stly— That you shall write to me of yourself—of the health wealth and welfare of all friends—but of *me* (*quoad me*) little or nothing.— 2dly—That you shall send me Soda powders—tooth-paste—tooth-brushes—or any such anti-odontalgic or chemical articles as heretofore "ad libitum" upon being re-imbursed for the same.— 3dly—That you shall *not* send me any modern or (as they are called) *new* publications in *English*—whatsoever—save and excepting any writing prose or verse of (or reasonably presumed to be of) Walter Scott — Crabbe — Moore — Campbell — Rogers — Gifford — Joanna Baillie—*Irving* (the American) Hogg—Wilson (Isle of Palms Man) or any especial *single* work of fancy which is thought to be of considerable merit.—*Voyages* and *travels*—provided that they are *neither in Greece Spain Asia Minor Albania nor Italy* will be welcome—having travelled the countries mentioned—I know that what is said of them can convey nothing further which I desire to know about them.—No other *English* works whatsoever.—— 4thly—That you send me *no periodical works* whatsoever—*no* Edin-burgh—Quarterly—Monthly—nor any Review—Magazine—News-paper English or foreign of any description——

[1] In *The Irish Avatar.*

5thly—That you send me *no* opinions whatsoever either *good*—*bad*—or *indifferent*—of yourself or your friends or others—concerning any work or works of mine—past—present—or to come.—

6thly—That all Negotiations in matters of business between you and me pass through the medium of the Hon[oura]ble Douglas Kinnaird—my friend and trustee, or Mr. Hobhouse—as "Alter Ego" and tantamount to myself during my absence.—or presence.——

Some of these propositions may at first seem strange—but they are founded.—The quantity of trash I have received as books is incalculable, and neither amused nor instructed.—Reviews & Magazines—are at the best but ephemeral & superficial reading—*who thinks* of the *grand article* of *last year* in any *given review?* in the next place—if they regard *myself*—they tend to increase *Egotism*,—if favourable—I do not deny that the praise *elates*—and if unfavourable that the abuse *irritates*—the latter may conduct me to inflict a species of Satire—which would neither do good to you nor to your friends—*they* may smile *now*, and so may *you* but if I took you all in hand—it would not be difficult to cut you up like gourds. I did as much by as powerful people at nineteen years old—& I know little as yet in three & thirty—which should prevent me from making all your ribs—Gridirons for your hearts—if such were my propensity.—But it is *not*.—Therefore let me hear none of your provocations—if anything occurs so very *gross* as to require my notice—I shall hear of it from my personal friends.—For the rest—I merely request to be left in ignorance.—

The same applies to opinions *good*—*bad* or *indifferent* of persons in conversation or correspondence; these do not *interrupt* but they *soil* the *current* of my *Mind*;—I am sensitive enough—but *not* till I am *touched* & *here* I am beyond the touch of the short arms of literary England—except the few feelers of the Polypus that crawl over the Channel in the way of Extract.——All these precautions *in* England would be useless—the libeller or the flatterer would there reach me in spite of all—but in Italy we know little of literary England & think less except what reaches us through some garbled & brief extract in some miserable Gazette.——For *two years* (except two or three articles cut out & sent by *you*—by the post) I never read a newspaper—which was not forced upon me by some accident—& know upon the whole as little of England—as you all do of Italy—& God knows—*that* is little enough with all your travels &c. &c. &c.—The English travellers *know Italy* as *you* know Guernsey—how much is *that?*—If any thing occurs so violently gross or personal as to require notice, Mr. D[ougla]s Kinnaird will let me *know*—but of *praise* I desire to hear *nothing*.——

You will say—"to what tends all this?—" I will answer THAT——to keep my mind *free and* unbiased—by all paltry and personal irritabilities of praise or censure;—To let my Genius take it's natural direction,—while my feelings are like the dead—who know nothing and feel nothing of all or aught that is said or done in their regard.—— If you can observe these conditions you will spare yourself & others some pain—let me not be worked upon to rise up—for if I do—it will not be for a little;—if you can *not* observe these conditions we shall cease to be correspondents,—but *not friends*—for I shall always be yrs. ever & truly

BYRON

P.S.—I have taken these resolutions not from any irritation against *you* or *yours* but simply upon reflection that all reading either praise or censure of myself has done me harm.—When I was in Switzerland and Greece I was out of the way of hearing either—& *how I wrote there!*—In Italy I am out of the way of it too—but latterly partly through my fault—& partly through your kindness in wishing to send me the *newest* & most periodical publications—I have had a crowd of reviews &c. thrust upon me—which have bored me with their jargon of one kind or another—& taken off my attention from greater objects. ——You have also sent me a parcel of trash of poetry for no reason that I can conceive—unless to provoke me to write a new "English Bards"—Now *this* I wish to avoid—for if ever I *do*—it will be a strong production—and I desire peace as long as the fools will keep their nonsense out of my way.——

[TO DOUGLAS KINNAIRD]   *25th. Septr. 1821*

My dear Douglas/—The enclosed letter is for Mr. Murray— which I pray you to forward or deliver and not to play me the trick which you did with my epistle to Miss Milbanke by *not* forwarding the same.—I leave it open that you may see that the Continents are of import to me—and at the same time—presentable.——

yrs. ever & truly & affectly
B

[TO COUNTESS TERESA GUICCIOLI]   [*26 Settembre 1821*]

[Added to letter of Lega Zambelli to Countess Guiccioli]

Eccellenza P[ettegola]—"E deserto il bosco &c. &c."—non v'è più comodo per il gatto.——Lega partirà in alcuni giorni—io verso il

1 o del mese venturo.—Voglio dare del'tempo per l'arrivo del convoglio e le varie bestie della mia storia Naturale di (*non* Buffon—ma) Buffon*i*.——Saluto teneramente la tua P[ette]lezza e sono colle solite riverenze alle altre due Eccellenze dell' Eccellenza vostra

umilissimo divotissimo oblig.mo &c. issimo Servitore

[Scrawl]

P.S.—Capisco poco del' odio vostro per una città dove non siete mai stata perseguitata—e dove foste nata.—Se *io* non amo il *mio* paese—v'è piu di una ragione, come la vostra E[ccellenza] sa bene. Per il resto io parto perche lo volete—ma vi prevengo che sarà ben' difficile che io non torno qui—colla prima occasione, e dopo poco tempo.——

[TRANSLATION]   [*September 26th. 1821*]

Goss[ip] Excellency—
"The wood is desolate," etc. etc.—there's no comfort left for a cat.
——

Lega will leave in a few days, I towards the first of next month. I want to leave in time for the convoy to arrive and the various animals of my Natural History—of, not Buffon, but Buffoon. I greet Your Gossip tenderly. I am, with the usual bows to the other two Excellencies,

Your most humble, devoted, obliged, etc. Servant

P.S.—I cannot understand your hatred for a town where you have never been persecuted and where you were born. If *I* do not love *my* country—there is more than one reason, as your Excellency well knows. As to the rest, I am leaving because *you* wish me to—but I warn you that it is very improbable that I shall not return here—at the first opportunity—and before long.

[TO DOUGLAS KINNAIRD]   *Septr. 27th. 1821*

My dear Douglas/—How am I to understand you? you have written to me letter after letter—saying that M[urray] offers too little—and when I decline an offer you write to me to accept it.—I think that you have not found me often acting contrary to your advice in matters of business—but could not you contrive to make it a little *consistent*? I have declined the offer—& I still think it inadequate.—Besides—I have since sent another poem ("Cain") which (barring accidents) may by this time have arrived.—You say I am not writing on a *"certainty"*[;] why no unpublished work ever can or will be other than a *chance* (like all other things) there is no lottery more hazardous than literature—but why did not *you* say all this before?—

The *former Juans* sold (I am *told*) very greatly—but perhaps this might be in the *pirated* editions—but *whose* fault was that? the *publisher's* for not putting *his* name on the title-page—an author may or may not put *his* own as he pleases but who ever heard of a bookseller taking the same liberty? This was Mawman's opinion himself a publisher—who called on me lately. What the *present Juans* may or may not do in the way of success I know not—nor is there yet *time* to know exactly—but you will perhaps find that they will not be thought inferior by the better judges—to the former—as to what you say of "the *women* &c."—did not this apply equally to those *before* published? Why *Murray* offered me *two* thousand for these *present cantos*!—& I let him *off* of my own account as far as regards *them*—without his asking it, but is *this* a reason that I am to do so about the plays too & the other poems?—or that he should sink *one half* of his own offer for the *Juans*? ——There is a difference between *one* & *two* thousand is there not? wide enough for us to have met in the interval without such a subsiding into units?——

I understand what you want—you want me to write a *love*-play—but this were contrary to all my principles—as well as to those of Aristotle.—I want to simplify your drama—to render it fit for the *higher* passions—& to make it more Doric and austere.—As to immediate *sale*—it is the steady *sale* of *works* by which a purchaser clears—& Murray's gains must be by the *former* purchasers buying new volumes to complete their sets.—Having said this much—I will nevertheless do as *you* like about the copy-rights—but do beg that you will put me in a *strait* line—your *present* letter is in contradiction to all the former.

D[ea]r D[ougla]s yrs ever & truly
Bɴ

P.S.—Address me at Pisa where I go to join the exiles.

P.S.—In one of your letters a few months ago—you say "M[urray] offers by far too little & when I say so—I have *good* authority for what I say—" this was of "the Doge" *after* publication—*now* you say that in any hands but *mine* it would *not* &c.——

[Beginning of letter missing]

I have just received a very inconsistent epistle from our friend *Douglas* K[innaird]—now all I ask is that he will not write contradictions of *himself* every two months.—

P.S.—Could you without trouble rummage out from my papers the first (or half) act of [a] tragedy that I began in 1815.—called "*Werner*"[1] —Make Murray cut out "the German's tale" in Lee's Canterbury tales (the subject of the drama)—& send me both by the post—they will come in a letter like the proofs—I am determined to make a struggle for the more regular drama—without encouragement—for Murray & his Synod do nothing but throw cold water on what I have done hitherto.—But they may be damned for aught that I mind them. —On the 11th. Inst. I sent a "Manfred" sort of thing called "Cain"— has he shown it to you?—Of course I write for the reader & not for the stage—so—no need of "Mr. Upton"[2]—I have also sent him a letter (enclosed to D[ouglas] K[innaird]) requesting him to send me no more reviews either of *praise* or censure—nor opinions of any sort from him or his friends—the fact is—that they irritate & take off one's attention which may be better employed than in listening to either libels or flatteries. I have begged this of him—under pains and penalties of another "English Bards &c."—my Bile could easily make Chyle of him & his—in such a production if they don't let me alone—or at least keep me in ignorance of their prate—let them chatter or scribble—so that I neither hear nor see them—which is not likely here till they send on purpose.

[TO JOHN MURRAY]   *Septr. 27th. 1821*

Dear Murray/—Give the enclosed to Moore when he comes over— as he is about to do.—It contains something for you to look at—but *not* for publication.—Address to *Pisa.*—I thought Ricciardetto was *Rose's*—but pray thank Lord Glenbervie[1] there*for*.—He is an old & kind friend of mine—if [it] be the *old* man you mean.—Is the young

---

[1] *Werner* was based on "Kruitzner, or the German's Tale" by Harriet Lee, published in a collection called *The Canterbury Tales* by Harriet and Sophia Lee.

[2] William Upton wrote songs for Astley's Circus. See Byron's ballad in his letter of April 11, 1818, to Murray., note 2 (Vol. 6, p. 27.)

[1] Lord Glenbervie translated *The First Canto of Ricciardetto* from the Italian of Forteguerri. It was privately printed, without the translator's name, in 1821, and was published with Glenbervie's name as translator in 1822.

one dead or alive?—I mean the "modern Greek"[2]—Frederick S. Douglas?—Moore & you can settle between you about the "Memoranda"—*I* can only do what I can to accommodate your arrangements —as fixed between you—which I shall do readily & Cheerfully.—

yrs. in haste
[Scrawl]

P.S.—Is "Cain" arrived?—He was sent on the 11th in *three packets*.—Did you get a new Italian account of M[arino] Faliero's Conspiracy for a note—sent two months ago by the post? & printed for the first time?——

[TO THOMAS MOORE]   *September 27th, 1821*

It was not Murray's fault. I did not send the MS. *overture*,[1] but I send it now, and it may be restored;—or, at any rate, you may keep the original, and give any copies you please. I send it, as written, and as I *read* it to you—I have no other copy.

By last week's *two* posts, in two packets, I sent to your address, at *Paris*, a longish poem upon the late Irishism of your countrymen in their reception of * * * [the King]. Pray, have you received it? It is in "the high Roman fashion,"[2] and full of ferocious phantasy. As *you* could not well take up the matter with Paddy (being of the same nest), I have;—but I hope still that I have done justice to his great men and his good heart. As for * * * [Castlereagh] you will find it laid on with a trowel. I delight in your "fact historical"[3]—*is* it a fact?

Yours, &c.

P.S.—You have not answered me about Schlegel—why not? Address to me at Pisa, whither I am going, to join the exiles—a pretty numerous body, at present. Let me hear how you are, and what you mean to do. Is there no chance of your recrossing the Alps? If the G.

---

[2] Lord Glenbervie's son, the Hon. Frederick Sylvester North Douglas, had published an *Essay on Certain Points of Resemblance between the Ancient and Modern Greeks* in 1813. He died in 1819.

[1] The caustic stanzas on Wellington were withheld by Byron from the third canto of *Don Juan*, but they were put at the opening of Canto 9, published by John Hunt.

[2] *Antony and Cleopatra*, Act IV, scene 13.

[3] Perhaps the story told in Moore's diary for August 23, 1821. Sir E. Nagle announced the death of Napoleon to George IV, saying, "I have the pleasure to tell your Majesty that your bitterest enemy is dead." The king replied, "No! is she, by God?" thinking he meant the Queen.

Rex marries again, let him not want an Epithalamium—suppose a joint concern of you and me, like Sternhold and Hopkins![4]

[TO RICHARD BELGRAVE HOPPNER]   [*Sept. 28? 1821*]

[Written on letter of the Prioress of the Convent at Bagnacavallo]
Apropos of Epistles—I enclose you *two*—one from the Prioress of a Convent—& the other from my daughter her pupil—which is sincere enough but not very flattering—for she wants to see me because it "is the fair" to get some paternal Gingerbread—I suppose.[1]—

[TO JOHN MURRAY]   *Septr. 28th. 1821*

Dear Moray/—I add another cover to request you to ask Moore to obtain (if possible) my letters to the late Lady Melbourne from Lady Cowper.—They are very numerous & ought to have been restored long ago—as I was ready to give back Lady M's in exchange—these latter are in Mr. Hobhouse's custody with my other papers & shall be punctually restored if required.—I did not choose before to apply to Lady Cowper—as ⟨the subject of⟩ her mother's death naturally kept me from intruding upon her feelings at the time of it's occurrence.— Some years have now elapsed—& it is essential that I should have my own epistles.——They are essential as confirming that part of the "Memoranda" which refer to the two periods (1812—& 1814) when my marriage with her niece was in contemplation—& will tend to show what my real views and feelings were upon that subject—which have been so variously represented.——You need not let *this motive* be stated to Ly. C[owpe]r—as it in no degree concerns *her* particularly!— but *if* they refuse to give them up—(or keep back *any*—recollect— that they are in *great quantity*) it would become the duty of the Editor and my Executors to refer to parts of Lady Melbourne's letters—so that the thing is as broad as it is long.——They involve also many other topics—which may or may not be referred to—according to the discretion of Moore &c. when the time comes.——

[4] Sixteenth-century versifiers of the Psalms.
[1] On the back of the Prioress's letter Allegra wrote in a large copybook hand: "Caro il mio Pappa—Essendo tempo di Fiera desidererei tanto una Visita del mio Pappa, che ho' molte voglie da levarmi, non vorrà compiacere la sua Allegrina che l'ho ama tanto?" ["My dear Papa—It being fair time I should so much like a visit from my Papa, as I have many desires to satisfy, will you not please your Allegrina who loves you so?"]

You need not be alarmed[;] the *"fourteen years"*[1] will hardly elapse without some mortality amongst us—it is a long lease of life to speculate upon.—So your Cent per Cent Shylock Calculation will not be in so much peril, as the "Argosie" will sink before that time—and "the pound of flesh" be withered previously to yr. being so long out of a return.—I also wish to give you a hint or two (as you have really behaved very handsomely to M[oore] in the business—and are a fine fellow in your line) for yr. advantage.—*If* by yr. own management you can extract any of my epistles from Ly. Caroline Lamb (mind she don't give you *forgeries* in my *hand*; she has done as much you *know* before now) they might be of use in yr. collection—(sinking of course the *names*—& *all such circumstances* as might hurt *living* feelings—or *those* of *survivors*—) they treat of more topics than love occasionally. ——As to those to other correspondents (female &c.) there are plenty scattered about in the world—but how to direct you to recover them— I know not——most of them have kept them, I hear at least that Ly. O[xford]—& F[rances] W[ebster] have kept theirs—but these letters are of course inaccessible—(& perhaps not desirable) as well as those of some others.—I will tell you—who may *happen* to have some letters of mine—in their possession—Lord Powerscourt—some to his late brother—Mr. Long of—(I forget the place) but the father of Edward Long of the Guards, who was drowned in going to Lisbon early in 1809. Miss Elizabeth Pigot of Southwell—Notts (she *may* be *Mistress* by this time for she had more years than I) *they* were *not* love-letters— so that you might have them without scruple.——There are or might be some to the late Revd. J. C. Tattersall—in the hands of his brother (half-brother) Mr. Wheatley—who resides near Canterbury I think.——There are some to Charles Gordon—now of Dulwich— and some few to Mrs. Chaworth—but these latter are probably destroyed or inaccessible.——All my letters to Lady B[yron]—before and since her marriage—are in her possession—as well as her own which I sent to her—she had not the courtesy to restore me *mine*— but never mind——though they were too much to my credit—for her to give them back—we can do without them.—

I mention these people and particulars—merely as *chances*—most of them have probably destroyed the letters—which in fact were of little import—most of them written when very young—& several at School & College.——Peel (the *second* brother of the Secretary) was a

1 Murray had written on Sept. 6, 1821, that the £2000 paid to Moore for Byron's Memoirs if placed in the funds, would become £4000 in fourteen years. The implication was that he had been generous to Moore.

correspondent of mine—and also Porter the son of the Bishop of Clogher——Lord Clare—a very voluminous one——William Harness (a friend of Jew Milman's) another—Charles Drummond (son of the Banker)—William Bankes (the Voyager)—your friend R. C. Dallas Esqre.;—Hodgson—Henry Drury—Hobhouse—you were already aware of.——I have gone through this long list[2] of the

> "cold, the faithless—and the dead"[3]

because I know that like "the curious in fish sauce[''][4] you are a researcher of such things.—Besides these—there are other occasional ones to literary men—& so forth—complimentary &c. &c. & not worth much more than the rest.—There are some hundreds too of Italian notes of mine—scribbled with a noble contempt of the grammar and dictionary & in very English Etruscan—for I speak Italian very fluently but write it carelessly & incorrectly to a degree.

[TO THOMAS MOORE]   *September 29th, 1821*

I send you two rough things, prose[1] and verse,[2] not much in themselves, but which will show, one of them, the state of the country, and the other, of your friend's mind, when they were written. Neither of them were sent to the person concerned, but you will see, by the style of them, that they were sincere, as I am in signing myself

Yours ever and truly,

B

[TO THOMAS MOORE]   *September—no—October 1, 1821*

I have written to you lately, both in prose and verse, at great length, to Paris and London. I presume that Mrs. Moore, or whoever is your Paris deputy, will forward my packets to you in London.

I am setting off for Pisa, if a slight incipient intermittent fever do not prevent me. I fear it is not strong enough to give Murray much chance

---

[2] Moore used this list as a guide when he was gathering letters for his biography of Byron.

[3] Scott, *The Lady of the Lake*, Canto I, stanza 33.

[4] Unidentified.

[1] The prose thing was a letter to Lady Byron, from which Moore printed extracts (See March 1, 1821, to Lady Byron.)

[2] On hearing that Lady Byron was patroness of an annual Charity Ball, Byron wrote some lines of verse complaining that "the saint keeps her charity back for 'the Ball' ". Moore (II, 540) printed two stanzas.

of realising his thirteens again. I hardly should regret it, I think, provided you raised your price upon him—as what Lady Holderness (my sister's grandmother, a Dutchwoman) used to call Augusta, her *Residee Legatoo*—so as to provide for us all: *my* bones with a splendid and larmoyante edition, and you with double what is extractable during my lifetime.

I have a strong presentiment that (bating some out of the way accident) you will survive me. The difference of eight years, or whatever it is, between our ages, is nothing. I do not feel (nor am, indeed, anxious to feel) the principle of life in me tend to longevity. My father and mother died, the one at thirty-five or six, and the other at forty-five; and Dr. Rush, or somebody else, says that nobody lives long, without having *one parent*, at least, an old stager.

I *should*, to be sure, like to see out my eternal mother-in-law, not so much for her heritage, but from my natural antipathy. But the indulgence of this natural desire is too much to expect from the Providence who presides over old women. I bore you with all this about lives, because it has been put in my way by a calculation of insurances which Murray has sent me. I *really think* you should have more, if I evaporate within a reasonable time.

I wonder if my "Cain" has got safe to England. I have written since about sixty stanzas of a poem, in octave stanzas (in the Pulci style, which the fools in England think was invented by Whistlecraft— it is as old as the hills in Italy) called "The Vision of Judgment, by Quevedo[1] Redivivus," with this motto—

> "A Daniel come to *judgment*, yea, a Daniel:
> I thank thee, Jew, for teaching me that word."[2]

In this it is my intent to put the said George's Apotheosis in a Whig point of view, not forgetting the Poet Laureate for his preface and his other demerits.[3]

I am just got to the pass where Saint Peter, hearing that the royal defunct had opposed Catholic Emancipation, rises up and, interrupting

---

[1] Byron chose for his pseudonym the name of the great Spanish satirist Francisco Gomez de Quevedo y Villegas (1580–1645), whose *Sueños* (*Visions*) ridiculed the vices and foibles of the Spanish court. Quevedo's first "Vision", *Sueno de las Cavalleras* is a story of the Last Judgment.

[2] *Merchant of Venice*, Act. IV, scene 1. Byron has brought together two separate passages, lines 221 and 340.

[3] The preface to Southey's *A Vision of Judgment*, his poet-laureate apotheosis of George III, contained an oblique attack on Byron as the leader of the "Satanic school" of poetry.

Satan's oration, declares *he* will change places with Cerberus sooner than let him into heaven, while *he* has the keys thereof.

I must go and ride, though rather feverish and chilly. It is the ague season; but the agues do me rather good than harm. The feel after the *fit* is as if one had got rid of one's body for good and all.

The gods go with you!—Address to Pisa.

Ever yours.

P.S.—Since I came back I feel better, though I stayed out too late for this malaria season, under the thin crescent of a very young moon, and got off my horse to walk in an avenue with a Signora for an hour. I thought of you and

> "When at eve thou rovest
> By the star thou lovest."[4]

But it was not in a romantic mood, as I should have been once; and yet it was a *new* woman, (that is, new to me,) and, of course, expected to be made love to. But I merely made a few common-place speeches. I feel as your poor friend Curran said, before his death, "a mountain of lead upon my heart,"[5] which I believe to be constitutional, and that nothing will remove it but the same remedy.

[TO DOUGLAS KINNAIRD]   *R[avenn]a Octr. 4th. 1821*

My dear Douglas/—All I can say is that yr. present opinion & counsels are opposite diametrically to what they were two months ago. —At present the face of the negociation is changed by the addition of the drama of "Cain" (supposing it to have arrived safely) sent the 11th of Septr. to A[lbemarle] Street.—By this post also another poem (which *you* will like—if nobody else does) will be forwarded—it is a "Vision of Judgment" in a Whig point of view to cut up the Renegade Southey, & his Nightmare, with the same title.—You sent by mistake yr. brother's letter—to *me*—with *Ravenna* on the cover—I opened it by mistake—but have forwarded it with an explanation.——

yrs. ever
[Scrawl]

P.S.—The funds—and the Attorneo? eh.—There is another way of settling the matter.——This would be to run the risk with the

---

[4] Moore's *Irish Melodies*, No. 1.

[5] In the depression of his last days, Curran, the Irish patriot, complained of having "a mountain of lead upon his heart". He died, Oct. 14, 1817.

publisher—and *divide* expences *hazard* & *profits.*—The booksellers always *discourage* this—& when it is tried—contrive to keep back the sale—and to so manage the accounts so [sic] as to make the authors ostensibly losers.—The duration of copyright is *eight and twenty years.*—I presume that *you* will not say—that if I had gone *halves* in expence & profit with the bookseller upon *my works since 1812*—that I should not have obtained much more than I *have* done—without counting the years yet to run (that is *twenty* more) of the copyright. ——It is true at first I should have received much less—but upon the *whole* what should I have made?—The price now offered me is not a *hundred* per year of the eight & twenty years.—Do you mean to say that I should not average this?—or let it be thus—*I* pay the expence— & take the profits?—— Is a *month's* sale of D[on] J[uan] a fair proof of the eight & twenty years profit?—& yet upon *this* you decide—not very positively—for your opinions vary——In all probability instead of the two thousand guineas I should not (between trick & damping the sale to force me into a contract) obtain *three hundred* for the first year—but if I only obtained *one hundred* a year for the eight & twenty —it is eight hundred more than the offer.—I will *not* accept this offer, unless *you* have *pledged* yourself for *me*—in that case I will—as in honour fitting & proper.—Recollect that there are now above fourteen thousand lines of mine unpublished (except the late Juans) in M[urray]'s hands—these will make *three volumes*—and no temporary damp nor trickery of *booksellers* will make me throw away my time or my talent, till I have a satisfactory reason.——Just think over what I have said calmly and *bankerly*—and compute what I should have made (barring *trickery*) by halving expences & profits with the publisher for the last *eight* years? and there are *twenty* more to run of the *oldest* copyright. The difficulty would be to get them to give a *true* account— & not to play tricks to force a contract—otherwise—as a man of business—*you* well know the result.—As it is—I will try the experiment rather than submit—though it will be a great temporary inconvenience.—As to the plays—you have not read but *one* & can't judge yet till they are published.

[TO LORD KINNAIRD]   *R[avenn]a Octr. 4th. 1821*

My dear Kinnaird/—The address of the enclosed will explain how it came here—& how it came to be opened.——There was no cover.— It was brought to me in bed with my other letters—& I had opened it at the same time with my eyes—without looking at the address.——

The first words showed me to *whom* it was directed—but not *where*—and I send it to Milan—still uncertain whether you are yet returned from Naples.——If you will let me have a line to say that it has had no further adventures—direct to me at *Pisa*—where I am going to join the Exiles from hence—as usual—they have been proscribed for having dreamt of *liberty*.——All my friends are amongst the number—and I am to join them there for the winter.—Let me hear that you prosper—and believe me

ever & truly yrs
[Scrawl]

[TO JOHN MURRAY]   *Octr. 4th. 1821*

Dear Murray/—I send you in 8 sheets and 106 stanzas (octave) a poem entitled a "Vision of Judgment["] &c. by Quevedo redivivus—of which you will address the proof to me at *Pisa*—and an answer by return of post.—Pray—let the Printer be as careful as he can to decypher it—which may be not so easy.——It may happen that you will be afraid to publish it—in that case find me a publisher—assuring him —that if he gets into a scrape I will give up *my name* or person. I do not approve of your mode of not putting publisher's names on title pages—(which was unheard of—till *you* gave yourself that *air*)—an author's case is different—and from time immemorial have published anonymously.——I wait to hear the arrival of various packets.

yrs. [Scrawl]

Address to *Pisa*.——

[TO DOUGLAS KINNAIRD]   *Octr. 5th. 1821*

P.S. 2d.—Excuse this [illegible word]—but I forgot to mention that there is a bill of Murray's for books & other things—which we will deduct at our next settlement.—Don't omit this.—The plan I hinted at in my letter would be best for a man of clear finances—but as mine will probably never be so (unless I survive Lady Noel) the former mode of selling the copyright may be the more eligible—particularly as the booksellers always do all they can to stop the sale in the other case—because the profits are not completely *their own* and *they* can *keep* back a sale—& forward one upon occasion—but this is one of *their* mysteries —which are manifold. You know *now*—what of mine is in M[urray]'s hands—and I wish to know what we are to expect for the whole, including "Cain" & what is sent by this post ("the Vision" which I wish *you* to look at—you and Hobhouse will like it—I think) and "entre nous"—the *next* poem I write—I shall publish anonymously & with another publisher————though probably with far *less* profit—at the outset;—but I am not *bound* to M[urray]—nor do I wish to burthen him with too many of my lucubrations—especially as by what he says and you hint—they are not likely to succeed as heretofore.———— I have had more than one proposition from respectable men of "the trade" before to-day————and shall turn my eyes that way—in my next attempts————but without my name as I do not wish to hurt M[urray]'s feelings in any way—and it might look like a curtness between us.————

My dearest Augusta/—Has there been nothing to make it grey? to be sure the *years* have not.————Your parcel will not find me here—I am going to *Pisa*—for the winter.—The late political troubles here have occasioned the exile of all my friends & connections—& I am going there to join them.—You know or you do *not* know that Madame La Comtesse G[uiccioli] was separated from her husband last year (on account of P. P. Clerk of this parish) that the Pope decided in her favour & gave her a separate maintenance & that we lived very quietly & decently—she at her father's (as the Pope decided) and I at home— till this Summer.—When her father was exiled—she was obliged either to accompany him or retire into a Convent—such being the terms of his Holiness's deed of divorcement.————They went to Pisa— by my recommendation & there I go to join them.————So there's a *romance* for you—I assure you it was not my wish nor fault altogether —her husband was old—rich—& must have left her a large jointure in a few years—but he was jealous—& insisted &c. & *she* like all the rest—*would* have her own way.—You know that all my loves go crazy—and make scenes—and so—"She is the sixteenth Mrs. Shuffleton".[1]————Being very young—very romantic—and odd—and being contradicted by her husband besides—& being of a country where morals are no better than in England—(though elopements and divorces are rare—and this made an uncommon noise—the first that had occurred at Ravenna for two hundred years—that is in a *public* way with appeals to the Pope &c.) you are not to wonder much

[1] In George Colman the Younger's *John Bull*, Act III, Shuffleton says: ". . . she is to be the fifteenth Mrs. Shuffleton".

at it;—she being too a beauty & the great Belle of the four Legations—
and married not quite a year (at our first acquaintance) to a man
forty years older than herself—who had had two wives already—& a
little suspected of having poisoned his first.——

We have been living hitherto decently & quietly—these things here
do not exclude a woman from all society as in yr. hypocritical country.
——It is very odd that all my *fairs* are such romantic people—and
always daggering or divorcing—or making scenes.——But this is
"positively the last time of performance" (as the play-bills say) or of
my getting into such scrapes for the future.—Indeed—I have had my
share.—But this is a finisher—for you know when a woman is
separated from her husband for her Amant—he is bound both by
honour (and inclination at least I am) to live with her all his days, as
long as there is no misconduct.—So you see that I have closed as papa
begun——and you will probably never see me again as long as you
live.—Indeed you don't deserve it—for having behaved so *coldly*—
⟨when I was ready to have sacrificed every thing for you—and after
you had taken the farther . . . always⟩—It is nearly three years that
this "liaison" has lasted——I was dreadfully in love—and she blindly
so—for she has sacrificed every thing to this headlong passion.—That
comes of being romantic—I can say that without being so *furiously* in
love as at first—I am more attached to her—than I thought it possible
to be to any woman after three years—⟨except one & who was she
you can guess⟩ and have not the least wish—nor prospect of separation
from her.—She herself—(and it is now a year since her separation a
year too of all kinds of vicissitudes &c.) is still more decided—of
course the *step* was a decisive one.—If Lady B[yron] would but please
to die—and the Countess G[uiccioli]'s husband—(for Catholics can't
marry though divorced) we should probably have to marry—though
I would rather *not*—thinking it the way to hate each other—for all
people whatsoever.——However—you must not calculate upon seeing
me again in a hurry, if ever.——How have you sent the *parcel*—& how
am I to receive it at Pisa?—I am anxious about the Seal—not about
Hodgson's nonsense—what is the fool afraid of the *post* for? it is the
safest—the only *safe* conveyance—they never meddle but with political
packets.

yrs. [Scrawl]

P.S.—*You* ought to be a great admirer of the *future* Lady B. for
three reasons. 1stly. She is a grand patroness of the *present* Lady B.—
and always says "that she had no doubt that she was exceedingly

ill-used by me["]—2dly. She is an admirer of yours—and I have had great difficulty in keeping her from writing to you eleven pages—(for she is a grand Scribe) and 3dly. she having read "Don Juan" in a *French* translation—made me promise to write *no more* of it—declaring that it was abominable &c. &c.—that *Donna Inez* WAS meant for Ly. B.—& in short made me vow *not* to continue it—(*this* occurred lately & since the last cantos were sent to England last year) is not this altogether odd enough?—She has a good deal of *us* too—I mean that turn for ridicule like Aunt Sophy and you and I & all the B's. Desire Georgiana to write me a letter I suppose she can by this time.—Opened by me—and the Seal taken off—so—don't accuse the post-office without cause

B—that's a sign—a written one where the wax was.

[Postscript to a letter from Lega Zambelli to Countess Guiccioli]

A[mo]r Mio—Saressimo partiti in questa settimana se non fosse per l'incertezza cagionata da questa voce adesso generale del' nuovo esiglio dei Romagnoli in Toscana che mi veniva anche detto dal Zio Cavalli.——Fammi sapere la verità—e come debbo regolarmi (si è vero) per trovarci insieme.—Credimi sempre

> tutto tuo
> [Scrawl]

My Love—We should have left this week, had it not been for the uncertainty caused by the rumour, which has now become general, about a new exile of the Romagnoli in Tuscany, which was told me by Uncle Cavalli.——Tell me the truth—and what I shall do (if it is true) so that we may meet. Believe me always—all yours—

Dear Moray/—Please to present ye. inclosed to Mr. Moore.——Also please to acknowledge by next post the arrival of a packet containing "the Vision" &c. which is sent to you with this—that is—by the same post.——Address to *Pisa.*

> yrs. [Scrawl]

By this post I have sent my nightmare to balance the incubus of * * * [Southey]'s impudent anticipation of the Apotheosis of George the Third. I should like you to take a look over it, as I think there are two or three things in it which might please "our puir hill folk."[1]

By the last two or three posts I have written to you at length. My *ague* bows to me every two or three days, but we are not as yet upon intimate speaking terms. I have an intermittent generally every two years, when the climate is favourable (as it is here), but it does me no harm. What I find worse, and cannot get rid of, is the growing depression of my spirits, without sufficient cause. I ride—I am not intemperate in eating or drinking—and my general health is as usual, except a slight ague, which rather does good than not. It must be constitutional; for I know nothing more than usual to depress me to that degree.

How do *you* manage? I think you told me, at Venice, that your spirits did not keep up without a little claret. I *can* drink, and bear a good deal of wine (as you may recollect in England); but it don't exhilarate—it makes me savage and suspicious, and even quarrelsome. Laudanum has a similar effect; but I can take much of *it* without any effect at all. The thing that gives me the highest spirits (it seems absurd, but true) is a dose of *salts*—I mean in the afternoon, after their effect. But one can't take *them* like champagne.

Excuse this old woman's letter; but my *lemancholy* don't depend upon health, for it is just the same, well or ill, or here or there.

Yours, &c.

Dear Moray/—You will please to present or convey the enclosed poem[1] to Mr. Moore,—I sent him another copy to Paris—but he has probably left that city.—It is doubtful whether the poem was written by Felicia Hemans[2] for the prize of the Dartmoor Academy—or by the Revd. W. L. Bowles with a view to a bishopric—your own great discernment will decide between them. By last post I sent the "Vision of Judgment by Quevedo Redivivus"—I just piddle a little with these trifles to keep my hand in for the New "English Bards &c." which I

---

[1] "Our puir hill folk" in Scott's *Waverley* were the Covenanting Whigs.

[1] *The Irish Avatar.*

[2] The sentimental poetess, who enjoyed much fame in her day, was frequently the butt of Byron's wit and sarcasm.

perceive some of your people are in want of—and which I only wait for a short visit to your country to put me more in possession of the nonsense of some of your *newer* ragamuffins—to commence.—I have *not* sought it—but if I *do* begin—it shall go hard—as Shylock says—"but I better the Instruction".[3]——

yrs. ever [scrawl]

P.S.—If there is anything new of *Israeli's*—send it me.—I like Israeli—1stly. he "having done the handsome thing by me" as Winifred Jenkins says,[4] when you showed him (you shabby fellow)! my marginal notes in Athens upon his essay—instead of being angry like a spoilt child of ink and paper—and 2dly. because he is the Bayle of literary speculation—and puts together more amusing information than anybody—& 3dly. he likes *Pope*.—Don't forget to send me my first act of "Werner" (if Hobhouse can find it amongst my papers) send it by the post (to Pisa) and also cut out Sophia Lee's "German's tale" from the "Canterbury tales" and sent [sic] it in a letter also.— I began that tragedy in 1815—but Lady Byron's farce put it out of my head for the time of her representation.—

By the way you have a good deal of my prose tracts in M.S.S. Let me have proofs of them *all* again—I mean the *controversial* ones— including the last two or three years of time. Another question? The Epistle of St. Paul which I translated from the Armenian—for what reason have you kept it back, though you published that stuff which gave rise to "the Vampire"[?] Is it because you are afraid to print anything in opposition to the Cant of the Quarterly about "Manicheism"? Let me have a proof of that Epistle directly. I am a better christian than those parsons of yours though not paid for being so.— Address to Pisa & acknowledge all packets by *name*—else it makes confusion.——

[On separate sheet]

Send. Faber's treatise on "the Cabiri"[5]

Sainte-Croix's "Mystères du Paganisme"[6]—(scarce perhaps; but to be found—as Mitford refers to his work frequently)

---

[3] *The Merchant of Venice*, Act III, scene 1

[4] At the end of Smollett's *Humphry Clinker*.

[5] George Stanley Faber (1773–1854) was an Anglican theologian. His *Dissertation on the Mysteries of the Cabiri or the Great Gods of Phoenicia* (2 vols.) was published in 1803.

[6] Guillaume Emmanuel Joseph Guilhem de Clermont-Lodève, baron de Sainte-Croix (1746–1809) published his *Recherches historiques et critiques sur les mystères de paganisme* in 1784. A second edition appeared in 1817.

A common bible of a good legible print (bound in Russia) I *have* one—
but as it was the last gift of my Sister—(whom I shall probably never
see again) I can only use it carefully—and less frequently—because
I like to keep it in good order.———Don't forget this—for I am a great
reader and admirer of those books—and had read them through &
through before I was eight years old—that is to say the *old* Testament
—for the New struck me as a task—but the other as a pleasure—I
speak as a *boy*—from the recollected impression of that period at
Aberdeen in 1796.

Any Novels of Scott or poetry of ye. same;—ditto of Crabbe—Moore
—and the Elect—but none of yr. damned common place trash—unless
something starts up of actual merit—which may very well be—for 'tis
time it should.—

Plutarch's morals[7]—&c. in the *old* English translation.—— Gillies'
Greece[8]—&c. and Interval between Alexander and Augustus (I *have*
Mitford) in Octavo if possible—I can't read quartos.——

"Life of Apollonius of Tyana,"[9] published (or translated) 8 or
nine (9) years ago.

"Leslie's Short and Easy Method with the Deists."[10] I want a
Bayle,[11] but am afraid of the carriage and the weight, as also of folios
in general.

"Burton's Anatomy of Melancholy."[12]

[TO DOUGLAS KINNAIRD]   *R[avenn]a Octr. 9th. 1821*

My dear Douglas/—By last post I sent to M[urra]y a poem called
"a Vision &c." which *see*.—By this post another—"the Irish avatar"
which *see* also—it will delight your radical soul.—You will find both

---

[7] Plutarch's *Morals* (or *Opera Moralia*) consisted of some sixty essays giving
advice on various subjects. There were several translations into English before the
nineteenth century.

[8] John Gillies (1747–1806) historical and classical scholar, published a popular
History of Greece in 1786.

[9] See May 28, 1821, to Murray.

[10] Charles Leslie (1650–1722), a non-juror and controversialist, first published
A Short and Easie Method with the Deists in 1698. Many editions followed.

[11] Pierre Bayle first published his *Dictionnaire historique et critique* in 1687.
Byron's copy, 10 vols., 1734, was sold at auction on April 5, 1816, before he left
England.

[12] Murray wrote on Nov. 14, 1821: "I have now sent you all the books you
wrote for, and amongst them your own copy of Burton, which I got at your sale."
(*LJ*, V, 392n.)

in Albemarle Street, (barring accidents)——In alluding to Murray's book-bill &c. in my last letter—I forgot to mention that it ought only to date from *Spring* 1818—it being then agreed to at *his own* request that the present of "*Beppo*" on my part—was to cancel all former stationery or book-accounts between us.—Perhaps *he* may have forgotten this—as you say in one of your *very consistent* letters—that he forgot that "the letter on Bowles['"] had been profitable—for which "he ought to have given me &c."——Whether he has forgotten or not he has never alluded to it—nor do I care.—I pray in your prosperity to think of the *funds* and of those therein and am

yours ever
[Scrawl]

P.S.—Address to *Pisa*—

[TO JOHN CAM HOBHOUSE]   ⟨*Septr*⟩ *Octr. 12th. 1821*

My dear Hobhouse/—I had written already to ask "Mr. Nisby what he thought of the Grand Vizier"[1] and of the Greeks our old acquaintances.——I think you have given Bowles his Gruel with your parody on Savage—which is certainly better than *his* parody on the *legitimate* Savage (I once saw somewhere a parallel between us) and must have put him into a fine tantrum—as for "*Argument*" "I never dispute your talents in making a Goose-pye Mrs. Primrose—so pray leave argument to me."[2]——As to the printer's errors—Oons!—what do you think of "*Adriatic* side of the Bosphorus"—of "*praise*" for "*pair*" "*precarious*" for "*precocious*" and "*case*" for "*chase*"——Mr. Murray has received a trimmer—I promise you—not without cause.— Our friend Douglas has also been seducing me into mercantile contradictions—1stly. by writing letter after letter to convince me that M[urray] never offered me *enough* for the past M.S.S.—and then when I had refused what was really an *inadequate* offer—turning round upon me and desiring me to accept it!——Now as Croaker says—"plague take it—there must be a right and a wrong"[3] and what is it?—Douglas contradicted himself so suddenly, I don't know.——However since

---

[1] These characters occur in Addison's essay in the *Spectator*, No. 317, March 4, 1711–12.

[2] *Vicar of Wakefield*, Chapter 6.

[3] Goldsmith, *The Good Natured Man*, Act IV. Croaker says: "A plague of plagues, we can't be both right."

that—I sent two more Poeshies to A[lbemarle] Street—"*Cain*", a tragedy in three acts—"a Vision of Judgement" by way of reversing Rogue Southey's—in my finest ferocious Caravaggio style—and a *third* entitled "the Irish Avatar" upon the late Irishisms of the Blarney people in Dublin.—All which I pray you to look at—I am mistaken if[these?] *two* latter are not after your own radical heart.——

Your infamous Government will drive all honest men into the necessity of reversing it——I see nothing left for it—but a republic *now*—an opinion which I have held aloof as long as it would let me.—*Come* it must—*they* do not see this—but all this driving will do it—it may not be in ten or twenty years but it is inevitable—and I am sorry for it.—When we read of the *beginnings* of revolutions in a *few* pages—it seems as if they had happened in *five* minutes—whereas *years* have always been and must be their prologues——it took from eighty eight to ninety three—to decide the French one—and the English are a tardy people.——I am so persuaded that an English one is inevitable—that I am moving Heaven and earth—(that is to say Douglas Kinnaird—and Medea's trustee) to get me out of the funds. ——I would give all I have to see the Country *fairly free*—but till I know that *giving*—or rather *losing* it—*would free* it—you will excuse my natural anxiety for my temporal affairs.——

Still I can't approve of the *ways* of the *radicals*—they seem such very low imitations of the Jacobins.—I do not allude to you and Burdett—but to the Major and to Hunt of Bristol & little Waddington[4] &c. &c. —If I came home (which I never shall) I should take a *decided* part in politics—with pen and person—& (if I could revive my English) in the house—but am not yet quite sure *what* part—except that it would *not* be in favour of these abominable tyrants.——I certainly lean towards a republic—all history—and experience is in it's favour even the French—for though they butchered thousands of Citizens at first, yet *more* were killed in any one of the great battles than ever perished by a democratical proscription.—America is a Model of force and freedom & moderation—with all the coarseness and rudeness of it's people.—I have been thinking over what you say of Italian tragedy—but have been rather surprized to find that I know very little about it—and I have so little turn for that kind of disquisition that I should only spoil your sager lucubrations.—I believe I said as much in a former letter.—

---

4 Major Cartwright, "Orator" Hunt, and Samuel F. Waddington were "Radical" politicians whom Byron considered rabble-rousers. Waddington had opposed the war with France and published Radical pamphlets.

You will make a better thing of it without me.——You enquire after
my health—it is as usual—but I am subject to great depression of
spirits—occasionally; without sufficient cause.—Preserve yours.——

yrs. ever
[Scrawl]

P.S.—Address to Pisa

P.S.—An anecdote is just come into my head—I don't know how.
Do you remember Madame Michelli at Venice?—When young she
took a fancy to Dragonetti the great fiddler——and whispered in his
ear to come to her at a certain hour on the morrow—*he* asked her "if
he was to bring his great fiddle"—& she was so shocked that she
[revoked?] her rendezvous.—Madame Benzon told me this—an
excellent authority on the *exploits* of her contemporaries.——I put
this nonsense to fill the vacant sheet up.—

[TO COUNTESS TERESA GUICCIOLI]   *R[avenn]a 12 8bre. 1821*

A[mo]r M[i]o—Ora che sei certo che vengo—la differenza di alcuni
giorni più o meno non può importare—nè dovrebbe inquietarti nulla.
—E' necessario che io aspetto un' altro ordinario (il *18* solamente) per
avere La risposta ad un' pacco spedito in Inghilterra nel' mese scorso.
—Io l'aspettava *jeri*—ma non essendo capitato—bisogna che l'attendo
questa settimana.—Se non arriva Giovedi—partirò l'istesso senza
aspettare oltre.——Per cinque giorni non abbiamo avuto che una
dirotta pioggia—altramente spedirei i miei cavalli la mattina—con
tutto ciò che le strade sono in un' stato pesante pei cavalli Olandesi—i
quali naturalmente il Cocchiere [tuo?] vuole conservare in buonà
salute [words torn out] Servitore già-Cocchiere—(ed ora non so che)
io [non p]rendeva mai impegno di riceverlo nel' servizio[mio]—nè posso
farlo senza cacciare dei miei—ciò che sarebbe un' ingiustizia—se
prima non mancono ai doveri loro.—Se questo uomo è ammalato io
farò il possibile per soccorrerlo——e poi egli sarà pagato per il
tempo che restò coi mobili—e per sue fatiche—ma non posso nè fare
nè promettere altro.—Saluta Papa e Pierino con tutta la cordialità ed
amicizia.—Sta Sana—e non esaggerare con quell'*ampollosa epistolare*
immaginazione di Santa Chiara (benedetto sia il Convento!) le cose
semplici e necessarie in mali e torti &c. &c. che non esistono se non in
tua testa romancesca o piuttosto *romantica*—poiche rovescia tutte le

regole del' pensare—per agire *alla De Stael*.—Perdonami questa predica;—nella speranza riverderti presto *sono, come son' sempre stato,* il tuo

a—a—in E.—

P.S.—Abandono Lega a tutta la tua degnissima indignazione e castighi meritati.—Farèmo di lui ciò che vuoi al' mio arrivo.——Egli partirà due o tre giorni prima di me—credo il 20mo. cioè Sabbato—ma dipenderà un' poco del' tempo per causa dei cavalli più fini.—Io penso di lasciare R[avenn]a Lunedi-otto—il 22o. del' corrente.——

[TRANSLATION]   *Ravenna. October 12th. 1821*

My Love—Now that you are certain that I am coming—a few days more or less can make no difference—nor should they upset you. It is necessary that I should wait for another post (only on the 18th) to have the answer to a packet sent to England last month. I expected it yesterday, but since it has not come, I must wait this week. If it does not arrive on Thursday I will start all the same, without delaying further. For five days we have had nothing but pouring rain—Otherwise I would have sent off my. horses this morning. With all this the roads are in an awful condition for the Dutch horses which the coachman naturally wishes to preserve in good health [torn] . . . man servant who was your coachman (and now I don't know what) I never made any promise to take him into my service and now I cannot do so—without turning out one of my own—which would be an injustice, unless first they had failed in their duties. If this man is ill J will do everything possible to come to his aid and then he shall be paid, for the time he has stayed with the furniture and for his work—but I can neither do nor promise anything more. Greet Papa and Pierino in all cordiality and friendship.

Keep well. And do not exaggerate with that turgid epistolar imagination of Santa Chiara—(blessed be the Convent) the most simple and necessary things into evils and wrongs, etc. etc., which do not exist except in your romanesque or rather *romantic* head. For it upsets all the rules of thought in order to behave *à la De Staël.* Forgive this sermon.' In the hope of seeing you again soon,

I am, as I have always been, your Friend and Lover for Ever.

P.S.—I leave Lega to your very just indignation and deserved punishment. We will do with him what you will on my arrival. He will start two or three days before me—I believe on the 20th, that is Saturday. But it will depend a little on the weather on account of the more delicate horses. I am thinking of leaving Ravenna on Monday week—the 22nd of this month.

[TO COUNT RUGGERO GAMBA] *Ravenna 19 8bre. 1821*

[Added to letter of Lega Zambelli to Count Gamba]

Caro Amico/—Con tutto ciò che Lega ha avuto due mesi 'per prepararsi'—è ancora in tutta la confusione di una *fuga* improvisa. Non ho mai visto un' animale simile per la lentezza se non sia la tartaruga. —Dentro la settimana vantata mi metterò in viaggio.——Salutate la Teresina e Pierino—e credetemi con tutta stima ed am[acizi]a

il vostro B———

P.S.—Pregate la Teresa bastonare Sigr. Lega *bene*—lo merita per tutte le ragioni.—

[TRANSLATION] *Ravenna. October 19. 1821*

Dear Friend/—For all that Lega has had two months "to prepare himself"—he is still in all the confusion of an unexpected flight. I have never seen an animal like him for slowness except for the tortoise.— Within the boasted week I shall set out on my voyage. Greet Teresa and Pietro—and believe me with all esteem and friendship

yours B———

P.S.—Ask Teresa to flog Signor Lega *well*—he merits it for every reason.

[TO COUNTESS TERESA GUICCIOLI] *8bre. 19. 1821*

Amor Mio+—Lega parte domattina senza altro.—Sarà accompagnato di tutti i Servitori della Scuderia—&c. coi cavalli e due legni. ——Io partirò dentro la settimana—verso Giovedi probabilmente. ——Ti assicuro che la lentezza e la confusione di Lega è una cosa sorprendente—oltra passando le mie idee non piccole di sue *qualità*.— Tu hai aggiunta ai varii dispiaceri che ho dovuto incontrare da qualche tempo—colle tue lagnanze &c. per la mia *non* partenza.——Io sono partito il momento che fosse possibile. Ti prego di risparmiarmi tali lagnanze che non sono nè giuste nè ragionevoli.—Sperando abbracciarti presto—sono di tutto cuore il tuo

a—a—in e.—
[Scrawl]

P.S.—Ti prego rimpro[verare] ed anche *darne* (con *quelle*) a Lega—*Bastonalo bene*—lo merita—se non fosse per la *mia insistenza* non sarebbe partito nè anche adesso.—

[TRANSLATION]   *October 19th. 1821*

My Love +—Lega leaves tomorrow, definitely.—He will be accompanied by all the grooms, etc. etc.; with the horses and two carriages.

I shall leave within the week—towards Thursday, probably. I assure you that the slowness and confusion of Lega is something astounding, surpassing my not slight opinion of his *qualities*.

You have added to the various troubles that I have had to encounter recently with your complaints, etc., about my *non*-departure. I left the moment it was possible. Pray spare me more complaints—which are neither just nor reasonable. Hoping to embrace you soon—I am with all my heart your friend and lover for ever.

P.S.—Pray scold and even *beat* (with those) Lega. Beat him well he deserves it—if it were not for my *insistence* he would not have started even now.

[TO JOHN MURRAY]   *Octr. 20th. 1821*

Dear Moray/—*If* errors *are* in the *M.S.S.*—write me down an Ass—they are *not*—& I am content to undergo any penalty if they be. —Besides, the *omitted* Stanza (last but one or two) sent *afterwards*— was that in the M.S.S. too?——Have you received a printed sheet or two from an old M.S.S.—as a note to the Doge? sent two months ago? —I am anxious about that.—As to *"honour"* I will trust no man's honour in affairs of barter.—I will tell you why.—A state of bargain is Hobbes's "state of Nature—a state of war."—It is so with all men.— If I come to a friend—and say "friend, lend me five hundred pounds!" he either does it or says that he can't or won't.—But if I come to Ditto—and say "Ditto,—I have an excellent house—or horse—or carriage—or M.S.S. or books—or pictures—&c. &c. &c. &c. &c. honestly worth a thousand pounds, you shall have them for five hundred["]——what does Ditto say?—Why he looks at them—he *hums*—he *ha's*—he *humbugs*—if he can—to get a bargain as cheaply as he can—because *it is* a bargain—this is in the blood & bone of mankind—and the same man who would lend another a thousand pounds without interest—would not buy a horse of him for half it's value if he could help it.—It is so—there's no denying it—& therefore I will have as much as I can—& you will give as little.—And there's an end.—All men are intrinsical rascals,—and I am only sorry that not being a dog I can't bite them.——So—Thomas M[oore] is in town incog.—Love to *him*.—I except him from my regretted morsures—for I have always found him the pink of honour—and honesty—besides I liked his country till it's late performance.—By the way did Mawman or Mawman's friend deliver to him the *two* M.S.S. Books—consigned for him?—*This* is *your* concern so anatomize Mawman about it.—They belong to your posthumous adventure—that is to say—to mine.——I am filling another for you with little anecdotes to my own knowledge or well authenticated—of Sheridan—Curran &c. and such other public men—as I recollect to have been acquainted with—for I knew most of them more or less.[1] I will do what I can to prevent your losing by my obsequies.—Acknowledge packets.—

[Scrawl]

P.S.—Address to Pisa.

P.S.—Acknowledge "Vision of Judgement by Quevedo Redivivus" sent on the 9th.—also "The Irish Avatar["] (for Mr. Moore)—put in the letter-bag afterwards—a day or two.—

[TO SAMUEL ROGERS]   *Ravenna. Octr. 21st. 1821*

Dear Rogers/—I shall be (the Gods willing) in Bologna on Saturday next.—This is a curious answer to yr. letter—but I have taken a house in Pisa for the winter to which all my chattels—furniture—horses—carriages—and live stock are already removed—and I am preparing to follow. The cause of this removal—is—shortly—the exile or proscription of all my friends, relations, and connections here into Tuscany—on account of our late politics——and where they go I accompany them.—I merely remained till now to settle some arrangements about my daughter—and to give time for my furniture &c. to precede

[1] This was Byron's notebook of "Detached Thoughts" begun on October 15, 1821. (See Vol. 9).

me.——I have not here a seat or a bed hardly except some *jury*-chairs
and tables and a mattress for the week to come—If you will go with
me to Pisa I can lodge you for as long as you like—(they write that
the House—the Palazzo Lanfranchi is spacious—it is on the Arno)
and I have four carriage[s] and as many saddle horses (such as they
are in these parts) with all other conveniences at your command, and
also their owner.——If you can't do this—we may at least cross the
Apennines together—or if you are going by another road—we shall
meet at Bologna I hope. I address this to the Post Office (as you
desire) and you will probably find me at the Albergo di *San Marco*—
if you arrive first—wait till I come up—which will be (barring
accidents) on Saturday—or Sunday at farthest—I presume you are
alone on your voyages.——Moore is in London *incog.* according to
my latest advices from those climates.——It is better than a lustre
(five years and six months and some days more or less—since we
met) and like the man from Tadcaster in the farce ("Love laughs at
Locksmiths") whose acquaintances including the cat and the terrier
"who caught a halfpenny in his mouth"—[1] were all "gone dead"—
but too many of our acquaintances have taken the same path.——Ly.
Melbourne—Grattan—Sheridan—Curran— &c. &c. (without reckoning the "οἱ πολλοί") almost every body of much name of the old
School.—But "so am not I, said the foolish fat Scullion"[2]—therefore
let us make the most of our remainder.——Let me find two lines from
you at "the Hostel or Inn".——

yrs. ever &c.
BYRON

[TO COUNTESS TERESA GUICCIOLI]   *8bre. 23. 1821*

Amor Mio—Lega partì Sabbato. La mia partenza è fissata per il
Sabbato venturo—cioè in quattro giorni.——Spero che sarai contenta.
—Lega debbe essere in Pisa prima di questa letterina—ma supponendo
che la rapidità di suoi viaggi corrisponde coi altri movimenti di
quell' uomo—potrebbe essere che il biglietto arriva prima del' balordo.
——Ho voluto darlo una settimana di tempo per fare il viaggio—se io
fossi partito il primo *egli* non sarebbe mai a Pisa.—Egli ha già
commesso un' delitto, nel' accordare troppo ad un' vetterino per due

---

[1] George Colman the Younger, *Love Laughs at Locksmiths*, Act. II.
[2] *Tristram Shandy*, Book V, chap. 7.

cavallo fin' a Lugo.—Ma non lo pagherò—quando veniamo ai conti della strada.—L'aiuto di questi cavalli era necessario—per risparmiare troppa fatica ai due Olandesi prediletti del' Cocchiere.—Saluto Papa e Pierino e ti abbraccio alla *Corinna*—Amami—Amor mio—sono sempre il tuo

A. A. in E.
[Scrawl]

P.S.—Mi dispiace la malattia del' domestico—Guarda che non manca niente di necessario per il suo stato.—Essendo di fresca età si puo sperare per lui.

[TRANSLATION] *October 23rd. 1821*

My Love—Lega left on Saturday. My departure is settled for next Saturday—that is in four days.—I hope you will be pleased. Lega should be in Pisa before this note—but supposing that the rapidity of that man's journey corresponds to his other movements—this note may arrive before the fool.———I have preferred to give him a week to do the journey—If I had started first he would never have got to Pisa. He has already committed one crime in paying too much to a coachman for two horses to Lugo. But I shall not pay him, when we come to the travelling accounts. The help of these horses was necessary, to save from too much fatigue the two Dutch horses, the coachman's favourites. —Greet Papa and Pierino for me, and I embrace you *a la Corinne*— Love me—my love—I am always yours

A. A. in E.

P.S.—I am sorry about the servant's illness. See that nothing necessary for his health is lacking. Being still young, we can hope for him.

[TO JOHN MURRAY] [*October 25?*] *1821*

Dear Moray/—The enclosed is for Mr. Moore.—Address you to Pisa—and acknowledge packets—various & sundry.—"A Vision of Judgement" and another poeshie, for Mr. Moore the latter.—— Rogers is at Venice—and has written to me to meet *here*—but I have been obliged to transfer to Bologna—because all my furniture &c. is now at Pisa—& I have no conveniences for a visitor.—On Saturday I expect to find him & myself there.—

yrs. truly [Scrawl]

Dear Moray/—I waited here another *week* to receive the proofs of "Cain" which have *not* arrived—though your letter announced them for next post.—I must start for Pisa on Saturday—so by this means there is a *fortnight* lost—for the proof must follow through cross posts. —Upon my word—you will provoke me to play you some trick one of these days that you won't like.——By this post I send you a *third corrected* copy of "Don Juan"——I will thank you to be more careful in future.

yrs. [Scrawl]

Please to acknowledge the "Vision of Judgement by Quevedo redivivus" and other packets.——

Dear Moray/—You say the errors are in the M.S.S.—now—excuse me—but this is *not* true—and I defy you to prove it to be true.—The truth is you are a fine gentleman—and negligent as becomes a mighty man in his business.—I send you a *third copy corrected*—with some alteration—& by this and the other *corrected* copies I request you to print any future impression.—

Byron

P.S.—Collate this with the other two copies both sent by the post. ——And pray when I send you a *parcel* or *packet*—*do* acknowledge it— I care nothing about my letters or your answers—I *only* want to know, when I have taken trouble about a thing that it has arrived.——*You* shall be the hero of my next poem—will you publish it?——

[Note written in copy of *Don Juan*, Cantos III, IV, V]

The Publisher is requested to reprint (provided the occasion should occur) from *this* copy—as the one most carefully gone over by the Authour.—The Authour repeats (as before) that the former impressions (from whatever cause) are full of errors.—And he further adds that he doth kindly trust—with all due deference to those superior persons —the publisher and printer—that they will in future—*less* misspell— misplace—mistake and mis-everything, the humbled M.S.S. of their humble Servant.

A[mor] M[io]—Post dimani me metterò in viaggio.——Il tempo non è molto favorevole ma ciò importa poco,—importava più pei cavalli Olandesi—che già debbono essere a Pisa.—Dunque speriamo rivederci fra poco—sta tranquilla—e credami il tuo

a. a. in e. [Scrawl]

P.S.—La Vittoria si sposa con uno di *Imola*—(mi vien' detto) la *Tuda* si *fa*—al' amore col' nuovo Vice-legato—(un' altra diceria forse) tutte le amorose di Pierino sono già provedute—vecchie e giovani—— dunque;—i nonni sono in campagna ancora—la Giulia qui.—Il Signor Nonno continua avere quella facilità inconveniente pei [bricioli?]—ma in tutto il resto sta bene.—I due ragazzi furono in città ma sono già tornati alla villa. Saluta le due altre Eccelenze.—

[TRANSLATION]   *October 26th. 1821*

My Love—The day after tomorrow I shall start. The weather is not very favourable, but that does not matter much—it mattered more for the Dutch horses, which must already be in Pisa.

So let us hope to see each other before long—be reassured and believe me yours

a. a. in e.

P.S.—Vittoria is marrying a man from Imola (I am told). Tuda is making love with the new Vice Legate (another bit of gossip perhaps) —all Pierino's loves are already provided for therefore; old and young; the grandparents are in the country still—Giulia is here. Grandfather continues to have that inconvenient facility for [crumbs] [tiny pieces?] but otherwise is well. The two boys were in town but have already returned to the Villa. Greet the other two Excellencies.

" 'Tis the middle of night by the castle clock"[1] and in three hours more I have to set out on my way to Pisa—sitting up all night to be sure of rising. I have just made them take off my bed-clothes—blankets inclusive—in case of temptation from the apparel of sheets to my eyelids.

Samuel Rogers is—or is to be—at Bologna, as he writes from Venice.

I thought our Magnifico would "pound you,"[2] if possible, He is trying to "pound" me, too; but I'll specie the rogue—or at least, I'll have the odd shillings out of him in keen iambics.

Your approbation of "Sardanapalus" is agreeable for more reasons than one. Hobhouse is pleased to think as you do of it, and so do some others—but the "Arimaspian", whom, like "a Gryphon in the wilderness," I will "follow for his gold"[3] (as I exhorted you to do before), did or doth disparage it— "stinting me in my sizings."[4] His notable opinions on the "Foscari" and "Cain" he hath not as yet forwarded; or, at least, I have not yet received them, nor the proofs thereof, though promised by last post.

I see the way that he and his Quarterly people are tending—they want a *row* with me, and they shall have it. I only regret that I am not in England for the *nonce*; as, here, it is hardly fair ground for me, isolated and out of the way of prompt rejoinder and information as I am. But, though backed by all the corruption, and infamy, and patronage of their master rogues and slave renegadoes, if they do once rouse me up,

> "They had better gall the devil, Salisbury.[5]"

I have that for two or three of them, which they had better not move me to put in motion;—and yet, after all, what a fool I am to disquiet myself about such fellows! It was all very well ten or twelve years ago, when I was a "curled darling,"[6] and *minded* such things. At present, I *rate* them at their true value; but, from natural temper and bile, am not able to keep quiet.

---

[1] Coleridge, *Christabel*, Part I, line 1.

[2] The suggestion is that Murray would try to pay Moore in pounds instead of guineas for Byron's Memoirs.

[3] *Paradise Lost*, Book II, lines 943–947.

[4] The Cambridge term for the ration of food and drink allowed by a college for poor scholars or sizars.

[5] *King John*, Act IV, scene 3.

[6] *Othello*, Act I, scene 2.

Let me hear from you on your return from Ireland, which ought to be ashamed to see you, after her Brunswick blarney.[7] I am of Longman's opinion, that you should allow your friends to liquidate the Bermuda claim.[8] Why should you throw away the two thousand *pounds* (of the *non*-guinea Murray) upon that cursed piece of treacherous inveiglement? I think you carry the matter a little too far and scrupulously. When we see patriots begging publicly, and know that Grattan received a fortune from his country, I really do not see why a man, in no whit inferior to any or all of them, should shrink from accepting that assistance from his private friends which every tradesman receives from his connexions upon much less occasions. For, after all, it was not *your debt*—it was a piece of swindling *against* you. As to * * * *, and the "what noble creatures! &c. &c." it is all very fine and very well, but, till you can persuade me that there is *no credit* and no *self-applause* to be obtained by being of use to a celebrated man, I must retain the same opinion of the human spe*cies*, which I do of our friend Mr. Spe*cie*.

[TO JOHN MURRAY]   *8bre. 30th. 1821*

D[ea]r Moray/—You say the errors were in the M.S.S. of D[on] J[uan].—but the *omitted* stanza—which I sent you in an after letter—and the omitted *notes?*—please to replace them.

yrs. [Scrawl]

I am just setting off for Pisa.
Favour the enclosed to Mr. Moore——Address to Pisa.

---

[7] See Sept. 17, 1821, to Moore, note 1.
[8] Moore's publisher Longman had told him that Lord Lansdowne had offered to contribute £1000 to liquidate the debt caused by the default of Moore's deputy in Bermuda. Other friends also offered to contribute, but Moore was too proud to accept.

LIST OF LETTERS AND SOURCES

Date	Recipient	Source of Text	Page
		1821 (continued)	
Aug. 31	J. Mawman	MS. Milton S. Eisenhower Library, The Johns Hopkins University	195
[Sept. ?]	Teresa Guiccioli	MS. Biblioteca Classense, Ravenna	195
Sept. 1	Douglas Kinnaird	MS. Carl H. Pforzheimer Library	195
Sept. 1	J. Mawman	Text: *LJ*, V, 354n	196
Sept. 3	Thomas Moore	Text: Moore, II, 521–523	196
Sept. 4	John Murray (*a*)	MS. Murray	197
Sept. 4	John Murray (*b*)	MS. Murray	197
Sept. 4	Douglas Kinnaird	MS. Murray	198
Sept. 4	Teresa Guiccioli	MS. Biblioteca Classense, Ravenna	199
Sept. 5	Octavius Gilchrist	MS. Henry E. Huntington Library	199
[Sept. 5?]	John Murray	MS. Murray	201
Sept. 5	Count Ruggero Gamba	MS. Biblioteca Classense, Ravenna	202
Sept. 8	P. B. Shelley	MS. Pierpont Morgan Library	202
Sept. 8	Octavius Gilchrist	Text: Copy in Murray Collection	203
Sept. 9	John Murray	MS. Murray	203
Sept. 9	Teresa Guiccioli	MS. Biblioteca Classense, Ravenna	204
Sept. 10	John Murray	MS. Murray	205
Sept. 11	Douglas Kinnaird	MS. Murray	205
Sept. 12	John Murray	MS. Murray	206
Sept. 13	Douglas Kinnaird	MS. Murray	208
Sept. 13	Augusta Leigh	MS The Earl of Lytton	209
Sept. 14	Lady Byron	MS. The Earl of Lytton	209
Sept. 15	Douglas Kinnaird	MS. Murray	211
Sept. 15	Teresa Guiccioli	MS. Biblioteca Classense, Ravenna	212
Sept. 17	Teresa Guiccioli	MS. Biblioteca Classense, Ravenna	213
Sept. 17	Thomas Moore	Text: Moore, II, 527	213
Sept. 19	Thomas Moore	Text: Moore, II, 527–530	214

FORGERIES OF BYRON'S LETTERS

May 5, 1821: To [John Murray?]. Bixby.

May 5, 1821: To Douglas Kinnaird. Schultess-Young, XVI, pp. 179–181.

May 12, 1821: To Douglas Kinnaird. Schultess-Young, XVII, pp. 181–82.

June 5, 1821: To J. Hoppner. Schultess-Young, XXX, pp. 204–5.

Aug., 1821: To Douglas Kinnaird. Schultess-Young, XIX, pp. 184–85.

Aug., 1821: To Douglas Kinnaird. Schultess-Young, XX, pp. 185–87.

Aug. 23, 1821: To Douglas Kinnaird. Schultess-Young, XVIII, pp. 183–84.

Aug. 28, 1821: To John Hanson. Schultess-Young, XXXVI. pp. 216–17.

Oct. 3, 1821: To [John Murray?]. Bixby.

Oct. 25, 1821: To Douglas Kinnaird. Schultess-Young, XXI, pp. 188–90.

Appendix III

BIBLIOGRAPHY FOR VOLUME 8

(*Principal short title or abbreviated references*)

Astarte—Lovelace, Ralph Milbanke, Earl of: *Astarte: A Fragment of Truth Concerning George Gordon Byron, Sixth Baron Byron.* Recorded by his grandson. New Edition by Mary Countess of Lovelace, London, 1921.

Bixby—*Poems and Letters of Lord Byron.* Ed. from the Original Manuscripts in the Possession of W. K. Bixby of St. Louis by W. N. C. Carlton, M. A. Published for the Society of Dofobs, Chicago, 1912.

Dictionary of National Biography.

Hodgson, Memoir—*Memoir of the Rev. Francis Hodgson, B. D.* By his son the Rev. James T. Hodgson. 2 vols. London, 1878.

LBC—*Lord Byron's Correspondence*, ed. by John Murray. 2 vols. London, 1922.

LJ—*The Works of Lord Byron. A New, Revised and Enlarged Edition. Letters and Journals*, ed. Rowland E. Prothero. 6 vols. London, 1898–1901.

Marchand, Leslie A.:—*Byron: A Biography.* 3 vols. New York, 1957; London, 1958.

Moore—*Letters and Journals of Lord Byron: with Notices of His Life.* By Thomas Moore. 2 vols. London, 1830.

Moore, Memoirs—*Memoirs, Journal, and Correspondence of Thomas Moore.* Edited by the Right Hon. Lord John Russell, M.P. 8 vols. London, 1853–56.

Moore, Letters—*The Letters of Thomas Moore.* Edited by Wilfred S. Dowden. 2 vols. Oxford, 1964.

Origo, Iris: *The Last Attachment.* London, 1949.

Poetry The Works of Lord Byron. A New, Revised and Enlarged Edition. Poetry, ed Ernest Hartley Coleridge. 7 vols. London, 1898–1904.

Smiles, Samuel: *A Publisher and His Friends: Memoir and Correspondence of the Late John Murray.* 2 vols. London, 1891.

[Wilson, Harriette]: *Harriette Wilson's Memoirs of Herself and Others.* New York, 1929.

INDEX OF PROPER NAMES

Page numbers in italics indicate main references and Biographical Sketches in the Appendix. Such main biographical references in earlier volumes are included in this index and are in square brackets.

Coolidge, Mr, of Boston, 146
Corneille, Pierre, *Polyeucte*, 94 and n
Cornwall, Barry *see* Procter, B.W.
Costa, Professor, 160 and n, 170
Cowley, Abraham, *Epitaphium vivi Auctoris*, 50 and n
Cowper, Lady, w. of fifth Earl, possessor of B.'s letters to Lady Melbourne, 226
Cowper, William, 93
Crabbe, George, 132, 219, 238
Croker, John Wilson, review of Keats's *Endymion*, 163n
Curioni, Alberico, 77 and n; recommended to Murray and others, 77, 86, 113–14, 129 and n
Curran, John Philpot, 230 and n, 245, 246
Cuvier, Léopold Chrétien, 'Essay on the Theory of the Earth', 216 and n

d'Albany, Comtesse, 14 and n
Dallas, Robert Charles, [*Vol. 1*, 274–5], 228
Dalyell, Sir J. G., *Shipwrecks and Disasters at Sea*, B.'s debt to, 186 and n
Dante, 39–40, 93, 130
Daru, Pierre Antoine, Count, History of Venice, 124 and n, 151
Davy, Sir Humphry and Lady, 29
Delaval, Sir F. B., 42
Devonshire, Elizabeth Duchess of, B. commends the Gambas, 154–5, 159, 161, 170, 204
Dibdin, Thomas, 68 and n, 133
Diodorus Siculus, 26, 27, 128–9, 129n
D'Israeli, Isaac, 77, 145, 237
Douglas, Hon. Frederick Sylvester North, *Ancient and Modern Greeks*, 225 and n
Dragonetti, Domenico, 241
Drummond, Charles, 228
Drury, Henry Joseph, [*Vol. 1*, *144n*], 228
Dryden, John, 101; in Johnson's *Lives*, 115 and n; *Aurung-Zebe*, 40 and n; *Absalom and Achitophel*, 164 and n; 'Huntsman's Ghost', 48; 'Theodore and Honoria', 48n
Dyer, Sir Edward, *Gronger Hill*, 94

Edgeworth, Maria, 29 and n
Edgeworth, Richard Lovell, f. of above, 30 and n; *Memoirs*, 29 and n, 42

Edleston, John, 24 and n
Ekenhead, Lt, swims the Hellespont, 80, 81, 83
Elise, 97n
Elisei, Giovanni Battista, 36 and n
Elliston, Robert W., and *Marino Faliero*, 64, 66, 112, 116, 119, 120, 129
The Etonian, 193 and n

Fabbri, Mrs Santino, 168
Faber, George Stanley, *Great Gods of Phoenicia*, 237 and n
Fabre, Françoise, 14n
Farquhar, George, *The Beaux' Stratagem*, 17 and n, 50 and n; *The Recruiting Officer*, 134 and n
Fawcett, John, 55 and n
Fearman, publisher, and *Don Juan*, 90 and n, 91–2
Ferdinand, King of Naples, 12 and n, 20
Fielding, Henry, 11–12
Fitzpatrick, Gen. Richard, 29 and n
Flahault, Mme de, 54 and n
Fletcher, William, 149
Florence, 151n, 157, 161 and n, 169
Forteguerri, Niccolo, *Ricciardetto*, 224n
Foscolo, Ugo, 69, 79, 151
Francis 1, 118
Frere, John Hookham ('Whistlecraft'), 193, 229
Frimont, Marshall, 122 and n

Galignani, Jean Antoine, 56, 60, 72, 105, 118, 191; B.'s French copyright, 72, 74; death, 84; *Literary Gazette*, 84; *Messenger*, 11
Galilei, Galileo, 53
Gallina, Vincenzo, 17–18
Gamba Ghiselli, Count Ruggero, [*Vol. 7*, *272*], 12, 14, 18; exiled, 105n, 151n, 154, 157, 179–80; B. and his repeal, 154–5
Gamba Ghiselli, Count Pietro, [*Vol. 7*, *273*], 12, 14; and the Revolution, 16–17, 17–18, 40, 43; exiled, 105n, 151n, 154, 157; B. and his repeal, 154–5
Gamba Ghiselli, Countess, 51
Gay, John, 148n; *Beggar's Opera*, 110 and n
George III, Southey's apotheosis, 229 and n, 230; as Prince of Wales, 71n

George IV, coronation, 143 and n, 144;
in Ireland, 213n; anecdote, 225n
Ghigi, Pellegrino, 71, 86; B.'s banker,
86
Gifford, William, 94, 110, 114, 128,
193, 219; likes *Sardanapalus*, 156,
168; dislikes new dramas, 218
Giganti, Giuseppe, 124 and n
Gilchrist, Octavius Graham, involve-
ment in Pope controversy, 111n,
199 and n; B.'s proposed defence,
111 and n, 116, 197; attacked by
Bowles, 111n, 199 and n; three
pamphlets, 199 and n, 200
Gillies, John, *History of Greece*, 238
and n
Ginguené, Pierre Louis, 14 and n, 41,
53
Glenbervie, Lord, trns. *First Canto of
Ricciardetto*, 224 and n
Goethe, Johann Wolfgang von, 25, 198
and n; *Edinburgh Review*, 164
Goldoni, Carlo, 15n
Goldsmith, Oliver, *The Goodnatured
Man*, 239 and n; *Vicar of Wake-
field*, 38 and n, 40, 92, 239 and n
Gordon, Charles, 227
Grammont, Philibert, Comte de, 148
Grattan, Henry, 219, 246
Gray, Thomas, *Elegy*, 53n; additional
stanzas, 50–1
Gretry, André Ernest, 41
Grey, Charles, second Earl Grey, 27,
28, 120n
Grillparzer, Franz, 26; *Sappho*, 25 and
n
Grimm, Friedrich Melchior, *Correspondence Littéraire*, 30, 31, 41 and
n, 46
Guiccioli, Count Allessandro, [*Vol. 6,
276–7*], 233
Guiccioli (née Gamba Ghiselli)
Countess Teresa, [*Vol. 6, 277–8*],
16; visited by B., 12, 13–14, 18,
23; quarrels with him over love,
26; separates from her husband,
34, 41, 233; appearance, 95; B.
on his love for her, 138, 160, 170,
177–8; dislike of *Don Juan*, 147
and n, 148 and n; goes to
Florence, 151n, 184; in danger in
Papal States, 159, 161; in Bologna, 168; B. on her future home,
184; divorce, 214; their love
affair, 234–5

Hannibal, 69 and n
Hanson, John, [*Vol. 1, 275*], Rochdale
mortgage, 62, 152 and n; re-
lationship with B., 72, 87, 208
Harlequin's Misfortunes, 117 and n
Harness, William, [*Vol. 1, 154 and n*],
228
Harris, Harry, 60 and n, 64
Hazlitt, William, 38
Heber, Richard, 207 and n
Hellespont, B. and swimming, 80–2
Helvetius, Claude Adrien, *Encyclopédie*,
42n
Hemans, Felicia, 236 and n
Hentsch, Mr, Jnr, banker, 157 and n
Herodotus, 189 and n
Hill, Aaron, 'Progress of Wit', 11 and n
Hoadly, Benjamin, *The Suspicious Hus-
band*, 14 and n
Hobbes, Thomas, 'state of Nature', 244
Hobhouse, John Cam (later first Baron
Broughton de Gyfford, [*Vol. 1,
275–6*], 81, 83, 121, 130, 145;
wants no Life of Byron, 11n; epi-
grams on Long, 24; to entertain
Curioni and Taruscelli, 84–5;
Latin version of *Hints from
Horace*, 88; defender of Queen
Caroline; 100n, 148n; acting of
Marino Faliero, 120 and n;
attacks Parliament, 120n, 121n; to
proof read *Don Juan*, 194–5;
collection of B.'s letters, 216, 226;
parody on Savage, 239; *Re-
collections of a Long Life*, 121n;
preface to *Rimini*, 218
Hodgson, Rev. Francis, [*Vol. 1, 276*],
228; 'takes up' Pope, 88, 112n;
indebted to B., 156; *Childe
Harold's Monitor*, 112 and n, 114
and n; *Saeculo-Mastix*, 112 and n
Hogg, James, 219
Holderness, Mary Doublet, Countess,
229
Holland, Lord, Lope de Vega, 14
Holland, Lady, w. of above, 164 and n
Holmes, James, painter, 95 and n, 135,
136
Home, John, *Douglas*, 143 and n
Homer, translations, 25n, 93, 148n
Homer Travestie, 22 and n
Hoppner, R.B., Br. Consul, [*Vol. 5,
294–5*], 75, 139
Hoppner, Mrs, w. of above, 98

267

Horace, *Ars Poetica*, 59 and n; *Carmina*, 31 and n

Hoste, Commodore, 54n

Hume, David, *History of England*, 75 and n

Hunt, Henry 'Orator', Radical, 240n

Hunt, James Henry Leigh, [*Vol. 2, 281–2*], 173

Hunt, John, prosecution, 181n; Canto 9 *Don Juan*, 225n

Imola, Count and Countess of, 184 and n, 249

Ingram family, 113 and n

Irving, Washington, 219; admired by B., 146; *A History of New York by D. Knickerbocker*, 53 and n, 173 and n; *Sketch Book*, 53 and n, 145

Jeffrey, Francis, Lord Jeffrey, 61, 102, 178; in *Hints from Horace*, 88

Jesuits, *Mémoires de Trévoux*, 140 and n

Johnson, Samuel, 74; *Lives of the Poets*, 21 (Dryden), 115; *Vanity of Human Wishes*, 19, 103 and n

Jonson, Ben, 57, 110

Jugurtha, King of Numidia, 14n

Julius Caesar, 47

Juvenal, *Satire*, 128 and n

Kean, Edmund, 60, 112, 181; *de Montfort*, 208, 210

Keats, John, 'killed by the *Quarterly*', 102, 104, 117, 162, 172, 173; B. on his poetry, 163, 166, 172; *Endymion*, 103, 163n; *Hyperion*, 163n; *Sleep and Poetry* (attack on School of Pope), 104 and n

Kemble, John Philip, 60

Kinnaird, Douglas, [*Vol. 2, 282–3*], 61, 63; to entertain Curioni and Taruscelli, 86; B.'s financial affairs, 91, 95–6, 122, 135, 143, 152–3, 171, 176, 180–1, 185–6, 230–1, 239; mercantile matters, 187; to proof read *Don Juan*, 194

Kosciusko, Tadeusz, 40 and n

La Rochefoucault, François, Duc de, *Reflexions Morales*, 41 and n

Lake Poets, 201

Lamb, Lady Caroline, [*Vol. 2, 283*], 217, 227

Lambton, John, first Earl of Durham, 121n

Langhorne, Rev. John, trns. Plutarch's *Lives*, 127 and n

Lansdowne, Sir Henry Petty-Fitz-maurice, third Marquis of, 111

Lawrence, Sir Thomas, 28

Leander, swims the Hellespont, 80, 81, 162

Lee, Harriet and Sophia, *The Canterbury Tales* ('Werner'), 224 and n, 237

Leeds, Duke of, 34 and n

Lega *see* Zambelli

Legnani, Luigi, 138 and n

Leigh, Hon. Augusta (née Byron), [*Vol. 1, 273*], 238; financial future, 89; possessor of B.'s Journal, 176, 217; poor state of nerves, 217

Lemprière, John, 102

Le Sage, Alain René, *Gil Blas*, 88 and n, 148

Leslie, Charles, *Short and Easie Method with Deists*, 238 and n,

Lewis, (Monk) Matthew Gregory, 54

Lockhart, John Gibson, 99n; *John Bull's Letter*, 145 and n

London Magazine, 99n

Long, Edward Noel, 23 and n, 24–5; death, 24, 227

Longman, publisher, 141, 251 and n

Louis XIV, apocryphal story, 119 and n

Manton, Joe, gunsmith, 31

Martin Marprelate, 127

Martinetti, Mme, 154

Matthews, Charles, death, 24

Maupertuis, Pierre Louis, 46 and n

Mawman, J., bookseller, 197, 207, 223; publishes *Hours of Idleness*, 195 and n; and B.'s *Memoirs*, 196n; recipient of 'paper books', 196 and n, 245; and Roscoe's *Pope*, 201

Melbourne, Lady, [*Vol. 2, 283–4*], 155, 246; B.'s letters to, 226

Mengaldo, Angelo (Chevalier), 81, 82, 131

Milman, Henry Hart, Dean of St Paul's, 193 and n, 207

Milton, John, 40, 109, 200; *Comus*, 23 and n; *Il Penseroso*, 19 and n; *Paradise Lost*, 68, 208 and n, 250 and n

Missiaglia, Giovan Battista, [*Vol. 6, 177n*], 70–1, 75

Mitchell, Thomas, trns. *Comedies of Aristophanes*, 132 and n

268